The Interpersonal Unconscious

THE LIBRARY OF OBJECT RELATIONS
Series Editors
David E. Scharff and Jill Savege Scharff

The Library of Object Relations provides an expanding body of theory for understanding individual development and pathology, human interaction, and new avenues of treatment. They apply to realms of experience from the internal world of the individual to the human community, from the clinical situation to everyday life, and from individual psychoanalysis and psychotherapy, to group therapy, couple and family therapy, and to social policy.

The Interpersonal Unconscious by David E. Scharff and Jill Savege Scharff
Unfree Associations, Updated Edition: Inside Psychoanalytic Institutes by Douglas Kirsner
Object Relations Brief Therapy: The Therapeutic Relationship in Short-Term Work by Michael Stadter
Object Relations Therapy of Physical and Sexual Trauma by Jill Savege Scharff and David E. Scharff
The Relational Origins of Prejudice: A Convergence of Psychoanalytic and Social Cognitive Perspectives by Ron B. Aviram
New Paradigms for Treating Relationships edited by Jill Savege Scharff and David E. Scharff
The Primer of Object Relations, Revised Edition by Jill Savege Scharff and David E. Scharff
Object Relations Individual Therapy by Jill Savege Scharff and David E. Scharff
Love and Hate in the Analytic Setting by Glen O. Gabbard
Containing Rage, Terror, and Despair: An Object Relations Approach to Psychotherapy by Jeffrey Seinfeld
Treating Borderline States in Marriage: Dealing with Oppositionalism, Ruthless Aggression, and Severe Resistance by Charles C. McCormack
Cruelty, Violence, and Murder: Understanding the Criminal Mind by Arthur Hyatt-Williams
The Sexual Relationship: An Object Relations View of Sex and the Family by David E. Scharff
On Freud's Couch: Seven New Interpretations of Freud's Case Histories edited by Irene Matthis and Imre Szecsody
A Prophetic Analyst: Erich Fromm's Contributions to Psychoanalysis by Mauricio Cortina and Michael Maccoby
Object Relations Brief Therapy: The Therapeutic Relationship in Short-Term Work by Michael Stadter

The Interpersonal Unconscious

David E. Scharff, MD
Jill Savege Scharff, MD

JASON ARONSON
Lanham • Boulder • New York • Toronto • Plymouth, UK

Published by Jason Aronson
A wholly owned subsidiary of The Rowman & Littlefield Publishing Group, Inc.
4501 Forbes Boulevard, Suite 200, Lanham, Maryland 20706
http://www.rowmanlittlefield.com

Estover Road, Plymouth PL6 7PY, United Kingdom

British Library Cataloguing in Publication Information Available

Library of Congress Cataloging-in-Publication Data

Scharff, David E., 1941-
The interpersonal unconscious / David E. Scharff, Jill Savege Scharff.
p. ; cm. -- (Library of object relations)
Includes bibliographical references and index.
ISBN 978-0-7657-0869-4 (cloth : alk. paper) -- ISBN 978-0-7657-0871-7 (paper : alk. paper) -- ISBN 978-0-7657-0870-0 (ebook)
1. Psychoanalysis. 2. Subconsciousness. 3. Interpersonal relations. I. Scharff, Jill Savege. II. Title. III. Series: Library of object relations.
[DNLM: 1. Psychoanalytic Theory. 2. Unconscious (Psychology) 3. Family Relations. 4. Interpersonal Relations. WM 460.5.U6]
RC489.S827S33 2011
616.89'17--dc23
2011022817

∞™ The paper used in this publication meets the minimum requirements of American National Standard for Information Sciences—Permanence of Paper for Printed Library Materials, ANSI/NISO Z39.48-1992.

Printed in the United States of America

Contents

Acknowledgments

Our thanks go first to Giulio Cesare Zavattini who commissioned our electronic article "The Interpersonal Unconscious" for *Funzione Gamma*, # 21, 2005, and to Claudio Neri who gave his permission for the print version in this book.

We gratefully acknowledge the collaboration of Shi Qijia, Vice-President of Wuhan Hospital for Psychotherapy in Hubei Province, who gave permission to include an article co-written with Jill Scharff "Social Change, Intercultural Conflict, and Marital Dynamics in a Chinese Marriage in Brief Concurrent Individual and Couple Therapy" in the *International Journal of Applied Psychoanalytic Studies* 5(4):302–321 (2008), reprinted in adapted form by permission of Wiley and Sons.

We are grateful to Taylor and Francis for permission to reprint with some modification our article "Using Dreams in Treating Couples' Sexual issues" from *Psychoanalytic Inquiry* 24(3):468-482. http://www.informaworld.com.

Many thanks go to Oliver Rathbone for facilitating permission to modify, adapt and re-use our article: "Marriage is a Strange Attractor: Chaos Theory as a Paradigm Shift for Couple Therapy" published in M. Ludlam and V. Nyberg (Eds.), *Couple Attachments: Theoretical and Clinical Studies*, pp. 189–220, http://www.karnacbooks.com/isbn/9781855754522, published by Karnac Books in 2007; and David Scharff's article "The Concept of the Link in Psychoanalytic Therapy" published in the journal *Couple and Family Psychoanalysis* 1(1): 34–48; and his book review essay on *The Work of Confluence: Listening and Interpreting in the Psychoanalytic Field* by W. Baranger and M. Baranger, http://www.karnacbooks.com/isbn/9781855757615, also published in *Couple and Family Psychoanalysis*

1(1): 146–149—all adapted and reprinted with kind permission of Karnac Books.

We are fortunate that living together accelerates our exchange of ideas. As a couple, we find ourselves at the crosshairs of the link—the vertical axis connecting us to the theories and techniques handed down to us from British Object Relations and American psychoanalysis, and the horizontal axis connecting us to contemporary chaos theory, attachment therapy, neuroscience, and link theory, in a fertile learning field with a remarkable group of psychoanalysts and psychotherapists at the International Psychotherapy Institute and the International Institute for Psychoanalytic Training. In discussion with faculty, students, and distinguished guest speakers there, too many to list and impossible to list just a few, we have found emotional support, intellectual stimulation, and inspiration. In that environment with those colleagues, we have a renewable source of energy, and our ideas have a home.

Earl Hopper awakened our interest in the social unconscious, and Pier Ferrari introduced us to mirror neurons. Chris Clulow and James Fisher helped us to appreciate attachment theory in work with couples. Editors Alberto Eiguer, Jon Carlson, Barbara Feld, Molly Ludlam, Anna Nicoló, Nadia Ramzy, Stewart Twemlow, bi-annual conferences of The International Association of Couple and Family Psychoanalysis, and the American Psychoanalytic Association Discussion Group on Family Therapy led by Richard Zeitner and David Scharff, bring our ideas on applied psychoanalysis to a wider audience. At the International Psychoanalytic Association Discussion Group on Family Therapy, we have enjoyed the invaluable help of Isidoro Berenstein (Chair), Roberto Losso, and Julio Moreno among others as we struggle to translate link theory and relate it to our theories based in object relations. Jean-Michel Quinodoz encouraged our early thoughts on the applicability of chaos theory to psychoanalysis and our interest in dreams. We hope that they realize how much all of them contributed to our final product.

We are profoundly grateful to our patients for trusting us to work with them, to Annalunes from Bilotta and Maribel Cano for keeping us afloat, to our children for the pleasure they bring us, to all our colleagues for giving us the confidence to write out our ideas, and to Jason Aronson for finding them worthy of publication.

Introduction

In recent years, many currents have joined to produce a tide of change in psychoanalytic theory and practice. It is exciting to work in a time when there is so much flux in the fields of psychoanalysis and analytic therapy, when psychoanalysis has moved from the grip of dogmatic schools with separated areas of knowledge towards more openness and mutual enrichment.

We began our thinking and writing from the perspective of British object relations, and that foundation has continued to serve us well. In the generation after Freud, the thinking of Fairbairn, Klein, Winnicott, Bowlby, and Bion formed a foundation that continues to work because, taken together, their independently conceived theories about development in the context of relationship form a loose-knit, open systems way of theorizing and working that learns and grows from experience and adapts to new input. We have not had to abandon that foundation in order to incorporate new ideas and even new paradigms drawn from advances in neuroscience, chaos theory, attachment theory, and psychoanalytic theory itself.

Fairbairn was the first to declare that Einstein's twentieth-century theory of relativity offered a better metaphor for a psychoanalytic model than Freud's early views modeled on nineteenth-century physics. The new model took psychoanalysis beyond the intrapsychic view of the individual as a closed predetermined system to the interpsychic understanding of the self learning and growing in a system of relationships. In this way of thinking, just as matter and energy were discovered to be inextricably related, so interactive mental processes and mental structure could not be separated. Process becomes structure and structure drives processes of interaction!

Fairbairn's student and biographer John Sutherland saw that open systems theory and information processing offered yet another paradigm shift towards a model of an autonomous ego that was an emergent structure, in open communication with the social environment and ever growing towards more complexity. Bion's writing also moves in this direction. Neither lived to see chaos theory, derived from the intersection of physics and mathematics, offer a new model for the complex processes they were describing, but with their foresight and the company of several contemporary writers, we can use the metaphor of chaos theory to update our earlier models.

Our life-long interest in the conjoint therapies, our work analyzing, writing, and teaching about families and couples, and our use of group process in teaching, have kept us always aware of the role of the family in the life of each individual, and the contributions of each individual to the couple, family, and groups of which the individual is a part. Slowly it dawned on us that the ideas we had about how family members interact required us to expand our views of development, our clinical theory, and our ideas on unconscious psychic organization. There are many threads to this story: Our continuing interest in ongoing discoveries about development, neuroscience and ethology, advances in attachment theory, and theories of the link and the field that originated in South America all give us new ways of seeing this process.

All of this culminates in the realization that we live in an unconscious field. Each of us contributes to it, and each is structured and enriched by it. Our own unconscious and affective mind is built from a mixture of what we are born with, what we are born into, and interactions we experience throughout the life-cycle with others—parents, siblings, extended family, teachers, friends, colleagues, and the wider social world. The unconscious is not individual as Freud thought: It is fundamentally interpersonal at the same time that it feels intensely our own. We are social creatures, not only in our behaviors and interactions, but in the deepest recesses of our minds. The exploration of how this is so, and what it means for individual growth and for the psychoanalytic therapies constitutes an exciting evolution of our field for the twenty-first century.

Chapter 1

The Interpersonal Unconscious

The dynamic unconscious is interpersonal in every dimension. It forms in an interpersonal matrix, it is constructed as a dynamic system of internal relationships, and it is expressed in personal choices, behaviors, and relationships. Clinical experience working analytically with couples and families and teaching and learning in groups forces us to this conclusion. We can no longer conceive of the unconscious as an individual property according to Freud's original topographic and structural theories. Even though my unconscious is unique to me, paradoxically it is also shared with intimate partners, work groups, and social groups as I engage with them in reciprocal interactions. In this state of mutual influence, their unconscious minds and mine are constantly under construction across the life cycle.

The unconscious mind develops in dynamic interaction with the unconscious field into which it is delivered. The field consists of the shared unconscious assumptions in the family and the society—repressed or ignored aspects of social life, culture, history, values, and family relationships. Infants are born into links to all that previous generations have suffered and repressed. They arrive in a nuclear family where each family member has multiple conscious and unconscious interactions with the other members in various shifting sub-groupings, and where parents interact exclusively as a couple at times. Being totally dependent, the infant has to attach to at least one parent for safety and comfort. This being necessary for survival, the infant's state of mind is intimately connected to the parent's mind and dependent on the parent's ability to imagine the infant's feelings and respond in ways to contain anxiety. The parent's capacity for imagining the baby's feelings and responding empathically are affected by the parent's unconscious feelings as a parent and an intimate partner in the present—and, as a child in the past, an early experience that comes to life again in caring for a child.

Gaze interactions, cooing conversations, cuddling, feeding, toileting, and putting to sleep are conscious behaviors filled with more or less well metabolized unconscious elements. The baby takes in these experiences, and to the extent that they were too frustrating, splits them off from good memories, and represses them. The unconsciously determined behaviors and rhythms of interaction that occur between infant and parent develop patterns that are instantiated as neural connections in the infant brain. These infant-parent patterns are broken up and attracted to new patterns as they come into contact with new patterns of relating provided by various family members and by the parental couple at various stages of development.

The parental couple holds the child in its shelter but excludes the child from its genital sexuality, which generates feelings of excitement, longing, and rejection in relation to the couple. To the extent that the parents have repressed problems at the emotional or sexual heart of the couple relationship, the child will pick up any areas of unconscious conflict and inhabit them to give life to the repressed. The parents then have to interact with that which they have wanted to avoid, and it is hard to do this when it appears in the form of the child they love and for whom they are responsible. The unconscious interaction drives experiences that create dynamic tension that affects the unconscious organization of the mind of the developing child and of the maturing parent. As the child grows to adulthood, chooses a partner and has a child, the cycle begins anew. The experiences of the previous generations and the nuclear family, recorded in mental structures that are expressed and modified within the new couple relationship, are handed down as the link into which the child is born.

This gives an outline of the concept of the interpersonal unconscious (D. Scharff and J. Scharff 2005). Now we must return to the original psychoanalytic view of the unconscious, and build from there. Gradually, we present our conception of the idea from object relations theory applied to groups and families, adding findings from link theory, chaos theory, neuroscience, and attachment research to elaborate and support our idea. Various chapters address these contributory elements in greater depth with many clinical examples to flesh out our concept of the interpersonal unconscious until the final chapter when we integrate all our ideas and apply them in a concluding clinical example. But first we need to acknowledge and define the unconscious mind originally conceived of as a dimension of the mind of the individual.

THE TRADITIONAL CONCEPT OF THE INDIVIDUAL DYNAMIC UNCONSCIOUS

Addressing the unconscious mind through studying slips, jokes, dreams, and hysterical symptoms, Freud developed his psychoanalytic view of the dynamic unconscious as a purely individual construction, as an area filled with somatic tension from the body and repressed thoughts and affects from the mind of the individual (Freud 1900, 1901, 1905a; Breuer and Freud 1893–1895). His classical followers continued to think of the unconscious mind as a property of the individual. True, his contemporary Jung (1953–1979) described the unconscious as only partly individual, the other part being collective, connected to the myths of the culture, but Freudian analysts did not subscribe to his collective idea of the unconscious. In the 1950s, Lacan (1977) returned to a study of the unconscious, and conceived of it as being complex and structured, but not connected to archetypal images, and definitely individual in nature.

Building on Freud's writings, a later generation of analysts began to study the unconscious as it affected the analytic relationship. The resulting object relations theory provided an elaborate view of how the influence of parents and the social environment on development became internalized as internal mental structure, but object relations was still essentially an individual psychology.

Freud's concept of the dynamic unconscious emerged first in *Studies on Hysteria* written with Breuer (Breuer and Freud 1893–1895) and was elaborated most famously in *The Interpretation of Dreams* (Freud 1900). In *Studies in Hysteria* bodily symptoms such as numbness, paralysis, and coughing were shown to be the physical expression of emotional distress arising from conflict between sexual and aggressive impulses located in the unconscious. Freud (1905b) thought that development proceeded along a predestined set of psychosexual stages as if this progress was not affected by the behavior of parents and significant others. His view of the unconscious was individual in origin and in nature. Freud thought that dreams represent individual wishes, and that each dream stands upon the legs of the individual's drives expressed in the various levels of psychosexual development. Dreams are constructed from wishes to express the drives, residues of daily experience, and memories of the individual's past encounters, blended into a dream narrative. However, Freud also found that hysterical symptoms arise from conflict over the expression and suppression of erotic feeling that has been stimulated prematurely by an unscrupulous adult or worse yet by a family member on whom the child depends. The child suffers from the emergence of the drives in the perpetrator, which color both the physical actions of the perpetrator and the ensuing dream narrative of the victim. Even though Freud described contributions from the interpersonal world to the construction of those pieces of evidence of unconscious functioning, his point of view remained focused on the individual unconscious.

Until now, analysts studying the unconscious not only thought of it as an individual construction, but tended to attribute it to the work of an individual—Freud alone. Yet in Breuer, Freud had had a partner in exploring the meanings of hysteria. In Freud's self-analysis, his basic tool for proving the wish-fulfillment basis of dreams, he was supported by the silent and at the time unknown correspondence partnership with Fleiss (Freud 1950). Thus the psychoanalytic elaboration of the unconscious mind has been attributed to the brilliance of one man. It is time to acknowledge that the concept of the dynamic unconscious mind was arrived at, not by one man, but by creative pairs developing their ideas together.

It was in interpersonal interaction that the psychoanalytic concept of the dynamic unconscious mind was developed, yet it was seen as a property of the individual mind, arrived at from discussion of self-analysis and demonstrated in individual analysis with hysterical patients at the turn of the twentieth century. By the 1950s, analysts were looking beyond the patient as an object of study to become interested in the unconscious quality of the relationship between analysand and analyst. Object relations theory was born, and with more attention to projective identification and countertransference, the ground was prepared for a two-body psychoanalysis, also being worked on in self psychology, relational theory, and intersubjectivity. Indeed "contemporary psychoanalysis is marked by a pluralism unknown in any prior era" with many different theories of therapeutic action (Gabbard and Westen 2003, p. 823). Whether analysts schooled in these theories conceive of therapeutic action as addressing conflicts, compromise formations, motives, defenses, links between thoughts and feelings, or parts of the self, and whether they most value interpretation or the provision of a new object relationship, a feature that their techniques have in common is that they create an interactive matrix and effect change by weakening nodes in a network of unconscious associational networks, whatever they think these nodes comprise (Gabbard and Westen 2003). It is time, more than 100 years on, to re-frame the unconscious as the product of interpersonal interaction, and as jointly held property.

Our own ideas stemmed from the clinical application of object relations ideas to couple and family analysis and to group teaching, and have since been enriched by the advances in psychoanalytic theory mentioned above, link theory, attachment research, neuroscience findings, and chaos theory. It was in family groups for therapy and stranger groups for mental health professional education that we became convinced of the interpersonal aspects of the unconscious. But it is to individual analysis that we look for our first example of the interpersonal unconscious. The second illustration is from family therapy, and the final one in this chapter is from marital sex therapy.

CLINICAL EXAMPLE FROM CHILD ANALYSIS: INTERPERSONAL TRANSMISSION OF UNCONSCIOUS AGGRESSION AND GUILT

The first example of the interpersonal origin of the unconscious shows a child is born into a link to the previous generation, how unconscious affect crosses generational boundaries, and how a parent's unconscious constellation affects the development of a child's unconscious mind.

Anne, a 10-year-old girl was in analysis with David Scharff while her mother, Janet, was in analysis with a colleague. Anne came to treatment for her paralyzing obsessive-compulsive disorder. She checked her room endlessly at bedtime for burglars, anxiously recruited her parents to soothe her and interrupt her rituals, and was preoccupied with undoing unfriendly thoughts lest someone die. She repeatedly reviewed her mistakes in schoolwork and tennis, saying, "The teacher doesn't like me. I won't pass," or "My tennis coach hates me."

In analysis, Anne's inner world remained opaque to me (DES) for some time. She attended eagerly, and showed the self she wanted me to see. An accomplished, devoted young tennis player, she often brought a racket in to the session and propped it by the door. She wrote her name in endless variations, coupled with pictures of tennis balls and rackets and sporting slogans, but gave little else. Anne opened up slowly, eventually using clay and occasional drawings, which extended the mode of her self-expression but not her range. Her initial drawings were quite stylized.

After several months Anne arrived at a drawing that pointed me to her fear of her own aggression. In the drawing (figure 1.1) a girl holding a small camera faces a cascading waterfall and behind her an expanse of water she describes as being as large as Niagara Falls. Out of the girl's sight there is a parachute with a small male figure below it above the water. When I said, "The parachutist falling in the water is interesting," she said, "Oh, no! Not interesting! I don't want to talk about that!" Anne did not want to face the aggression she had shown in putting the parachutist in position to land in the falls, unseen by the girl. This gave me, if not Anne, a clear picture of her fear in connection to her own aggression.

This drawing gave me a way of talking to Anne about anger. She admitted to frequent irritation with her brother, but I realized that he was a screen. I became convinced that her symptomatic obsessive-compulsive symptoms were fundamentally defensive against hidden anger in an anxious relationship with her mother. Her father was almost entirely spared.

Figure 1.1 Anne's Drawing

In parent sessions with me near an approaching holiday visit from Anne's grandparents, Janet, her mother, showed anxiety about seeing her parents, and resentment of Anne's mother came through. Janet told me that she had become more conscious of this anger in her own analysis, and now felt guilty about it. Like Anne, Janet had spared her father, even though she had reason to object to his minimizing her considerable childhood musical accomplishments and talent as a tennis player.

In subsequent parent sessions, it became clear that Janet also held a current grudge against her husband Bob, Anne's father, for failures and limitations similar to her mother. She did not let him off the hook the way she spared her father. Bob earned her anger by various displays of thoughtlessness and self-centeredness, even though they were mitigated by his care for Janet and the children. He was the target for Janet's lifelong anger at a maternal figure.

Now I began to see Anne's small figure of a parachutist (represented in many other ways in other sessions) as a free fall from an earlier generation, an unconscious transmission of her mother's theme: The relative failure of a parental figure that became the target of frightening unconscious anger. Just as Anne's mother had harbored a lifetime's resentment at her mother whom she also loved, Anne resented her mother, also while valuing her highly. Then, frightened to confront her mother with her anger, Anne sacrificed another internal figure, a small and inconsequential male, the parachutist who represented her brother. But the guilty unconscious recognition of the murderous effect of her anger haunted her every day, making her fear that with one slip her anger could literally kill the objects of her love. Now I could see that the constellation of diminishing and killing off a male as a substitute for anger at a mother was an unconscious constellation shared by mother and daughter.

We must ask the question of the link between these two similar patterns of guilty mother-daughter resentment. How was it transmitted, when Anne's mother was so caring of Anne, so good with her in so many ways? The answer lies in Janet's wish to avoid the realization that Anne is coming to hate her the way she unconsciously hated her mother. Janet let Anne run roughshod over her while conscientiously doing all the things for her that she felt her own mother had not. Because of unconscious guilt, Janet saw the threat of retribution from Anne, and Anne must have seen that fear in her mother's eyes. The projective identification of resentment and guilt took hold in Anne and evoked the very behavior in Anne about which Janet herself felt guilty.

The image of the parachutist provides the link between the top of the page and the bottom, and symbolically between the generations. As a male parachutist, he is an envied boy, free of the daughter's dilemma with her mother, the butt of Anne's jealous rage, independent and daring, yet going to his fate, much as her father became Anne's mother's sacrificial target. Anne's father and brother, males together, are also unconsciously blamed for not compensating for failures in mothering.

Unconscious states of mind are passed transgenerationally, identified with, and shared painfully by parent and child. Recurrent interactions imbued with parental anxiety create a battleground in which parent and child become the source of each other's misery in current life. Healthy families also share unconscious fear but learn to negotiate, accept, develop mutual holding, and transform the embedded objects to clear paths of development. Families without such resilience need therapy to resolve their battles.

Freud extrapolated his theoretical position from the interplay between his creative mind, his experience as a neurologist, and his work with individual adults under hypnosis and later in psychoanalysis. Since then psychoanalysis has extended its reach. We are now able to treat children and infants, and to apply analytic theories to the study and treatment of couple and family dynamics. This gives us a broader base for examining unconscious influences on communication and behavior, and the cycle of mutual influence on the formation of individual and family structure.

Working as analysts and family therapists, we have come to understand that all aspects of mind are constructed in the crucible of interpersonal and intersubjective interaction. Parents lend their minds to their newborn infant, whose brain, with its profusion of neurons, is hard-wired to make full use of interaction with the adult mind. The infant brain responds to parental affect by neurological receptive activity that leads to neurologically mediated muscular activity to express affect, and this response cycle creates neurological links that build the infant's mind (Schore 2003a). In fact, it seems the infant brain is structured not only to receive signals but also to reach out and seek the adult input, and use it to organize at progressively higher levels. The brain and developing mind are built to be proactively interpersonal (Freeman 2007).

The infant brain is born with a surfeit of neurons. Healthy brain development results from pruning the number of neurons while increasing connectivity in an endless chaotic cycle of feedback in multiple interactional sequences. The brain matures when the rich complexity of neuronal growth is firmly connected to the components of the brain. While maturation occurs in this way at the neurological level, at the psychological level the mind differentiates by splitting into specialized parts that then interconnect to form a disseminated, dynamic system.

Long before we had access to brain scan studies, Fairbairn (1952) wrote that the infant was born with a pristine ego, which then became split in the process of development in response to experience that was felt as good (and therefore desirable) or bad (and needing to be pushed away), but the interaction between these split parts of the mind always tended towards higher levels of integration. This was Fairbairn's way of describing the opposing yet collaborating forces of deconstruction and construction, a necessary paradox that we can see at every level from brain architecture up to the maturation of the mind and its ability to conceive of self and otherness (Schore 2003a). The interpersonal environment is crucial to this development. That environment consists of the constant interplay of the mind with other minds, at intimate levels and at every stage of development. Each individual mind is built to reach out to other minds that then infuse the brain structure and mental architecture of each individual mind.

It has been obvious that language and logical thinking evolve from discourse with others, that parents who speak more to their infants have children with larger vocabularies and capacities for abstract thinking. But only in the last quarter century, thanks to the research on neurological growth and affect regulation, do we know that the same is true for emotional growth. Now we know that the parents' rich and continual interplay with the infant produces, in the first instance, enhancement of growth in the right brain where the affective range and emotional intelligence of the child are potentiated.

The *left* brain, seat of the verbal and logical mind, which we have always known grew from the stimulation of being spoken to by parents, does not catch up until 18 months of age. Joining the image to the word stimulates activity in the corpus callosum, the brain structure that connects the two hemispheres, and promotes integrated mental functioning.

The optimal situation for the growth of the infant's *right* orbito-frontal cortex, the executive of the emotional brain, is a positively toned parent-infant relationship. And we now think of this part of the right brain as the headquarters of the Freudian unconscious and of unconscious modes of thinking and processing experience (Schore 2002).

In their studies of emotional development during early attachment, Fonagy, Gergely, Jurist, and Target (2003) describe the infant's move from initially needing the parent to regulate the infant's emotional state (for instance by soothing the overexcited, comforting the fearful, or stimulating the apathetic) until the child can become capable of autonomous regulation of affect, a capacity inherited from experience with the parents and always imbued with the resonance of its origins in a partnership of co-regulation.

Severe anxieties in the attachment relationship, neglect, and trauma during the growing years shut down the process of development of the brain and mind, and actually produce smaller brains. The right brain shows impoverished and constrained connectedness, and the emotional mind located there operates on a reflex basis, with little flexibility or modulation. More specifically, with repeated experience of threat and danger, leading to a chronic heightening of fear, the right amygdala, the seat of the fearful response reflex, is seriously over stimulated. The amygdalae fire off automatically before the orbitofrontal cortex can check what is happening and modulate the reflex to an appropriate level of response (Schore 1994, 2003b). So the individual is left with an impaired capacity to delay, review experience, and respond thoughtfully. The result is an emotional short circuit to fear, a rapid move to defensiveness against incoming information from the interpersonal world.

CLINICAL EXAMPLE FROM ANALYTIC FAMILY THERAPY: UNCONSCIOUS CONFLICT AND INCESTUOUS DESIRE

In the next example, a child's symptom of cheating in school calls attention to unconscious conflict over a parent's secret enactment of an incestuous desire and leads to confusion in the family as a defense against recognition and pain. Confused thinking appears to blur the issue, and is so powerful that it becomes shared unconscious confusion in the countertransference. This example of family therapy with David Scharff shows the unconscious being constructed interpersonally and countertransference interpretation enabling the therapist to point out how the interpersonal unconscious has been a factor in learning disability.

Mick came to treatment because he had been caught cheating on a final exam in his senior year in high school, a seemingly gratuitous act since he was already accepted in college and had a good grade in the class in which he cheated. Mick's attention deficit and hyperactivity disorder, learning problems, and difficulty making friends had marked his earlier development, but in the last two years at a regular school he had done well.

When I (DES) met with Mick, his parents, and his sister for family treatment, it took me some time to discover that Mick was not the only one cheating. Growing up as an only child in a well-to-do professional family, Mick's father had been an underachieving cut-up, always a disappointment to his own prominent father. Then in adulthood it had taken him a long time to address his alcoholism successfully. So he had been personally invested in Mick's serious attempt to overcome his learning disability and social awkwardness.

Mick was puzzled by his cheating, and his only hypothesis was that he was driven to it by his mother's saying, "It's not acceptable to do badly on your math exam." He felt it was hard to satisfy his mother, by whom he felt pushed.

The discussion soon turned to the battles between Mick's parents. These ostensibly exclude Mick, and yet they are a matter of grave concern to him. He often intervenes to get his parents to stop, sometimes stepping in to take on his mother about something else in order to draw fire to himself. Mick and his father frequently align against the mother, while Mick's sister, Mary, sides with her mother. Father said he never saw his own parents fight—but then Mother reminded him that was because his parents were hardly ever with him, while he was raised by nannies. He had shrouded his parents in a mist of idealization, and could not see what they or he had truly felt.

Father then talked about how his wife's accusations would cause immense pain. Yet the substance of the argument was forgotten by the next day. For instance, she said she didn't know how she could be married to him after what he had done. But what he had done was completely obscured. Mother alluded to some upsetting things that father had brought out inappropriately. Or did she mean that it was the thing itself that was inappropriate? I could not tell. It was unclear what they were actually talking about. The children looked bored and dazed. I began to feel I could not think clearly. In the midst of this obfuscation I asked the children what they were hearing. Mary said that she really zones out, but she's learned that is just because of her learning disability. Mick said he was really confused about what his parents were trying to say, but that's because, like Mary, his learning ability makes him zone out.

Fighting confusion, I grew slowly aware that I was experiencing a shared unconscious state. The children had experienced the state and retreated from it, attributing it to their learning disabilities. I felt that the parents created this confusional state in the family by their intentional vagueness and refusal to speak clearly, presumably because they were afraid of what they might say. I now said that I thought they had been obfuscating to defend themselves from knowledge. Mother said that my language had confused her, and asked me to translate. I explained that "obfuscating" means throwing mud over a situation so that it can't be seen clearly. I said that in this session the parents were talking about something far wrong but not saying what it was, raising anxiety and creating confusion. I added that it could be that the children's learning disabilities, which they claimed as the cause of their "zoning out," may have been learned by taking in this confused climate between the parents. Mick looked interested, alert, and focused on the discussion for the first time. I asked if this pattern of allusion and obfuscation characterized the parents' fights. They said that this might well be so, but that they thought the children did not understand what they were fighting about, and therefore would not be affected.

Mary interjected in defense of her parents, "No! It's in my brain. It's a brain pattern."

"True," I said, "but the brain is responsive to interactions around it."

Father seconded me. "I've read new research that says the brain is plastic and molds itself into new patterns and that attention centers can get stronger with different experience." He looked meaningfully at Mary.

Turning to the parents, I asked, "What is it exactly that Father has done that makes Mother say she doesn't know if she can be married to him?"

The question hit home. After a pause, Mother said, "We've never told the children about it, and I don't like to say it."

Father interrupted, "I'd better say it. Our marriage almost broke up ten years ago. I had gone to New York to check on my wife's niece who had run away from home. I found her lap dancing at a strip club. I was still drinking a lot then, and I came on to her. I've been deeply remorseful for that, and realized immediately I had to stop drinking. My wife has never trusted me since then. Getting her to trust me has been so important to me, but I often feel I just don't pass the test."

"You and Mick are both in the situation of trying to pass a test that is important to Mother but impossible to do," I said. "Mick and Mary have shown the kind of confusion that develops in the atmosphere of not being able to discuss the dangers to the family. This one event didn't cause everything, but not talking about it makes learning difficult. It is part of a shared unconscious attitude that danger to the parental couple must be obfuscated. You assume clear thinking will lead to danger rather than to safe solutions. Fighting between parents is too dangerous to face, and so the children zone out and have trouble concentrating because of their need to protect their parents' relationship."

On her way out Mother said she was going to look up "that word obfuscation." She would like to understand it more clearly.

In this session, we see a core moment of shared unconscious confusion among family members and therapist, which represents the family's chronic way of dealing with their internal danger. The children's difficulty learning, and Mick's pointed symptom of cheating to avoid failing the test, organize the family-wide unconsciously maintained style of not thinking clearly. The moment of Mick's anticipated departure from the family represents a crisis about whether he can pass the test, and he echoes his father's "cheating" when looking for a lost soul, threatening the family's ability to trust his competence.

This is certainly not the whole story of Mick's symptomatic act and his learning difficulty, but it shows the significance of the system of unconscious interpersonal communication among family members that defines the functioning of his unconscious and the form of the expression of his compromise formations. The example shows that the members of a family cooperate to induce a state of mind in one another and produce symptomatic behavior in Mick that draws attention to a hidden problem. Mick's solo cheating episode both expresses and reinforces a shared family unconscious state of mind about men who fail the test and, in their anxiety to pass it, turn impulsively to cheating. This unconscious family organization is echoed in each family member in a different way—in the learning difficulty of both children, in mother's almost paranoid checking up and mistrust, and in father's desperation to prove himself and in his anxiety over the children's success. Finally, we see that the confusion the therapist felt and then worked his way out of, was an unconscious experience he shared with the family, a countertransference that enabled him to make the interpretation vivid, immediate, and therefore understandable.

Our argument for the interpersonal origin of all aspects of unconscious affect is in keeping with the modern view developed by Schore (2003) and others that the right brain is the seat of Freud's unconscious, and that its highest level executive functions are housed in the right orbitofrontal cortex. Fonagy et al. (2003) and Freeman (2007) show us that the entire brain, but especially the affective right brain, is interpersonally constructed and interpersonally regulated, and that this interpersonal aspect is maintained to some extent throughout life. We are all emotionally primed and educated to read others' minds. How does this happen? We used to say it must be communicated by micro behaviors or possibly pheromones, all too imperceptible for scientific detection. With the benefit of brain research, we can now say that this communication occurs at the neurological level through the action of mirror neurons (Rizzolatti, et al 2006; Rizzolatti and Craighero 2004; Gallese 2009). Rizzolatti and his colleagues noted that when person A observes person B doing something, neurons in A that are sited next to, and that fire alongside, A's motor neurons, now also fire as if A were active motorically, even though A only passively observes the action. Similarly if A notices affective behavior in B, the neurons that would produce the feeling in A fire off. Thus there is brain activity in the mind of an observer that instantiates the action state of the person observed—and emotions are experienced through internal body action.

We are built to know things about one another in non-verbal, primarily affective ways—that is, through our constant keen right brain interaction and communication, which happens ten times faster than left brain, verbal communication (Schore 2003a and b.) This communication is heightened with individuals in an analytic therapeutic relationship, where the task is to study problems in affective communication. Right brain communication is the basis for analytic listening, resonating with affect, empathy, and knowing the patient. It is at the core of the increasing use of transference-countertransference interaction as the principal global positioning system of analysis. Its importance was acknowledged in Strachey's (1934) plea for employing transference interpretation as the main agent of therapeutic action, but it was not until Winnicott (1947), Heimann (1950) Racker (1968), and others studied the role of countertransference that the ground was set for recognizing reciprocal unconscious communication in psychoanalysis (Scharff and Scharff 1998b.) Now the analyst must not only tune her receptive unconscious toward the patient like a radio receiver (Freud 1912) to listen to the unspoken messages generated by the patient, but must also verbalize the messages, a new way of making unconscious conscious, of bridging the cross-brain gap between right and left minds, between secondary and primary process.

How are these messages sent and received? Freud noted projection as a defense for getting rid of an unwanted idea (1911) and identification as a way of holding on to the lost object (1917). But it was Klein (1946) who saw that infants identify with what has been projected, good or bad. Her idea was that the constitutionally-determined death instinct poses a threat to the viability of the self and gives rise to annihilation anxiety. Too much of that anxiety, and the infant has to deflect the death instinct and project the resulting anxiety into the mother to get rid of it. Then the projection colors the mother with that anxiety and makes her seem persecutory. To cope with fear and rage now felt to be emanating from the mother, the infant resorts to introjective identification with the persecutory object evoked in her, to take it inside the self and control it there. Fortunately the hope-filled force of the life instinct creates positive images of the mother that counteract the terror.

Klein (1928) also held that the infant's perceptions of the parents as a couple were the beginning of the Oedipus complex. Infants deal with unconscious fantasies about the nature of their parents' coupling by projective and introjective identification. Depending on the projection of life or death drive material, they imagine the parents locked in endless bliss like a feeding frenzy, or in a tussle to the death. These unconscious fantasies arouse feelings of greed, envy, longing to merge with them, and hatred for being excluded. From this they develop a mental concept of themselves in relation to a couple, and that will determine their future choices of intimate partners in adulthood.

Like Freud, however, Klein maintained an individual focus on the powerfully driven infant, and wrote little about the influence of the actual mother or the parental couple on the baby. This bias was corrected with the contributions of Winnicott and Bion. Winnicott (1947) wrote about the mother's role in detoxifying hate. Bion (1970) developed the concept of containment, the mother's capacity to introjectively identify with her infant, sense the infant's experience, subject it to process and review, and so understand the infant in depth and give back to the infant a capacity for managing experience. These developments led to the realization that projective and introjective processes are interpersonal, mutual and in constant unconscious interplay in all intimate relationships.

In the therapeutic relationship, processes of projective and introjective identification provide the basis for empathy, sustained alliance, transference and countertransference, and therapeutic action. In the intimate couple relationship sexuality brings an exquisite physicality that recalls the intense experience of being held and handled during the infant years. Sexual interaction leads to the unconscious projection of images drawn from early experience into the partner via bodily communication, creating a state of shared unconscious communication. Then unconscious fantasies resonate and are introjected in ways that bring an integrative pleasure, build the couple's bond, and produce growth. When the projections do not fit, are refused, or are overwhelmingly destructive, and when the couple lacks a good containing function, the projective-introjective identificatory process becomes stuck and the couple relationship is then in a painful unconscious stalemate that stultifies growth.

Freud's early description of an infant powered by the pleasure principle, expending energy in relation to various bodily zones at various psychosexual stages was followed by Klein's version of the anxious infant who expends energy by off-loading excesses of constitutionally given aggression. Then came Winnicott's (1960a) description of the infant employing a false self (a more conscious self) to guard the true self (an inner, unconscious self) against the assault of the other's demands. Recent work on the mother–infant attachment has described the way an intrusive mother can be introjected as an alien object installed inside the self where it constantly threatens the self from inside (Fonagy et al. 2003). Freud and Klein believed that what is happening in the unconscious life of the child turns on the idea of there being a constitutional structure that determines what will happen. They held that this structure is centrally involved in dialogue with the structures of other people and develops in relation to them.

More recently, researchers point to the activity of the "unrepressed unconscious," those aspects of mental activity that function outside of consciousness. Automatic skills like riding a bicycle, catching a ball, or making love are non-conscious and rely on implicit knowing (Stern 2004). This kind of competence is distinct from both conscious verbalized knowledge and the dynamic unconscious. But it is not only motor skill that operates in the non-conscious sphere. Stern also writes that, "knowing how to be with others resides in implicit knowing" (Stern 2004, p. 115). This is "a form of procedural knowledge regarding how to do things with intimate others, knowledge we call 'implicit relational knowing'" (Lyons-Ruth 1998, p. 282). Stern and Lyons-Ruth and their colleagues of the Boston Process of Change Study Group trace the origin of implicit relational knowing to repeated interactional processes from birth onward.

Trevarthan (2009) suggests that the psychobiology of human meaning is rooted in cooperative rhythms and communications between infants and their parents. This can be seen to rest on what Gallese (2009) has termed *embodied simulation* in which the mirror neuron system instantiates our experience of others deep in our brains, and differentiates others based on their importance to the self. Ammaniti and Trentini (2009) have conducted fMRI research showing the activation of the mirror neuron system of parents in response their infants' emotional situations. This points to the discovery of a primary intersubjective system not only with mother and child, but with fathers and in the family triad as well (Fivaz-Depeursinge and Corboz-Warnery 1999, quoted in Ammaniti and Trentini). Emde (2009) suggests that there is a primary sense of we-ness, attributable to the beginnings of social referencing in the second six months, a sense of being part of a pair, a sense of *we-go* rather than *ego*. Taken together, these findings suggest that the interpersonal aspects of development are primary close to the beginning of life, and that interpersonal experience informs all levels of emotional and mental development including that of the unconscious.

Clinical Example from a Couple Relationship: Sex Embodies Internal Object Relations

Any solo motor act, including sexual function, desire, and response, is the property of the individual, which does not gainsay the fact that aspects of these skills had to be learned interpersonally. Even masturbation is interpersonal in that it usually involves erotic fantasies of others as loved ones or desired images (D. Scharff 1982). In mature sexuality, the individual motor act of sexual function is expressed in relation to a significant other, and so becomes a dual act of mutual pleasure in which motoric and receptive sensory experience, self and other, are in harmony.

In this final example of a couple therapy assessment with David and Jill Scharff, we want to illustrate that a couple's sexual relationship, including both its emotional and physical configuration, expresses unconscious elements that belong jointly to the couple. Then, these are communicated through the couple's shared projective identification to therapists in the clinical situation. We view sex as the physical aspect of emotional intimacy, imbued with all the coloring of the partners' internal object relations, fantasies, hopes and fears, based on their resonating with unconscious conflict in the family of origin. In a couple, intimate relating creates a meld of their unconscious structures and a re-organization in the marital joint personality. The sexual relationship converts individual and shared emotional unconscious issues into shared bodily interaction, and any problems in the sexual relationship are intimately expressive of the couple's shared unconscious.

Larry and Rachel, now in their mid 50s, had been married 25 years when they came to see us. They loved and respected each other, but they had not had sex in 10 years. In the first meeting, Rachel gave the story at length and with full emotional expression while Larry sat looking immobile and depressed. Rachel said, "I don't want to end our marriage but the problem is that Larry thinks he will die if he stays in the marriage."

Jill cut in to say, "Rachel has been giving the story so far. I want to be sure Larry doesn't die right now in this session. You've been silent, Larry, so where are you in this meeting?"

Larry said, "I do want to be in the meeting, but not in the marriage. I want to move out and live three blocks away from Rachel and the family, and visit Rachel if she'll have me." He did not want away from Rachel. He wanted away from the sexual expectations of the marriage.

Their marriage had been mostly a-sexual. Larry felt he was intimidated by women, stemming from the time his father abandoned the family when he was 11, leaving Larry with his exhibitionistic mother and two voluptuous older sisters. Years in therapy had not changed his fear of women, and especially of Rachel's impervious control. He said, "I feel Rachel is a Teflon Woman. She takes my complaints about her and turns them back on me to prove there is something wrong with me. I'm not a bad person. I'm decent and loving. Rachel is loving, too, but she's a schoolmarm who wags her finger at me. I feel subtly rebuked. I feel like a visitor in my own home. And I am still affected by the affairs she's had, the first with her boss while she was pregnant with our daughter. So I still can't enjoy a lovely photo of her with our daughter because I think of the affair. Then anger blocked my desire. Sex became a problem that it hadn't been before. We had sex maybe five times after that, and then it was finished. Then there was another affair four years ago with an employee under her management." Turning to Rachel, he said, "Sorry to expose you here."

Rachel said it had to be talked about with us, but after Larry described a bit more of the situation, she corrected the way he described the affairs (making us think she did indeed criticize him easily). She continued, "It was totally humiliating. Both the affairs were kind of abusive, but the worst was that after the second one, I was exposed and fired. Although I got another job, it was a terrible public ordeal. It was horrible for Larry, too."

Larry said, "I know I must be responsible for Rachel's unhappiness, and in that sense for the affairs, too. She had promised after the first one never to have another, and then she did it with an employee. But she was so humiliated and in so much trouble, there was no question of leaving her. And then her father died. I couldn't leave her then."

Rachel volunteered, "He was very supportive through all that."

As they continued the story, there was a note of pathos, mutual suffering, loving, and losing. Rachel explained, "Larry's loss of interest in sex was a powerful blow. I was alone and desperate. The affairs came from that. It wasn't what I thought I was signing up for—he had been excitingly sexual when we courted. I saw him as sexually sophisticated, much more so than I. He was into Playboy stuff, and I thought I would learn from him. But once the commitment was made, he just turned off. I remember one time I tried to be playful with a Playboy centerfold, but he felt I was making fun of him. It was a total fizzer."

"I don't remember it that way," Larry said. "I remember laughing like hell and tickling you. I remember liking the joke, but I don't remember whether there was sex."

David said, "This difference in the memory seems to be the point. Rachel remembers it as a spoiled attempt to appeal that typifies the sense that Larry can't get it right. Larry remembers it as a good time, whether it led to sex or not. This difference in the memories is part of what troubles you and we need to understand."

Jill asked Rachel about her growing up, wondering if something abusive in her history accounted for her involvement later in abusive affairs. At first Rachel described her parents as happy together, but then revealed that her mother was totally dependent on her father, who looked to Rachel in turn to take care of her mother. "I've always taken care of her, and now I take care of everyone."

"Who took care of you?" Jill asked.

Rachel shrugged, "I did."

"So when Larry couldn't deal with your needs, just as your mother failed to, you took care of him, and turned to someone else to meet your needs," Jill said.

"I did, just like in the affairs. And this last affair led to public humiliation. But I was desperate. I had no one to turn to. I was so lonely."

Larry interjected, "That's the dead elephant between us."

David said, "The lack of sex was the elephant in the room of your marriage."

Jill said, "True, but Larry said, the 'dead elephant' which makes me think of death. I see a man dying over and over as if at this moment I am you over and over facing the scene of your father leaving."

Larry ignored this, and went on to discuss how their previous therapist had understood him to have a "Madonna-whore complex." He said, "I do feel sexual desire and I masturbate to erotic pictures, but I feel no lust for Rachel."

When the interview was drawing to a close, David said, "I'm thinking of how unhappy you have both been for years, and how you, Larry, feel you're dying in this marriage but can't leave. I feel you stayed for your children."

"I would die for my children!" Larry said.

David said, "I think you did die for your children!"

Larry looked stunned. "Thank you!" he said. "That's absolutely right!"

Rachel said, "I feel accused of being the agent of the death of the marriage and of killing Larry."

Jill said to Larry, "I think it's a second death. Larry, you died when your father left. Then, when you slept close to your mother and sister in a tiny apartment, you killed your sexual desire to keep them safe from you without having to leave them. You had to kill the manly desiring part of you. Since then you've given Rachel the feeling of always being left by her man, over and over, just as you were left by your father. You put your pain about that abandonment by your father into her, and then she has put it back into you through her affairs. Since then, sex has stood for the pain of mutual abandonment."

Larry said, "The irony is that after I left home, my father actually came back. He had been rejected by the woman he left for, and had lived alone in a rooming house for years. My mother took him back, and they lived together until he died."

David said, "But it was too late for you. Only when you didn't need him, and after you had missed him all those years, he came back, not for your sake but to depend on your mother. Now you're afraid to depend on Rachel, to come back to her. And the plan you have is to live in a rooming house near her. That echoes your father's sad life. On your side Rachel, you felt your mother abandoned you by not taking care of you, by making you the mother, and by your father who expected you to mother your mother. Now that scenario repeats in sexual terms: Larry is not caring for you sexually and asking you to do the caring of him anyway."

Larry said, "We love each other. We are good partners in everything but this. It seems hopeless. It's so sad."

David said, "The sad feeling as we near the end of this session stems from desperately wishing for, and not finding, the care from each other that has been missing all your lives."

"Yes," said Jill. "Rachel you lived out your desperation in the affairs. Larry has died a thousand deaths. You both share the unfulfilled longing for a person who seems dead to each of you—the dead elephant in the room."

The sense of death of love after years of unfulfilled longing had permeated life for both Larry and Rachel. Sex in the beginning of their relationship had offered fulfillment, but from the moment of commitment, their repressed rejecting, painful objects had come to the fore in a dramatic to-and-fro that began, perhaps, with Larry's feeling threatened by episodes of Rachel's acting critically, followed by his withdrawal, resulting in her feeling unloved, her mounting resentment, his increasing withdrawal, her desperate attempt at repair with the affairs, his increasing hurt. And so, in an accumulating death spiral, they had collaborated unconsciously to produce the dead elephant that occupied almost the whole room of their marriage. In this way, the unconscious sharing of a legacy of feeling unloved (by his father and her mother) and feeling impinged on by each of their mother's demands, combined over time to push out the hopes that sexual love and all it conveyed could repair the sense of death. They came to share a resonating unconscious image of death and futility, spoken for by the dead elephant image in the session.

The work of the session involved taking in the feeling of their difficulty directly, and then working from inside our own experience to make conscious what was at first unconscious to us. First we opened our selves to allow unconscious communication, coming thereby to share a mood in resonance with them. Then we each became alert to hidden meanings in Larry's phrase, "the dead elephant," and worked to make sense of our feeling of sadness and longing, and to find out what his slip meant to us and to them. Allowing the affective tone and the slip to affect us unconsciously, and then using the slip to make the underlying situation conscious, we could arrive at understanding which gradually became conscious to all of us.

When we ended the session, we understood that Larry still had every intention of leaving. So we were surprised when, a week later, the couple called. The session had, they said, brought new hope for a life together, and they asked to begin couple therapy. The therapy began, and as it did, it developed a pattern of lively, engaged sessions alternating with dead time. As soon as we connected and got moving on a theme, absences interrupted the flow of the work, but at the same time delivered into the treatment the very problem of the relationship, the death of love and hope by unmetabolized dead objects.

The couple conveyed their enormous longing in their body language and in the quality of their emotional expression, more than in their well chosen words. The therapists began to resonate emotionally with their mutual frustration, sadness, and futility. The depth of their unconscious suffering and the structure of their relational difficulty had been instantiated in us through projective and introjective identification conveyed at a basic level through our mirror neurons (Gallese 2003b, 2009).

We have presented this and other examples to show how unconscious fantasies people the individual unconscious with images of significant object relationships. The death and life instincts—or the aggressive and libidinal forces—and the projective and introjective identificatory processes do their work hand in hand—like balancing activity of the neurons connecting furiously and at the same time pruning themselves—to create balanced images of the good and bad aspects of self and mother, self and parental couple, perceived under the influence of the instincts.

The family is an intimate small group held together at its core by mutual projective and introjective identification at all levels of psychic organization—from the marital couple at its centre to each individual, there being many possible relationship combinations among parents, children, siblings, and extended family. In couples and families deprivation and trauma narrow and distort the capacity for an accurately resonating projective identificatory system, whereas positively toned interactions promote growth in the capacity to tolerate negative experience and affect even as they install a secure background of optimism and potential for growth. The positive family develops a shared unconscious that is able to communicate in a fluid way with the conscious life of the family, giving it life and color, movement, and affect. This supports the individual family members to grasp opportunities for learning from good experience and so nourish parts of the self that need to grow and reintegrate into the whole personality.

In communication with that family unconscious, and with the unconscious life of the couple relationship, the individual unconscious forms and keeps on forming at the various stages of development. In health, the dynamic unconscious communicates with and supports the functioning of the autonomous self (J. Scharff 1996). When the child or adolescent seeks play-mates and peers, or the adult chooses friends and colleagues, the unconscious pieces must fit and yet be dissimilar enough for there to be room for new learning and growth. When the adult eventually commits to a life partner, it is the quality of the unconscious that determines the nature of the choice. A couple relationship is born, two individuals ready to nurture children in the bosom of their shared unconscious. So the cycle repeats.

SUMMARY

The Interpersonal Unconscious is interpersonally constructed, expressed, and maintained. It is constructed from infancy onward via spoken and unspoken communication between infant and parents. It is interpersonally expressed in interaction with family, friends, and colleagues throughout life and interpersonally experienced in intimate relationships, including psychotherapeutic ones. It remains interpersonally active as it continues to grow and learn from the wider social environment.

Chapter 2

The Link

In the last 60 years, most English-speaking psychoanalytic writers interested in the mutual influence of people on one another in couples, families, and groups were looking to and contributing to the literature of object relations theory. Meanwhile, a parallel literature on the theory of *"el vinculo"* translated as *"link theory"* was developing. It thrived at first in South America, developed from contributions by Pichon-Rivière in Argentina in the 1950s and more recently from Kaës and others in Europe. Link theory and object relations theory explore closely related concepts. In examining the overlap between them, we hope to spark a dialogue between the English-speaking focus on the object relations and the European and Latin preference for the link, and so extend both literatures.

First, the term *link* needs some more elaboration. English-speaking analysts might think of *link* as a ring connecting two other rings, signifying the link between two people, each of whom is a subject and not merely the object of the other. This meaning is suggested by translating *vinculo* as *bond*, but bond refers to an attachment, which does not do justice to the complexity of the idea of *vinculo*. The link is not only the bond but also the space and all the connections within which the bond forms. It is closer to the meaning of *vinculo* to imagine a chain link, each link connecting to other links in many directions along the fence. This gets us closer to the complexity of the concept of the link. So, in this chapter, we use the word "link," which is the usual translation of the South American *vinculo*, and we reserve the word "bond" for its usual English common-sense meaning.

At this point, we need to distinguish between the English language and South American uses of the word "link." In psychoanalytic literature, the word "link" is used in the sense intended in the writing of Klein and Bion.

Klein (1975a, 1975b) described the interaction between male and female elements in the baby's perception of parental intercourse, and between breast and baby in connection to the link between thought and feeling or its absence. In the Oedipal period—which begins very early for Klein—the joining of male and female elements represents an advance over earlier modes of splitting of perception and thinking, and is part of the growing child's capacity to tolerate the idea of parental intercourse (Klein 1945). This integrative capacity is a feature of the depressive position in which the child becomes able to experience whole objects with ambivalence and gratitude. For Klein, the word link refers to the joining of elements, and the linking of ideas that belong together, as happens in the interpretive process. Then in his influential paper "Attacks on Linking" (1967a), Bion took English-language ownership of the word "link" by describing the connecting of thought and affect in the healthy development of mind, and their disconnecting when attacked by mental processes invaded by the death drive.

Although arriving by different routes and in different languages, internal object relations theory and link theory were both well established by the late 1960s and do overlap, although they differ in specifics. Object relations emphasizes the construction of internal dynamics from formative interpersonal experience and their separate, subsequent influence on external relationships. The link emphasizes the intermediate area, the mutual construction of a shared organization resulting from the simultaneous contribution of interacting individuals to the shared interactional pattern, and, at the same time, the role of that shared pattern in organizing the individuals. It is not until the 1960s and later that object relations theory began to address the same area as the link: analysts applied object relations concepts to couple and family therapy, developing such concepts as the "joint marital personality" of Dicks (1967) or "the analytic third" of Ogden (1994), "unconscious basic assumptions" of Bion (1961), the "social unconscious" of Hopper (2003), and "intersubjectivity" (Stolorow and Atwood 1992; Beebe and Lachmann 2002). These English language terms refer to overarching patterns that are in the same territory as the link, but the link concept and the complexity it embraces came first. Link theory encompasses the family, the social group, the preceding generations, and the individual. It fleshes out object relations studies of the intergenerational transmission of relational patterns, as seen for instance in studies on the transmission of attachment patterns or the transmission of trauma between generations (Faimberg 2005; J. Scharff and D. Scharff 1994, 2006).

On the other hand, in the English-language literature on object relations, the close study of the early mother–infant relationship as a foundation for internal and external development, and the use of transference and countertransference in the clinical setting bring in-depth understanding of the centrality of early relationships and holding environments. We believe that as we bring the two literatures into closer approximation, they complement each other in generative ways.

THE WORK OF PICHON-RIVIÈRE

Building on ideas of Fairbairn and others, Pichon-Rivière introduced the concept of "*el vinculo*" translated as "the link." For Pichon-Rivière, the individual's psyche is built on the twin pillars of the constitution of the internal world and the influence of the social. He defined the link as expressing *both* internal object relations and the external interactions of people or subjects with each other. Whereas the earliest English-speaking psychoanalytic studies of the individual had a single focus on *either* the influence of internal object relations on the person's relations with the external world *or* the effects of the external world on the internal object relations, Pichon-Rivière's interest was, from the beginning, a dual focus on the two-way, complex, mutual influence of the internal world on external relations and of the external world on internal object relations throughout life.

Pichon-Rivière developed his ideas from his reading of Fairbairn some years earlier than Dicks's elaborations of Fairbairn and Bion's elaborations of Klein. He taught a lot, but he wrote little, and nothing is translated in English yet, and so we have to construct our understanding of his ideas from secondary sources. Here is the concept from Pichon-Rivière as we understand it: The link is the connection between people, activated by infantile needs for love, nurturance, care, feeding and knowing. It consists of subjects in interaction taking each other inside through introjective and projective identification to form the interior world of each of them. Individuals are born into and shaped by a field that has two organizational dimensions, which Pichon-Rivière described as a vertical axis and a horizontal axis. The vertical axis links each person to previous generations and to the history and culture into which they are born. The horizontal axis links each person to family and wider current social groups, for instance the "village" in which each person lives. These links are formed by infantile need—the needs for love, care, understanding, containment of frustration and aggression, and sexual expression and fulfillment—and they persist throughout life. The link forms a super-ordinate structure, fed by interpersonal interaction. In this way, mutual conscious interaction sets the stage, but unconscious interaction plays the more powerful and continual role.

Internal and external worlds are joined by the link, which therefore has a transitional quality between these two worlds. For Pichon-Rivière the link originates in individual need (a concept that he uses to replace drives). Like Fairbairn (1952; D. Scharff and Birtles 1994) Pichon-Rivière saw needs as acquiring meaning in the relationships that shape the individuals. Needs have qualities, including goodness and badness, that characterize particular links. These qualities color aspects of truth, falsehood, deception, integrity, attack, perversion, healing, scapegoating, and so on. In given cases we can characterize particular links according to their function in the field in which they operate.

The link is expressed in all individual and interactive productions: dreams, symptoms, acts towards others, and bodily experiences. Even those acts or symptoms that seem to be most distinctly individual contain aspects of relatedness. For instance the dream seems to be an individual production but it also expresses both internal object relations and communicates aspects of current relationships.

In object relations theory, the terms "internal" and "external" objects have been used specifically to differentiate between what goes on inside a person and in relationship with others. More than that, object relations theorists have had a dual focus on the communication between external and internal object relations, shown in Klein's concept of projective and introjective identification, Bion on containment, and Fairbairn on introjection, splitting and repression, but none of them focus specifically on the space between. Winnicott does focus on the potential space and on transitional objects but not on the quality of the space in connection to earlier generations. Writing in the tradition of object relations theory but with access to family and couple therapy, we have contributed to the study of how each person's primary objects both influence and are influenced by internal object relations, or to be more exact, by the continuing dynamic constellation of internal relations between self and object (D. Scharff 1982, 1992; D. Scharff and J. Scharff 1991, 1987; J. Scharff and D. Scharff 1998c, 2006.)

Each person in a family is a subject of the link and subjected by the link. The link is in the space between the family members and in the space between the nuclear family and the other generations. Tension between the child's drives for love, nurture, and safety and the capacity of the outer world to meet and regulate those needs creates the link and determines the structure of the child's psyche. The child's psyche is molded by the legacy of the previous generations and current experiences of the family and social world, or to put that in link theory terms, it lives in the links on the vertical axis between the generations and on the horizontal axis between the child, the family, and the social world.

Elaborations of the Concept of the Link

The concept of the link is being further developed by in Argentina by R. and A. Losso (2006) and R. Losso (2009), Berenstein (2009, 2010), and

Moreno (2010) among others, and in France by Kaës (Kaës 2007; Kirshner 2006), and Nicoló (2009) in Italy. Work better known in English, such as Faimberg's (2005) work on the telescoping of generations, also derives from it. In Chapter 3, we will elaborate the concept of Baranger and Baranger (2008, 2009) on the psychoanalytic field, a closely related concept because it addresses the linking of complex patterns. Current concepts of the link expand its role in unconscious transmission and show how individuals within an interpersonal field are shaped by it.

The main point of link theory is that each person is born into links and lives in links: Through the link, what is interactive or interpersonal becomes intrapsychic, and what is intrapsychic becomes interpersonal or, to use a more recent term, interpsychic (Bolognini 2010). The concept of the link emphasizes that the ongoing bond between two people is built by their interaction, while at the same time it influences the internal world of each of them. In each of these cases, one pattern of organization joins with other organizational patterns to produce a new, overarching higher-level pattern that could not be predicted from knowledge of the interacting components that produce it. In chaos theory, this kind of overarching pattern is understood to develop from subsidiary organizations in interaction, and is referred to as a "strange attractor" (Gleick 1987; Scharff and Scharff 1998a). In English language psychoanalysis, this overarching pattern is the analytic third produced by the interaction of patient and analyst (Ogden 1994). In marriage it is the joint marital personality (Dicks 1967). In groups it is the unconscious bond shared by members of the group as basic assumptions that organize them (Bion 1961).

Link Theory and Dreams

Following Fairbairn (1952), we think of dreams as short versions of internal reality of the individual dreamer. But dreams also communicate aspects of that interior reality to the people who are currently in relationship to the dreamer, while they equally express the effect of those relationships on the dreamer. When dreams are told, they are delivered into interpersonal space and express interpersonal and intersubjective themes. At the same time, they are potential interpersonal communications in psychoanalysis, in psychoanalytic couple and family therapy, and in institutions, as we will demonstrate in Chapter 6 (J. Scharff 1992; D. Scharff and J. Scharff 2004).

What the concept of the link adds is that dreams also express the current influence of those external relationships on the continually developing unconscious organization of the individual, and that such a dream is both a record of that interpersonal influence and is itself part of the process of mediating the internalization of the link. Before learning about the link, we wrote about the use of dreams in the process of individual, couple, and family work, but we did not yet get the point that a dream is more than a film of individual psychic structure or a communication of personal reality among parties. A dream is a live record of the process of the link that transforms the individual in a generative relationship, and, at the same time, is a marker of the transformation. The dream *is* the process.

In life, dreams communicate to life partners about each other and about their relationship. In analytic therapy, they communicate to therapists about the ebb and flow of the therapeutic relationship. In the treatment situation, countertransference is the road to understanding the relationship between patient and therapists, not only the patients' intrapsychic constellations. But countertransference as a term no longer does justice to the situation we are trying to understand. The term countertransference denotes the therapist's intrapsychic experience, which is made up of the combination of her own psychic set and her reception of the encounter with her patient. But the link is the shared pattern, not only her experience of it. The link is between patient and therapist, shared and not owned individually by either participant (or by any one of the participants in the situation of a larger group).

Since links are always co-constructed, how they reflect the therapeutic relationship must always be considered along with consideration of what a current link says about the links in general. Individual subjective fantasies, dreams, affect, speech patterns, and unconscious patterns of interaction all play a role in interpersonal interaction. Overarching patterns (or "attractors" to borrow again from chaos theory) are formed by interactive transformations of internal object organizations of each person involved. In turn, these patterns are in constant communication with, and continually modify the internal object relations of each individual within the relational pattern. The organization of each person's interior world is constantly influenced by others, and by the social and cultural context.

We have described this situation in Chapter 1 as the matrix in which each individual unconscious is formed, so that each subject's individual unconscious is inherently and inextricably interpersonal. What we have said about the unconscious being fundamentally interpersonal also applies to other aspects of conscious functioning in the individual: the non-repressed unconscious and procedural memory are also interpersonally shaped (Kaës 2007). In the literature about the link this interactive product itself becomes the focus of study. Such links are of many kinds, but they all are formed by the joining of forces from each or all of the individuals so connected and interdependent. They partake of all the forces of each individual, whether we think of these as life and death drives; libido and aggression; or love, hate and the search for knowing (Bion 1962).

Bion's basic assumptions (1961) are overarching unconscious organizations of groups (and by analogy, family groups) in which various individuals speak at differing times for different aspects of links. Klein's "internal couple" is an internal organization resulting from the Oedipal child's view of the envied and feared parents' relationship. "Joint marital personality" (Dicks 1967) and "shared family assumptions" (Zinner and Shapiro 1989) express unconscious couple and family organizations made up of many participating links that add up to varying overarching organizing patterns, seen in family therapy as focused and contextual transferences and countertransferences (D. Scharff and J. Scharff 1987). The predominance of any one of these patterns shifts with time and circumstances because all the possible links are present in overt or hidden forms in every group.

In life, experience of links provides the material from which each person constitutes all internal groups, from internal dyads to internal social groups. What is originally interpsychic becomes intrapsychic (Kaës 2007; Bolognini 2010). This process constitutes what Pichon Rivière called "the internal group." The first and most important of these internal groups is the internal family, which includes the internal couple.

THE WORK OF RENÉ KAËS

The most extensive investigation of the link that we have found in English is the recently translated *Linking, Alliances, and Shared Space* by René Kaës (2005, 2007). Kaës's ideas have become foundational to many European writers on analytic family and group therapy, but until the publication of this book, they were not available in English. Exploring the quality and operation of links through close study of groups, he describes the two areas of the psyche as the individual unconscious and the intersubjective field structured by three elements—individual sexuality, speech, and intersubjective linking. Links transform identifications and alliances: individual and group are in a relationship of constant mutual influence. There are primary groups (the family) and secondary groups (peers, colleagues, and institutions). The mediators of the groups are borne by the processes of the speech bearer, the symptom bearer, and the dream bearer. The group (including the family and the analytic treatment group) has common and shared dream space, in which there is polyphony of dreaming, that is of overlapping, multiple sleeping and waking dream processes and images that express and influence both group and individual. Unconscious alliances and resistances form facilitating and interfering pathways and barriers. There is therefore a common area of identity that all members of the group use to realize what is impossible to realize individually. Ogden's (2009) recent writing on intersubjective dreaming in analysis and teaching explores similar territory. In Kaës's conception each person is the subject of the individual's unconscious and the subject of linking. Offensive alliances positively express themes and defensive alliances resist themes. We can see this for instance in adolescents who oscillate between expressing family themes and combating them.

The concept of positive and negative alliances is also expressed by Berenstein's (2009, 2010) idea of radical differences and field interferences that run counter to the positive expression of a link. The force of "alterity," that is the alien otherness of the other subject in a relationship between two (or more) subjects, and especially the undeniable otherness of the other person's body, opposes the tendency of the individual to continue psychic existence without modification. The concept of field interference is also expressed in the idea of the "the work of the negative" (Green 1999). Moreno's (2010) description of "associative" and "connective" processes gives another useful language for the flux between the conservative forces of the inner world—the associative processes—and the stream of connective processes from the outer world that challenge and interrupt them (Cairo 2007). The interplay between the two forms a never-ending tension between conservation of inner pattern and openness to external experience that constantly restructures each person.

The positive expression of links is structuring of the unconscious, while the defensive alliances operate against such structure and toward individual and group splitting and fragmentation. But the work of the negative, the negative alliances, radical differences, and field interferences, also play a crucial role in structuring the mind. The person is more than simply the passive recipient of the sum of influences that he or she takes inside. While these influences may be destructive at times, at other times they move each person towards autonomy within relational bonds and are therefore crucial to growth in the capacity to encounter the external world. The presence of the other in psychic life is fundamental to growth and shaping of personality.

Kaës also writes that within the intersubjective field, the individual overall psyche and the unconscious are subject both to structuring and potentially alienating forces of others, which can have a myriad of influences from felicitous shaping to perverse antagonism. The individual's inner world does not belong solely to the intrapsychic realm, but equally to the influence of others—primary others such as parents, spouses, and children, and secondary others in the social world. The tension of influence in the shared space of family and stranger groups is always present. Thus, in a paradoxical way, the unconscious belongs to the individual and yet also belongs to the group—at first the family group and later other social groups in which each person lives, loves and works. In this way the individual is both a subject in her own right, and is subjugated by the significant others who variously offer influences of alliance, support, alienation and mutual shaping.

Kaës and Berenstein explore the territory of mutual influence in describing the tension between the expression of individual identity and the need to establish a separate identity in relation to other subjects. This creative tension exists in all primary relationships, and remains open to the constant risk that individuals will become alienated from themselves. This is not only a problem: it is most importantly a necessary force for structuring individuals in link relationships. It applies not only to parent-child relationships, but also to all intimate relationships: sibling, marital, extended family, mentoring, therapy or important work relationships. In the less intense links of relationships not thought of as particularly intimate or structuring, the effects and dynamics are weaker, but this does not mean they are unimportant, since weak links in life have the capacity to be organizing when existing psychic organizations loosen as disorganizing forces come into play.

Kaës writes that there are two qualities of subject in each person: the subject of the individual unconscious, and the subject of linking. In this way, the personal subject can be subjected to and subjected by the link. Such subjection is structuring of the individual unconscious in ways that can be positive or negative. The process adds up to the growth of individual identity captured in the formula WE + THE ONE →THE I. What this means is that living both as a member of the couple (WE) and as an individual (THE ONE), I become something other than I was before being in a couple, and so I conceive of myself differently as an individual (THE "I"). If this restructuring is to remain faithful to my sense of self, I need some degree of freedom from the alienating other and from its internalization in me as an alienating internal object. I need the presence of the other to require my mind to redefine my self and develop its range, but I need enough distance from the other to stay true to who I am.

Kaës stresses that linking contributes to both the repressed unconscious (internal objects in unconscious conflict with self) and the unrepressed unconscious (procedural aspects of relating that are not conflictual but that represent intergenerational transmission of relational configurations). For instance, it is common to describe a person as having mannerisms, facial expressions, gestures or speech patterns based in bodily gestures that are like those of a parent or spouse. These things are transmitted unconsciously but are not subject to dynamic repression and are not usually matters of internal conflict.

CLINICAL EXAMPLE: UNCONSCIOUS TRANSMISSION OF THE LINK BORNE IN A DREAM

Mercy is a 27-year-old American in psychoanalysis with Jill Scharff. Mercy was born in Romania and immigrated to the United States with her mother when she was 8 years old, her father and brother joining them a year later. Mercy now works as an economist in an international grant-giving organization. She has been married for a year to Harry, an American-born executive who is strong, reliable, and the leader in their relationship. Mercy is pleasant, respectful, and attractive but careworn and easily thrown in to depression. Mercy and Harry share ideals of public service to developing countries and look forward to a life of travel and foreign exchange. When Mercy was sent to Kenya to research the economic impact of one of the company's programs, Harry traveled to meet her on the return leg to spend a week in Romania, where her grandparents and uncles and cousins still live. Mercy was really looking forward to introducing her husband to her family and their culture. So when they met up in Romania after being apart for two weeks, Harry was totally surprised to find Mercy remote and listless, upset to see her grandparents getting older, and unable to connect to her family. He assumed she was upset by the shock of her grandparents' aging. They made their excuses and left early for the United States.

Back home, however, Mercy got even more withdrawn, physically slowed down, and depressed. Her therapist put Mercy on anti-depressants with little success, and referred her and her husband for a couple consultation. The couple therapist noticed that Mercy was deeply depressed, and reported to her individual therapist that her presentation was trance-like. A couple of months went by with no progress. Finally Mercy confessed that she had had an affair during her trip.

Infidelity seemed completely out of character for her. Harry and Mercy's individual therapist could not understand it. Mercy regretted her mistake and felt certain of her renewed commitment to Harry, but Harry left the home because he had lost confidence in his wife's love—and in her therapist. Mercy's therapist, also shocked that this could have happened while Mercy was in treatment and that she had withheld the truth from her for two months, realized that her treatment was not going deep enough, and transferred Mercy to more intensive therapy with me (JSS). This decision reassured Harry enough that he returned home on a trial basis.

Reconstructing What Had Happened

Over the weeks in analysis Mercy told her story. Since her marriage to Harry whose self-assured manner she admired so much, she had felt second best. She felt that her personality was subsumed in his; her family seemed dysfunctional compared to his, and she herself felt better being with his American-born parents than with her immigrant parents. As a couple Mercy and Harry followed Harry's pursuits, visited his family most often, and socialized with his friends. Once out from the hold of her marriage when on her business trip, Mercy felt free to be herself again. She felt empowered and inspired in her professional role evaluating the program in Kenya. She felt acknowledged and appreciated by the program director. She spent hours in excited conversation about life and work in Kenya, and experienced a growing sense of intimacy with him until it culminated in intercourse, followed by a sad parting. She experienced the unfolding events as if they were happening to her, but she also acknowledged that she had been the one to seduce him the night before she was to leave. As soon as she saw her husband again she lost all sense of empowerment and fell into a silent depression, filled with remorse, guilt, and loss of her powerful sense of agency, her only remnant of power resting on her withholding of information needed to explain her state of mind.

Applying link theory and focusing on the horizontal axis, we can see that as an individual (THE ONE) becoming a couple (THE WE) with self-assured, self-reliant Harry (an admirable, envied alienating other) Mercy developed a diminished sense of self (The "I"). Born into and shaped by a field in which her family was suffering from cultural dislocation and feelings of inferiority, Mercy identified herself as inferior in relation to her husband, her family as less than his. She came to the marriage with a need for love, nurturance, and knowing that would build her sense of self as an American, and a woman. A tension arose between the expression of these needs and her husband's capacity to tune in to her and meet them. She used her sexuality to reassert her sense of herself as a free and powerful individual and renew her capacity for intersubjective linking. Then the speech bearer aspect of herself shut down as the symptom bearer spoke through her depressed affect and psychomotor retardation. The dream bearer was not yet in evidence.

Mercy began by recalling the excitement of the affair, and, feeling remorse for her husband's suffering, eventually renounced her temporary lover, and tried to make reparation. She also worked on her subservience in the marriage prior to and after the affair, and connected it with her bending herself to suit her parents' need for her to thrive in the United States and do better than they could do. Sensitive to her immigrant parents' long-suffering attitude about working below their educational level, hints of emotional pain, and unacknowledged feelings that she cannot ask about, she feels guilty around them, and overly concerned about what they are feeling and thinking. She feels obliged to telephone her grandparents in Romania because she feels bad for them that her parents do not keep in touch with them, even though she dreads the calls because she feels constantly drawn in to their unexplained sadness. Dealing with her parents and grandparents, she feels that she goes into a state of inarticulate irritation at what is not being said, as if in a trance to avoid the impact of the atmosphere they generate.

In terms of link theory, we see here a response to the link on the vertical axis. Again the speech bearer is shut down.

Six months later, when Mercy confided in her mother about the trouble in her marriage because of her brief affair, her mother was sympathetic and uncharacteristically open. She told Mercy that she had had an affair the year that she and Mercy were in America before being joined by her father and brother, and that it had been a sore spot for Mercy's father for years. At the same time, Harry's mother told him that she too had had an affair, and that his father had forgiven her. Mercy and Harry were amazed. Neither of them had any inkling of these histories and no recollection of events that might relate to the revelations. For Mercy it explained some of the feeling of mystery and suffering that she sensed with her parents. For Harry, it gave rise to a tremendous rage at his mother for what she had done to hurt his father, and a sense of betrayal by both parents for presenting him with an apparently ideal marriage that was in fact flawed. Mercy described how, as the weeks passed, he continued to act as an ideally strong husband, but after each of his therapy sessions he fell into a withdrawn state or erupted in anguish about whether he could be betrayed again. I had the impression that he was recreating his impression of his parents' marriage as robust but now as having been agonized, and expressing their deep hurt and its impact on him alongside his current anguish over Mercy's betrayal of him.

Mercy's affair had left her in a trance-like state, which gave me the idea that the affair had occurred in a trance. My hypothesis was that she became vulnerable to infidelity in a moment outside of her reality in the United States, as a direct unconscious, unverbalizable intergenerational transmission from her parents' fracturing experience between two countries, as an enactment of a secret she had been searching to unravel, and as a protest against her husband's apparent security.

To put it in terms of link theory, the couple relationship lay at the crosshairs of a link on the vertical axis, connecting Mercy to her grandparents' unexplained sadness and on the horizontal axis connecting both members of the couple to their parents' marital histories. All Mercy could imagine was that her grandparents were sad because her parents left for the United States, to avoid the austerity and Communist repression in the 1980s.

Beyond that, Mercy was unaware of a possible connection between her grandparents' state of mind and the cultural history of Romania losing sovereignty and coming under Soviet control when lands were seized for collectivization, and torture and executions occurred to secure compliance with the new values. She did not know the history and she felt that she could not ask. On the horizontal axis, she was connected through her education, and her life in the United States to a middle class life of education and opportunity, a life of greater security and hope for recognition than her parents enjoyed. Both of them educated professionals, her parents lost their careers because they were unable to be licensed, and so they worked on the estate of a wealthy family, grateful and uncomplaining despite being abused by overwork. A year into analysis, the dream bearer appeared. Mercy's dream functions as a record of interpersonal influence and a means of reworking it. The function of speech usefully enters the dream too.

Mercy had been working with me on trying to understand her current problems in relating to earlier experience in her immigrant family and their social setting and their history as Romanians. Mercy said, "I had a terrible dream. Harry and my grandmother who seemed younger than now were both in the dream. I was in a room looking at a door. Something was happening behind that door that I couldn't understand. I pushed the door but it wouldn't open. I saw that there was a slit under the door that I could look through, and when I bent down to look under the door, I saw another room and I could almost see another door. I looked under the first door at the second door many times but I couldn't quite see because the second door was too far away, the slit was too small, and the angle not quite right. But whatever was happening behind the second door was the explanation for a big discovery. A whole lot of spiders kept heading for the first door and going in under it to the space beyond. Then the angle changed, and I saw them all go in behind the second door, and that was like, 'Aha, that explains it!'

"Grandma came in to the room, and so did Harry. I had all the things I was holding—candy, a book, many random items. I found it hard to hold on to them all, and I kept dropping some of them and would have to pick them up. Grandma was trying to take some of them, and I really didn't want her to. So I reorganized them to hold on to them. I hid two candies in the pages of the book. She really wanted them, and I said, 'No you can't have them; this is the one thing you can't have.'

"I knew what was happening within the second door, and I didn't want to tell her. So I just said a piece of nonsense: 'Oh that soup was ....' Actually I yelled it. This doesn't make sense now, but in the dream, it was a way of letting her know that I knew what she knew. I wanted to show her I knew but didn't tell her. She yelled back, 'Just those two candies.' It was all about wanting the two candies. Harry wasn't asking for anything."

After telling the dream, Mercy said, "It is also the way I feel when I am talking with my mom: I can't say what I feel. In the dream, I had trouble speaking, and it came out as nonsense and a shout. It took so much of my energy to say anything, and not a lot was coming out. It was like a dream of running fast: trying to but not being able to, finding yourself running in slow motion, pushing, and it takes so much energy to run even a little faster.

"For instance, when I answered her about the two candies and said, 'No you can't have them,' it was so hard to say it, but I only had to say it once about this one thing, these two candies. I was adamant. I said to myself, 'No, you can't let her have them, and you can't feel bad about it.' It was so weird. I remember Grandma as strong and speaking clearly—not how I think of her since her stroke, and not how she was the last time I saw her. I was thinking all week that I would make myself call her this weekend and not let her get away with saying stuff and me ignoring it, and when this weekend came, I put it off and didn't do it. When I do call, then it's like, 'Okay that's done, and I don't have to face it for another few weeks,' and then it's coming up again. I dread it. Grandma feels she can't complain to her local family so she complains to me because I allow it. It gets so tiring. I've said to myself, 'Just deal with that. Just go with it.'

"It's very similar to talking to Mom and not wanting to hear what she wants to complain about. I hate it. I don't want to feel that every time I talk to her. It's stressful. How anxious I feel! I can't find a way to make it not like that for me. I want to keep in touch, but I've stopped talking to her every day. I control the frequency, and that helps. She's getting along better with my dad, and that helps—but I don't control that. I don't know if I should bother calling my grandparents because I can't talk to them about how I feel about what they say. I can't tell them that they make me feel bad and guilty. I feel blocked. I can't get through to what it is that they aren't saying. If I don't call them I feel bad, and I don't want to do it, but I feel I have to."

I said, "You know there is a block but you aren't sure you want to get beyond it, just like in the dream you find a way to see past the first blocked door to the second blocked door, but not what's behind it."

Mercy responded, "It feels as if there is a secret that would explain me. Am I just making it up? This secret?"

I said, "It is a powerful hidden thing you don't feel entitled to see yet but have to deal with whether you alone made it up or not. What you are clear about is your refusing Grandmother's wish to have the two candies. What occurs to you about them?"

Mercy said, "Nothing comes to mind. They can't just be candies, because I don't care that much about sweets. I can't figure it out."

I wondered whether to say what was in my mind. Would it be subsuming her personality to do so? I realized I was in the same dilemma that she faced about whether to address what she saw before her in life and in the dream, both of us caught in an overarching pattern. I decided to speak about what was coming through to me, something she can't do with her family. I said, "I think the two candies you guarded from her stand for the couple of you and Harry."

Mercy replied, "Like, saying to myself, 'You have your own life now, don't worry about this other stuff now.' Dad has actually said that to me. But it still offends me that I'm agonizing over the calls to Grandma. I say I don't need to get into that. This is my life now. But why did I have to shout at her?"

I said, "You were urgently trying to protect yourself and Harry from the effects of the past."

She said, "I'm not sure what I'm protecting us from. How can the past affect Harry and me?"

I said, "It already did. Your parents and Harry's parents both had a painful problem with affairs, and that pattern re-emerged in your marriage. Even though you had no conscious knowledge of it, the need to solve an emotional problem was transmitted from both families to you as a couple having to deal with infidelity and the hurt it caused."

She said, "That's possible, given how much sense some of this has made, and how I've felt. So let this be the explanation, the context for my depression and my affair. But what about my grandparents? Am I trying to create this thing for myself that isn't really there? So let me ask them, and it won't be something to agonize over. I might be able to tell by what she says. (Here 'she' refers to her grandmother but it seems to me to apply to the mystery of dealing with her mother as well.) I feel it physically. My heart is in my chest. I'm so anxious. I need to give myself a push."

This reminded me of her pushing the door in the dream, pushing herself to speak loudly, and pushing on in the analysis even when she suffered so much. I recognized the door as a reference to my office with its double doors, and therefore to the analytic process of protected exploration. I saw her transference to me as the grandma who must be kept at bay and who does not give out information. I saw myself in the spiders as many versions of me scurrying around the doors of her unconscious mind. I thought that the first door represented the problem of unconscious communication with her parents, especially her mother, a door which she had begun to open in analysis, and the second door would lead to exploring with me the impact of the previous generation, for which she was now preparing the way.

Mercy tried to speak to her grandmother in person, and not surprisingly the old woman could not provide the information that Mercy sought. But Mercy did notice the anxious attachment between her grandmother and her uncle who lived near her, and that helped her understand her parents' avoidance of their families and guilt at getting away. Mercy did not get the level of personal revelation she was hoping for, but her mind opened to the likely effects on the family of the social upheaval in Romania, and her grandmother's evasive responses and anxious attachments confirmed Mercy's impressions of a time of pain and secrecy from which her parents had to escape but to which she had been drawn. Her inner world resonated with the outer world of then and now. Recognizing the message of her dream, the powerful hold of the secrets of the past, and the limits to any hoped-for resolution to the mystery, Mercy was freed to create her own reality. She moved on to improve her relationship with her mother, secure her marriage, and enroll in further training to advance her career. She and her husband did work through their hurt and secured their marriage, and moved towards buying their first home with room for a family when they were ready.

The dream had done its work of revealing to Mercy the transgenerational transmission of trauma and marking her wish to transform its effects on her. The dreamwork enabled her to confront the troubling uncertainties of the previous generation, and leave them in the past.

SUMMARY

The link is an apparatus for the origination, management, and transformation of individual psyches. The link forms and informs the psyche. It is an apparatus through which individuals form and manage the affective, largely unconscious organization in the process of internalizing groups of which they are a part, and through which they manage their external relationships in those groups. The link focuses on the intermediate zone that we now understand to have its own overarching organization that is constructed by the subjects and that organizes each of their psyches. We are born into such links, we live in them, and through them we express to others our being, our thoughts, and our innermost longings and fears.

Chapter 3

The Link, the Field, and Object Relations

We approach the concept of the link from our vantage point in the British object relations tradition (J. Scharff and D. Scharff 2005). So now, we will look more closely at precursors to ideas of the link and to current object relations concepts that overlap with the link, and then give a clinical illustration of the link in the next chapter.

The concept of the link specifies the quality of conscious and unconscious interactions among members of a family, group or analytic dyad, and so connects to the concepts of object relationships, transgenerational transmission, and the interaction of persons and social culture. For instance, the concept of the link facilitates an exploration of how superordinate patterns, such as joint marital personality, group basic assumptions or shared family assumptions, are contributed to by the individuals involved and in turn contribute to individual psychic structure and the expression of the link in intimate partnerships, family life, and social relationships (D. Scharff 2011b).

So what is a link, as opposed to an object relationship? Object relations theory and its application to the clinical situation focused at first on the internal configuration of conscious and repressed or dissociated components of self and object (Fairbairn 1944, 1952, 1963). The second step was to describe how the individual object relations set of the individual is unconsciously taken in through introjective identification and transmitted through projective identification to form a cycle of mutual unconscious communication in intimate relationships (Klein 1946). This communication happens from the beginning of life between parents and infants, and continues throughout life in the formation of intimate bonds between parent and child, spouses, and intimate friends. As we said in the first chapter, we think of this continuous unconscious transmission as foundational, from its role in shaping and growing the child's brain and mind, to its continuing role in all emotional communication.

The concept of the link elaborates on the psychoanalytic mechanisms of such transmission. As we have seen, Pichon-Rivière, who introduced the term *the link,* drew from Fairbairn and Klein's ideas, but he had his own unique perspective. He saw the expressions of the link in three spheres: the emotional, the bodily and the social world of interpersonal action. Body, mind and action are inextricably joined, and always carry the potential for transformation between realms. Emotion belongs equally to body and mind: the subjective experience of emotion is only possible when there are hormonal and neuronal experiences that embody action sequences in the body (Schore 2003a). In this way, body, mind and action in the world are inextricably tied together and rooted in each other, and so it makes sense that they should share a common vehicle for the transmission of their emotional content.

The idea that a link is expressed through the body fits with the more familiar concept of psychosomatic expression of mental contents. We tend to think of psychosomatic symptomatology as representing failures of psychic function (McDougall 1989). But by focusing on the normal bodily aspect of links, we can begin to see that the body is a healthy instrument for expressing emotional experience throughout life beginning in infancy. We feel things in our bodies—joy, arousal, excitement, tension, fear. We cry when sad (or happy), we scream in horror, and we startle when suddenly afraid. It is by startling that we recognize a threat. We may feel pain or queasiness in our abdomen, a sensation that expresses our fear—or alerts us to it. We may feel a backward propulsion in our stomach and throat if we are disgusted. Various people may feel the same bodily response but for different emotional reasons, depending on their end-organ sensitivities. Such normal bodily expression becomes the vehicle for psychosomatic illnesses, including sexual disorders, in conditions of stress that attack the body. But we should not forget that the bodily expression both of the link and of emotion is mainly normal and usual. The normal mind-body connection establishes the pathway which is then subject to the exaggerations inherent in emotional and psychic pathology.

Pichon-Rivière also deals with the social aspect of the link. He thinks of the person as a full inhabitant of the social world—not as an individual in isolation, but inevitably as a member of family and social groups. Family, couple and group therapy follow naturally from this point of view. When we fully incorporate the social link in our thinking, individual psychotherapy or analysis can not be conducted as though individuals are isolates. In the recent English language literature, the concept of the social unconscious (Hopper 1996, 2003, 2011) has introduced the view that individuals and groups are joined to the social world at every level, and that this social link is present in every group and individual therapy to an extent not previously appreciated. We will revisit this concept in Chapter 5.

Action expresses the unconscious social link in facial expressions that signal affective meaning (Tompkins 1995), speech that communicates emotion (Fonagy and Target 2007), and behaviors such as breast feeding, a slap in the face, a parental caress, or a sexual advance that communicates intimacy. All such interactional events convey unconscious affects such as desire, fear, contempt, or envy in complex ways that are layered, dynamic, constantly changing in meaning, and always, to some degree, in tension with whatever motives are consciously intended by the actor.

Faimberg (2005) and Losso and Losso (2006) developed another implication of the link concept. They noted the continual expression of vertical linking in horizontal linking. This is to say that the intergenerational roots of our minds are always present in the expression of bonds with our families, friends and social groups. In turn, while the literal or objective history that could have been recorded from outside personal experience in these historical bonds cannot be changed, the meaning each person makes of personal history does change and evolve in the light of current experience. It must be so: how else could ordinary growth or new relationships allow for continuing development, both positive and negative? How could therapy alter the meaning of a person's early history and especially its actual effect on current life? It is essential to emotional growth and health that the meaning of a person's history can be re-written.

COMPARING THE LINK AND OBJECT RELATIONS THEORY

The basic tenets of object relations theory lend themselves to comparison with the ideas of link theory. In Klein's (1975a) version of development, young children have unconscious fantasies about the penis and breast as objects of desire, fear, and envy. The child then experiences these objects in exciting and threatening pairings and introjects the combined image as a dynamic interaction of internal objects and parts of self (D. Scharff and J. Scharff 1987, 1991; J. Scharff and D. Scharff 1998c). This is referred to as the internal couple. Similar internalization of family and group relationships leads to the formation of internal families and internal groups. Klein's description of the infant's early experience of the interaction of body parts shows how bodily interaction perceived under the influence of developmentally normal fantasy is taken inside to organize mind. Klein's (1946) concept of projective and introjective identification, the displacement of unconscious mental content into the caring partner and its reinternalization serves purposes of self defense and communication about little realized parts of the self (J. Scharff 1992). When the person projects mental experience outside the self, it becomes the material from which unconscious links are made.

The theory of the link drew on Fairbairn's concept of object relations and now extends it. Fairbairn described the construction of the inner world through identification with introjected objects, the dynamic splitting of objects and the self, and the process of externalization of the inner object relations that results in treating external interactions in the light of internal organization (Fairbairn 1952; D. Scharff and Birtles 1994). Fairbairn's emphasis on the internalization of interactional experience gives us a vehicle for understanding how the link is taken inside to become an organizer and component of psychic structure. The concept of the link extends our understanding of the quality and organization of interaction that continually redefines the person and the internal identifications, the family, and the social group of which the person is a part.

We look to Klein's description of projective identification and Fairbairn's description of introjection to provide the twin arms of give and take that both construct and feed on the structure of the link. Then we look to Winnicott and Balint for attention to the links in the space between objects.

Balint (1968) realized that some people feel safest in the open spaces between people. He called them *philobatics* while those who cling to their objects for security he called *oncnophils*. For philobatics, security exists in the space between people where distance gives protection from fear or hatred of, or desire for, the object. In examining the quality of experience offered in the space between, Balint was in the territory of the link theory. Winnicott's study of the mother–infant relationship includes many elements of the link, including for instance the mother's state of mind as the infant uses her ruthlessly for the infant's growth. For Winnicott, all of this happens in the potential space that is the area of transitional phenomena (Winnicott 1951, 1971). What is inside one person is put into transitional space, and from there, it is taken in by the other. Primary needs are transformed into object relations. This potential space in which each individual is created and creates herself, is the area of the link, where speech, action and interaction form link processes. Winnicott (1960a) describes an area of individual development that is posited on there being links that need to be used and links that have to be resisted. Each person has a benign "false self" that uses given links to mediate with and relate to forces of the outside world. The individual has an inner core that is inviolable, a "true self"—the sanctum of individuality that resists the influence of links, and so protects itself, aided by the false self and its links. It is necessary for survival and for development to relate to other important figures and to the outer world in general, but this has the ever-present potential to violate the individual's true self. The system of links into which we are born functions both as a security and a constraint. Each person has to have the true self that resists alienation and a false self that relates to, and even embraces, otherness as a means to growth.

Winnicott's idea of true and false self is echoed in Berenstein's (2009) thoughts on radical difference and the intrusion of otherness. Moreno's (2002) concepts of associative and connecting elements in links describe the tension between personal continuity and the interruptive elements of the outer world. Kaës (2007) thinks the individual's unconscious is subject both to structuring and potentially alienating forces of others, which can have myriad influences from felicitous shaping to perverse antagonism. Kaës, Berenstein and Moreno explore the territory of mutual influence in describing the tension between group identity (including family group identity) and the need to establish a separate identity in relation to others. The individual's inner world, including the unconscious realm of internal object relations, does not belong solely to the intrapsychic realm, but equally to the influence of others.

More recently, attachment research has described specific patterns of bonding between parents and children that connect the generations (Main 1995; Fonagy 2001). Attachment style describes a context rooted in parents' histories and the inner world organization of each parent, a context into which a child is born and develops. In this way attachment is a link. Attachment theory resonates with link theory and has the advantage of providing specific descriptions of links and their consequences. The experience that an attachment bond can be reorganized in subsequent relationships—for instance, someone with an insecure attachment can move to an "earned secure attachment" through better relationships such as that with a good teacher or spouse or therapist—is an example of evolution of personality within the link. However, at the same time, attachment theory is limited because it does not consider the link *between* those parents, siblings, and the extended family. It also does not consider the social links that support or interfere with the parents and family. This is not meant as a criticism of attachment theory—adding such complexity would in all likelihood make matters too difficult to research, and attachment theory is first and foremost a research paradigm. We do want to credit its groundbreaking reach while acknowledging its limits. Attachment ideas overlap considerably with theories of the link, but cannot realize the full context of links and the way they organize and are organized by the wider family.

Volkan's (1981, 2006) concept of *linking objects* and *living linking objects* overlaps with the idea of the link. Originally developed in his discussion of the concretization of internal psychological objects in external objects that are clung to in pathological mourning, he later broadened the concept to include creative solutions to mourning as well. Even though his idea is not an interpersonal or interactive one, it connects to link theory in that it refers to the closing down of transitional space and the distortion of transitional objects in that constrained space.

We now turn to Bion's ideas. His study of groups demonstrated that various individuals speak at different times for specific *shared unconscious assumptions* because of their emotional valency to both resonate with and combine with others to drive the issue. In studying valency, Bion addresses which aspects of links such spokespersons carry (Bion 1961). The resonance of the particular link with the internal object relations constellation of the person is what drives the *valency* of each person to speak for a link at a particular moment (Scharff and Scharff 1998c). This is indeed a description of a group link. However, Kaës goes further in personalizing the links as the speech bearer, the symptom bearer and the dream bearer. Kaës's focus adds specifics about the quality of interactions—conscious and unconscious—to our capacity to study the object relations of members of a family, group or analytic pair.

Bion's later works on thinking (1967a) and especially his description of *attacks on linking* (1967b) describe attacks on mental process that have corollaries in attacks on, and attacks from, linking relationships in the external world. Perhaps his work most overlaps with theories of the link in his use of the symbols L, H and K (standing for Love, Hate and Knowledge) as internal desires for love, hate and knowledge that support thinking, and –L, –H, and –K (standing for the lack of those desires). –L, –H, and –K are as intrinsic to development as +L, +H and +K: For instance, a person dominated by –L cannot think about loving or libidinal thoughts, one dominated by –H cannot conceive of aggression, and –K defines impaired emotional capacity for knowing. Positive and negative working together in various combinations together shape and prune mental structure and personality. Bion does illustrate these ideas in analytic vignettes that show that they correlate with interactive links but his formulations on the thinking mind are confined to the intrapsychic realm. Bion does not describe external relationships influencing or being influenced by intrapsychic processes, and so his ideas on linking do not correspond fully with link theory.

However, Bion (1970) does move much closer to the territory of the link in his theory of *container/contained* in which he describes the processing function of the mother's mind as she unconsciously takes in the baby's unthought and primitive anxieties, detoxifies them through her "reverie" or unconscious resonance with her own mind, and feeds them back in more structured, less toxic form. In this way, the baby's mind is formed and matured. This mental processing occurs through the mental mechanisms of projective and introjective identification. A similar process applies to all intimate, growth promoting relationships, including the healthy marriage and good psychotherapy. Here Bion is describing a specific and crucial component of the action of links in which the analyst or parent's mind has to contain primitive and unstructured mental process.

But while Bion illustrates such processes and their failure, he does not join specific external object relationships with their implications for intrapsychic structure. Except for an occasional vignette about analysis, he does not describe interactional patterns that form the outer world component of links, and so he leaves that entire area for us to imagine. Kaës (2005, 2007) and Berenstein (2009) describe more specific qualities of unconscious links that organize groups than Bion. Working from Bion, we see the work of Kaës and Berenstein as enabling us to see that the negative forms of links inside the mind bear a correspondence to and derive from negative links in the interactive mental field. They both interfere with internalization and provide evidence of having been internalized. In this way, Kaes and Berenstein show that Bion's –L, –H and –K are not simply destructive by nature, but also contribute to the process of mental structuring.

MADELINE AND WILLY BARANGER: EL CAMPO (THE FIELD)

At this point, we introduce a discussion of the Barangers' seminal paper "The analytic situation as a dynamic field" (2008) and a collection of their analytic writings from the 1960s, *The Work of Confluence* (2009) recently made available for the first time in English (D. Schardd 2011a). Their concept of *el campo,* translated as *the field,* belongs in this extended discussion of the link, because the field is the territory in which links exist and act. The Barangers were close students of analytic literature, schooled by, among others, Pichon-Rivière, and they were well read in Lacan, and the British School (but not apparently Fairbairn). They in turn have informed the contributions of Ferro, Eizirik, Bolognini, and Kaës, and others whose work is not translated into English. Indeed, Ferro's ground-breaking book, *The Bi-Personal Field* (1999) takes its name directly from their writing.

The Barangers' concept of *el campo,* the field and more specifically the bi-personal field, refers to the totality of the analytic situation, the structure of analysis, the associations of the patient, and the unconscious structure of both patient and analyst. The field is structured by the individual unconscious and the intersubjective dialectic. It is not symmetrically intersubjective, however, because the patient's only task is to put his conscious and unconscious material into the analytic situation. The analyst, on the other hand, has to be available to be influenced by this in an immediate way, including falling ill from the shared effect of what the analytic pair has constructed, and at the same time the analyst has to monitor the process. The field is composed of the structure of the analytic contract, the material of transference, and the coming together of patient and analyst's unconscious fantasy. The analyst listens from a position of *neutrality* which, far from being like a blank screen, is rife with the analyst's unconscious fantasy life, which, however, the analyst must monitor. These ideas are reminiscent of Searles' (1965) writing about countertransference as the essence of psychoanalysis. Searles recommended the analyst fall ill in order to fully understand the patient, and to accept that his face belongs to the patient and is used by the patient to come to know herself. He was contemporary with the Barangers, and many of his ideas overlapped with theirs, but, writing in English, his ideas derived from different traditions.

The Barangers draw on Pichon-Rivière's idea that psychoanalysis is a spiral process, proceeding from various repetitions over similar territory, as patient and analyst together move into *bastions of impasse* that are the product of their shared, largely unconscious, interaction. Each bastion is a joint construction of resistance, counter-resistance by the therapist, and impasse—each construction unique to each analytic pair. Interpretation, followed by insight, breaches the bastions, and moves the analytic project forward. Unlike the analysand, the analyst has a dual role of being both in the field, and taking *a second look* at the development of bastions, over and over. That is to say, the analyst must also strive to look from outside the field, looking from *outside* the link *at* the link in process. Analytic process consists of developing insight, increasing shared understanding, experiencing and confronting impediments. If the field is armed against understanding, *perversity* can develop. The Barangers prefer the concept of *shared impasse* to the concept of *negative therapeutic reaction,* which in their view seems to blame the patient.

In the Barangers' clinical approach, the analyst interprets at *points of urgency* (a technique they derive from Pichon-Rivière). These are points in time when the field requires and is susceptible to understanding. There is a temporality to the field, and interpretation may address the here-and-now but will always encompass the past history of the analysand and the future implications of what is happening in the treatment. The Barangers wrote that Pichon-Rivière had altered the idea of *here-and-now* to *here-and-now-and-with-me*—an unconscious joining of analysand and analyst. Here we can see that the link includes an emotional link that is specific to the therapeutic pair. Thus the here-and-now situation includes the arc of the patient's life, past and future implications, the past and future of the therapist, and the past and future of the treatment. The link extends to the past history and future of both, and to the society and culture in which they exist. Treatment thus is a project of restoration within the spiral of treatment and of the patient's life. The analysand's growth has been interrupted by the developmental impasses of life. The bastions re-present in treatment, but the form of the bastion takes in treatment is uniquely determined by the melding of the unconscious of this particular patient and this particular therapist.

For the Barangers, the analysis of countertransference is the essential tool in understanding, interpreting, and lysing bastions in the field. In this respect, they anticipated much later writing on the use of countertransference in entering into, and coming to understand, the bi-personal field. The therapist gathers experience, becomes ill with the illness of the bi-personal field, and then initiates working a shared way out of it through interpretation. The patient can interpret and show leadership, but it is up to the therapist to carry the torch and show the way, and this differentiates the place of the analyst from the humanity-in-connection that the two of them share. The Barangers believed that interpretation leads to opening up further material and recognition of impasse. They also explored how interpretation can be used defensively to stop progress and maintain shared bastions. They were skeptical of the idea of *deep interpretation*, preferring to focus interpretation on that which the patient can recognize and own. The depth of the interpretation is defined not by the degree of primitiveness or by reference to infantile material, but by the quality of recognition by the patient, or the increment of understanding that accrues.

The therapist works as an interlocutor who sets the conditions of the work in the dynamic field of the two subjects who are working together and yet are separate. Words are the vehicle of exchange between them. The therapist's mind belongs to the intersubjective situation and speaks out at points of urgency in the field. Whatever is said may represent either a discontinuity or a coming together since both are crucial in the therapeutic process.

For the Barangers, analytic treatment is a two-body, a two-person project. But they also see that the unconscious internal object set of each subject in the analytic pair fills the bi-personal field with oedipal dynamics. They note that unmourned *dead/alive objects* can crowd out the vitality of internal object life and produce bastions of resistance to growth. This is particularly likely in situations of trauma, in which the creative re-writing of a patient's history can be brought to a standstill. The Barangers' idea of dead-alive objects is reflected in contemporary work on unresolved mourning and in Green's (1986) concept of *the dead mother.* The Barangers distance themselves from the idea of imposing theory on understanding based on the one-body theory focused on the analysand's pathological interactions.

The process of treatment is a re-imaging of the patient's history within the bi-personal field. This does not mean that memories are necessarily recovered, but that the conjunction of the minds of the patient and therapist lead to new understandings in which the arc of growth is re-instated.

"Interpretation aims at transforming the burden of fate into an element of creation" (Baranger and Baranger 2009, p. 43). In this way, analysis is not an encounter but a construction. The individual is not in a situation because of his history; he *is* his history, and so these encounters offer the possibility of constructing new ways of being. In this construction, we can see the way that the Barangers's work on the field embodies the process of drawing from the link that imbues that field with meaning, and that each person in the analytic field draws from and contributes to the evolution of that link, and therefore of the field.

OVERLAPPING ISSUES BETWEEN CONTEMPORARY PSYCHOANALYSIS, OBJECT RELATIONS, AND THE LINK

The central place of unconscious communication is being re-emphasized in contemporary analytic literature, and in ways that move it toward an interpersonal, interpsychic dimension. Parsons (2006, 2007, 2009), Ferro (2009), and Ogden (2009) focus on the joining of the unconscious processes of analyst and patient in a creative waking-dreaming, or shared unfolding alpha process of making new narrative and new images, that is unique to each analytic pair. This unfolding process, which is beyond the conscious and preconscious functions of the analyst and the transference-countertransference dialectic, is essential to move the analytic process forward and reveal new ways of relating for both patient and therapist.

Among contemporary writers, Ferro (2009) works most centrally in the overlap of object relations and the link. Drawing on the Barangers' concept of the field (Baranger and Baranger 2008, 2009) and on Bion (1970), he blends ideas from across the two cultures to craft a creative way of working both with object relations and in the link. In his review of the Barangers' work, Ferro emphasizes the evolution of his own idea of the field to include working continually with the vicissitudes of transformation of thought as Bion described. "[T]he analytic field is then that "unsaturated waiting room," where we can find emotions, proto-emotions and characters before they can be led back to their saturated course, through the relationship or a construction" (Ferro 2010, p. 426). Like Ogden (2009) and Grotstein (2007), Ferro privileges the process of mutual waking-dreaming as the process through which transformation is exercised within the field on the unprocessed elements. It is the field's capacity to hold and contain these unprocessed elements that is the most important element for success in analytic work. The extension of Ogden's (1994) concept of the analytic third to include waking dreaming fits with Kaës' concept of the "dream bearer." These ideas fit with our view of night-time dreaming as an interpersonal process, something we have written about previously in family and couple therapy, and will take up again in the light of our current thinking (D. Scharff 1992, D. Scharff and J. Scharff 2005) (see Chapter 6).

SUMMARY

Object relations theory (broadly developed in the English speaking analytic literature) and the theory of the link and the field (mainly investigated in Spanish, French and Italian) overlap with, expand, and illuminate each other. The concept of the link offers an extension of object relations theory in all realms of study and treatment, from individual and family, to groups and institutions. As we strive to form a link between object relations and the link, we find that the emphasis in one body of thought can enrich the other and so broaden and deepen our perspectives as theorists and clinicians.

Chapter 4

The Link in Family Dynamics

To show how link theory can augment our ability to conceptualize a family's experience, we will revisit one of David Scharff's sessions from a complex concurrent couple and family treatment that we previously described at length (Scharff and Scharff 1991).

CLINICAL EXAMPLE FROM FAMILY AND COUPLE THERAPY

The couple had originally come to me (DES) for treatment of sexual dysfunction. The wife, Velia, disliked sex and the husband, Lars had sexual urgency and premature ejaculation. They also asked me to see their middle child, Alex, aged 5 ½ who was soiling and wetting by and by night. I diagnosed Attention Deficit Disorder (ADD) with behavioral and learning difficulties. There were also two other children, Eric, aged 7 ½ and Jeanette, aged 3 ½. Eric was the sturdiest of the children, but was prone to depression when frequently the target of his mother's disapproval for failing to be the mature child. Jeanette, early in oedipal development was sweet and spontaneous, but too sexy for her years.

The Initial Family Assessment

In the initial family assessment session, the parents discussed the way that their sex life (which in this setting they discreetly referred to as their "conjugal difficulty") left them feeling frustrated and full of anger of which their children were aware. While the parents were referring to their conjugal difficulty, Jeanette and Alex had constructed a long building they said was a firehouse. Driving the fire truck through it, Jeanette knocked the firehouse down. Meanwhile Eric had drawn a picture of a war between enemy space ships and a good "mother ship." It had been unclear for a long time whether good would triumph, which, in the session, it ultimately did. Much of Alex's play was disruptive, especially at moments of family tension. Jeanette had made a spaceship with blocks in which she placed a large baby doll "mother" and a small "father." Lars winced as he saw the huge mother doll effectively smother the father doll.

We have tried to give just enough description of this initial family session to suggest that the children's play provided an echoing narrative of the parents' difficulty, as expressed in the sexual symptomatology. The children's play formed moving pictograms and naremes (Ferro 2009) of the inner family narrative, of the living link that was being expressed and played out. In the language of the link, we can say that the sexual symptom expressed the bodily difficulty in linking for husband and wife. While it used the failure of a psychosomatic link in the wife for this symptomatic expression, it was at the same time emotional and interactive between husband and wife. The sexual symptoms occupied the whole range of expressions of difficulty in linking, giving expression to the alienating, fearful and defensive aspects but also expressing desire and its vicissitudes.

The therapy that followed with the family revealed many transformations of the link, as described by Bion. To review what we developed in Chapter 3, Bion (1962) used the symbols L, H and K, as a shorthand way of referring to how love, hate and knowledge form links in thought and therefore in relating. Each link has a positive form (+L, +, H, +K to indicate the presence of love, hate, and knowledge) and an equally important negative form in which the capacity for love, hate, and knowledge is blocked or given negative emotional value (indicated by –L, –K and –H). A person or couple with a significant –H link would be organized against experiencing hatred in its various forms and degrees. Where a couple's sexual love life is blocked (indicated by –L) their relationship may become filled with aggression as a result of frustration (indicated by +H). For Lars and Velia the aggressive link was magnified in this way. Their various H, L and K links were played out within the whole family in ways we can begin to see and guess at even in this first family session. The +H link, that is excess aggression, was funneled into Eric's relationship with his mother because of the overflow of her frustration and anger at her husband and her fear that Eric would become passive and underachieving like him (and it turned out, like her own father). In a more disorganized way, the parents' frustrations were projected into Alex in several forms, including his unfocused, disruptive play. Mentally, Alex had incorporated the –K link present in the family interaction into his hyperactivity and inability to concentrate, which Lars also had. Somatically, Alex had introjected the psychosomatic disruption in his development of encopresis and enuresis. Both parents had repressed unrealized reservoirs of +L from the frustration of their sexual link, and this was being projected into Jeanette because, being in the Oedipal stage and being personally cute and charming, she was receptive to, and evocative of, the projection. She had a valency to contain the +L link to excess.

We have seen how the children's personalities lent themselves to the expression of these mental links. We can also see that aspects of the nature of the parental bond were being reacted to and played with in the children's play, where we might say a narrative was being constructed by the family within the holding and containment of the therapist even in this first session. This family was unusually able to work analytically, to show plenty of evidence of alpha function (Bion 1962; Ferro 2009). Given the slightest opportunity in treatment, they begin to construct complex narratives that might potentially address problems in the links and in failures of narrative transformation.

At this moment early in the session, Alex and Jeanette played the excitement and danger of the fire truck in the endangered container, while Eric drew a picture of the trouble in aggressive aspects of the family link in terms of an intergalactic battle in which the forces of good were on their mettle to defend the mother ship against evil invasion. Eventually in her play, Jeanette got the good mother to manage the spaceship, while the father was taken off in a cement mixer. Seeing that image, Lars winced and held his head, but he was smiling, too. Eric decided by the end of the session that the good guys had won and the mother ship was safe.

There were progressive, potentially healing forces in play in the family. So in this family interaction, we begin to see the outlines of family links: the trouble with the danger of loving and sexual links, fears about knowing, and difficulties with bodies that are family-wide concerns. Difficulty in the parents' bond fuels difficulties in the children's development and interaction, and in aspects of their thinking. At the same time, the children's interaction already informs the therapeutic link so that the therapist learns a great deal about the vicissitudes from their play and the parents' reaction to it. The children do not know the details of their parents' sexual life and histories, but they hear them alluded to in the session, much as they hear the rows in the parents' bedroom from their own rooms. The family constellations around these facts of life, whether known or not known, contribute to the fracturing of links on many levels.

Referral and Return to Treatment

I (DES) did not have open hours to take the family into treatment but I referred them. Over the next 2 ½ years, Velia saw a colleague for intensive psychoanalytic psychotherapy, mostly four times a week, for treatment of her borderline personality disorder. Although she was frequently depressed and had rages inside the family and out, she also showed intelligence and strength. Lars was discovered to have an adult learning disorder and probably adult ADD, but did not progress well in individual therapy. Alex improved on a psycho-stimulant, but, like his father, was unresponsive to individual play therapy. A year later, I offered weekly couple treatment to the parents for their sexual dysfunction and weekly family therapy for the whole family group.

Sex Therapy for the Couple

Couple therapy for Lars and Velia's sexual difficulty provided behavioral exercises at home followed in the next session by analysis of their intimate experiences (Kaplan 1974; Scharff and Scharff 1991). This method slowly helped the couple to move forward and understand their situation in ways that we will signify using Bion's terms. Velia soon found that her fear of sex (–L) with which she had presented, covered an underlying intense longing (+L), which inevitably was frustrated and switched to lifelong rage when she could not achieve orgasm (+H). Lars's learning difficulty that we might formulate as (–K) also affected his ability to learn and make connections in therapy, but he did gradually learn increased patience and forbearance. The situation for the family improved, albeit at a snail's pace. Suddenly, the couple recovered more complete memories of childhood that had been blocking the security and pleasure of their relationship.

A Couple Session

In a couple session shortly before the family session detailed below, Velia remembered for the first time that she had been the victim of direct physical abuse from her father, whom previously she had remembered as delivering only verbal abuse. There had been sporadic instances of sibling sexual play, which we had come to understand as occurring in compensation for her father's verbal abuse and her mother's helplessness to protect the children. When Velia remembered the physical abuse, Lars said that he also remembered abuse from his father. Early on, he had said that his father was arrested for public homosexual behavior when Lars was 17. The parents divorced and, after time in jail, his father had lived in a stable homosexual partnership. But now Lars suddenly remembered that on one occasion as a pre-teen he had asked his father about sex and his father had said, "Here, I'll show you," and had sodomized him. Subsequently, Lars had sodomized his younger brother. Their shared physical and sexual traumas have hurt the couple's sexual relationship, affecting Velia's sexual responsiveness and mood regulation, inhibiting Lars's sexual performance, and limiting his intellectual competence and therefore his promotion at work.

In terms of establishing narratives about links, we can see that the links that had been buried were now moving out of hiding and being expressed in the next generation, albeit in more subtle and less primitive ways. A shared way of treating +H, –L and –K links by this couple was built on treating their internal object relations history the same way: that +H events and –L events while they were growing up had been carried along as features of their primary links, but to cope with them, they shared an unconscious transformation: H was denied and so became –H most of the time, bursting out occasionally. +L was expressed toward the children, but –L was expressed in the conversion symptom of sexual dysfunction—the psychosomatic expression of their sexual bond. The couple's valiant shared effort not to perpetuate abuse by necessity required a considerable degree of denial of H, that is the expression of –H, which itself carried the burden of holding back +L. And to all this, we can add that seeking for knowledge (+K) was impaired. There were a great many things that could not be known or acknowledged, so there was a family-wide –K, most expressed in Lars's pseudo-stupidity as an adult, but also in Alex's inability to learn how to manage bodily functions and intellectual learning, and in some aspects at the upper reaches of Eric's more advanced development.

A Family Session after an Absence

At the time of this family session, I (DES) had been seeing the family and the couple in concurrent treatment for about 1 ½ years, and had returned from a 2-week vacation. The family session came earlier in the week than the couple session. Usually family sessions focus on the children's play, and the adult conversation keys off that. In this session, however, while I watch the children play out of the corner of my eye, my focus is drawn to Velia who has a migraine and looks depressed. Velia holds her head in her hand. Lars looks non-plussed. Jeanette is building a small containing structure out of blocks with a paper airplane inside and saying, "Here's his hiding place, Mom." Eric is playing with two fighter airplanes that chase each other in a dogfight. Alex is constructing block buildings. The children continue to play as the parents talk about their difficulties, and

Alex and Jeanette go on to play about a boat (actually a toy bathtub) in the sea and a helicopter overhead going away. Jeanette's doll, waving from the boat/bathtub, calls out, "Bye, bye. See you tomorrow."

For the first half of the session, Velia's headache and frustration become the "selected fact" for me (Bion 1962, p. 73). I engage in much more conversation with the couple about the causes of her headache and depression than usual. She says that things have not been going well sexually for the couple in the last two weeks, and Lars agrees. I infer that the failures are with his functioning but I do not ask for specifics in the presence of the children, it is not clear. I pursue the connection between my absence and their difficulty. While Velia can see the connection, Lars cannot. I connect this to his general difficulty in making links to his emotional experience with his wife, and with his father. I referred only obliquely to his recently revealed history of asking his father for support and getting something painful instead, not wishing to reveal the event of sodomy to the children. I interpret to him that he has collapsed in my absence because of the lack of my presence and support.

At this point in the session, the children's play reorganizes, and our focus returns to their play and discussion of the themes that they present. Eric takes the lead in playing with a pig hand puppet, that he has loudly grunting and saying, "Is there any food around here? I'm hungry." The other children join in with furry puppets of their own who dramatically complain about their hunger and the lack of enough food to eat. They then close in on me, hand me a purple puppet with big ears, and begin to attack my puppet, playfully but forcefully "honking" its nose. The feeling is ambiguous: aggression tamed by a kind of loving playfulness. Lars and Velia look on, both smiling. I comment that the children might not be the only ones who want to beat me up. Velia says she could imagine herself tweaking my nose, and she makes a gesture of doing so. Lars grins, and teasingly asks her why she doesn't just go over and tweak my nose. Watching the video afterward, I see myself draw back reflexively, defensively, as if to fend them off. I say, "No, why don't you just talk about it?" as though they weren't already doing so. A moment later, Jeanette marches noisily away, her heels clip-clopping on the tile floor, and returns to playfully tweak my puppet's nose again. I ask, "Where have you been?" She answers, "We've been honking someone's nose." "Why would you do a thing like that?" I ask in playful innocence. In a succinct interpretation, she answers, "Because he's been mean to us, so we're being mean to him."

As the session progressed, the elaboration in play and talk became more specific about the aggression that had been engendered in response to my absence. Each family member expressed in an individual way their own particular combination of longing, disappointment and anger—the children in their play and drawing, Velia directly in words, and Lars in his blocking and not knowing. At the same time, the children made it explicit that they liked coming to the sessions, and that their anger for my abandoning them was contained within that overall feeling.

Towards the end of the session, I asked Lars directly how my absence had affected him. Lars replied, "You don't even notice," implying that *I* had seemed not to notice *him*, he corrected his "slip" to clarify that he meant to say that *he* had seemed not to notice *my* absence. Lars fended off any meaning behind his slip, and fended off my interpretation that his falling apart sexually and losing self-esteem were due to his wish to reverse an unconscious perception that my temporary absence meant that I no longer noticed him or the couple's needs. But Velia got it. She playfully slapped him on the leg, and chimed, "Ha, ha, ha. You got caught in a Freudian slip! Nyah, nyah, nyah!" She then re-stated my interpretation. With a grudging laugh, Lars took in insight from Velia when he had so far been able to fend it off from me.

The final sequences of the session were led once again by the children's play. Eric took a toy ambulance and disrupted play that Jeanette and Alex had organized. Lars, functioning better now in role as a father who could set limits, told Eric to stop, and Velia, now functioning well as an ordinary mother again, countered Eric's assertion that he wasn't doing anything wrong. I asked her what she thought was happening, and she answered, "It's very clear. The ambulance-slash-doctor was tearing everything apart." In saying this, she made a slashing gesture with her hand, illustrating the slash in ambulance/doctor.

I saw what seemed to me to be a kind of interpretation in the form of her complex pun, and so I said, "I like the part about the 'ambulance-slash-doctor!' "

"Oh, yeah," she said. Again gesturing a slashing motion, she laughed, "Slash the doctor!"

It was time to stop. As the family gathered up their coats to leave, Jeanette whined, "I want to still stay."

The session marked many of the family's gains, and it was not long thereafter that the couple recovered intimacy (which was discussed in the couple therapy but not in family meetings) and the children seemed freed enough from their symptomatology that termination could be planned.

Discussion of the Operation of the Link

What we intend to illustrate in this story of this session is the complex of links that operate in all directions within it. When David Scharff used the word "link" with Lars, he was referring at that time to Bion's paper "Attacks on Linking" (1962) to mean the linking of thoughts that make sense together of experience. He had in mind that Lars' difficulty with linking thoughts and feelings echoed the couple's difficulty in connecting their bodies in pleasure via their sexual link. Lars's difficulty in thinking was exacerbated at that moment by Lars's feeling that his absent therapist had not noticed him.

However, in the Pichon-Rivière tradition, we can now see how the link between the spouses has been disturbed and is now in the process of transformation. Their link contains the marks of vertical or historical links to each spouse's parental generation. Presumably the grandparental generation had disturbed linkages with the generations before them that cannot be specified because we do not know their histories, but whose marks are unmistakable in the traumatogenic traces they have left. These disturbances are factored into the emotional, psychosomatic and interactive aspects of the couple's current system of links, and it is these that we examine in their couple therapy, emotionally, psychosomatically and interactionally.

At the same time, the couple's bond forms the material out of which each child's unconscious is formed, and to which they each react, so we can see elements of the continuation of this vertical link to the next generations in play in these sessions. The multi-directional links within the family are the building blocks of the children's internal links as they develop, and at the same time, each child (along with each parent) contributes to the family-wide system of linkages. They are in a tension of being formed by, subject to, and subjected by the individual unconscious of each parent and by the attractor formed by them as a loving, fighting, struggling pair. There is a constant tension between each child and the parents, among the children as a sibling group, and between the group of children and the parents. All this forms a field of almost infinite complexity. Finally, the difficulty with mental and sexual links that the therapist commented on is a direct result of these links in the broader sense, and at the same time, it influences and contributes to those links.

Participating in discussion, in play, and emotional interaction, the therapist's mind, actions, and words form a destabilizing force on the family group's patterns of interaction and unconscious communication. This takes us again to the territory of Berenstein (2009) and Kaës' (2007) *alienation* from the self—for each individual and for the family as a group. But it is this very force of alienation that offers to let the group and each individual reorganize towards growth in the areas in which each has been stuck and frustrated. Put in chaos theory terms, we are in the realm of chaotic disorganization and of tuning forces operating in the service of emergent self-organization at higher levels (Gleick 1987) (see Chapter 7).

In this case, the therapist's absence has removed him as a stabilizing and growth-promoting factor in the expanded family group. His absence replaces positive L, H and K with –L, –H and –K. The unacknowledged and un-experienced, split-off anger now blocks communication and effective function, more so for the parents than the children. The session puts that block—which had been expressed through the psychosomatic links of mother's headache and father's erectile difficulty—squarely into discussion, and then the children's play works to restore the link to the discussion that, without their help, had been running into Lars's mental brick wall and Velia's somatic internalization of difficulties in the link. When aggression emerges in the emotionally expressive play of the children, it reorganizes the family. The aggressive link is confirmed and expressed, and with it, the loving link. The link that supports knowledge and exploration (and growth) is also freed for expression. In the session, I could see the pain of Velia's migraine ease (the somatic link is transformed) as she smiles and even revels in the children's playful aggression, which enables her to express her own aggression, also with humor, and for Lars and Velia to teasingly join in expressing their anger at me. I learned in couple therapy the next week that their sexual link had also returned to the level achieved prior to my vacation. In the weeks that followed that session, Velia became orgasmic in sexual interaction with Lars, for the first time in her life.

The session demonstrates the living out in psychosomatic, emotional and interactional spheres a variety of symptoms that are vehicles for difficulties in vitalizing links. The therapist taps into these difficulties by his persistent destabilizing probing. He is an *alienating* force, a *field interference*—a *destabilizing tuning force* in terms of chaos theory. Then the session shows how the family members, by joining with the therapist in exploring and expressing impediments to the link, are able to use their own links in new creative ways to repair impingements that free up and reorganize their internal object relations, and improve their interactional functioning.

When we focus on the quality of the links as they are expressed initially in this session, then cultivated in various ways (verbally, in play, and in interplay by and with the family) we can see that the quality of link changes and brings an increment of growth to each member of the family. We can see how the links organize each member of the family, and how each of them contributes to the overall family pattern as it changes, especially in this session late in the family's treatment. Velia's depressed migraine changes to humorous acknowledgment of disappointment and anger; Lars's know-nothing blocking of linkages in thought alters to humorous participation and to more active parenting; Eric's play becomes more explicit and related—and more humorous and creative, too; Alex's somewhat disruptive and isolated play becomes more cooperative and thematic; and Jeanette's play becomes pointedly focused on me and on expressing the family-wide complex transference—disappointment, anger, and, at the same time, real concern for me.

SUMMARY

In terms of object relations theory, we see a family operating in the depressive position, linking thought and affect, and showing concern and gratitude. In terms of chaos theory, we see the emergence of higher levels of differentiation and of organization. In terms of link theory we see a couple metabolizing the persecutory impact of the vertical link to the previous generation and creating a better horizontal link for themselves, and so improving the vertical link for their children. The couple relationship is caught in the crosshairs of the vertical and horizontal axes. In general, we note an increment in the family's self-sufficiency, in the parents' containment of their internal objects even in the absence of support from me, and in the family's readiness to continue on the path of group and individual growth.

Chapter 5

The Social Unconscious

We have presented our theory of the interpersonal unconscious and the theory of the link. We have said that the individual is born into the link, and that the couple forms at the crosshairs of the link, at the intersection of the vertical axis (from the previous generations) and the horizontal axis (from the family, society, and culture). Now we will focus on the impact of that aspect of the link that features culture and connect it to the concept of the social unconscious. We will take one example from Chinese culture to illustrate the penetration of culture into the unconscious life of a couple.

Working with Chinese psychotherapists in the last few years has given us examples of the action of the link and the effect of the social unconscious, which are particularly vivid because of the immense cultural shifts in China in the twentieth century (D. Scarff 2011c). Drawing from writing Jill Scharff did with our colleague Qijia Shi on a case treated in his hospital, we begin with a comparison of attitudes toward concepts of the good husband and the good wife before 1911, from 1911–1980, and from 1980–2011, the era of social and economic reform, which includes openness to psychoanalytic thinking in China (Shi and J. Scharff 2008). We present Dr. Shi's example of a Chinese mixed-culture marriage, a Han-Uyghur couple, to show how conservative and contemporary values create conflict in a Chinese marriage, in this case expressed in both spouses' somatic disorders: the husband's painful throat and the wife's terrifyingly suicidal reaction to a pregnancy. We discuss the case both from a socio-psycho-somato-dynamic perspective derived from Dr. Shi's experience in China and Western Europe, from our object relations perspective derived from experience in Great Britain and the

United States, and from our study of community health and the social unconscious (Savege 1973; Hopper 1996). We hope to show how shifting economic policies and Western influence (including psychoanalysis), social change, and personal dynamic factors interact as the present and the past come into conflict within marital relationships.

FROM INDIVIDUAL TO SOCIAL SYSTEM

By the time Freud had constructed his structural theory (1923), he had realized that the individual psyche is composed from "subject-matter-memory traces of the experience of earlier generations" (1939, p. 99). He was keenly aware of the mutual influence of social and personal dynamic factors in the creation and functioning of individual personality as well. He wrote, "the events of human history, the interactions between human nature, cultural development and the precipitates of primaeval experiences . . . are no more than a reflection of the dynamic conflicts between the ego, the id and the super-ego . . . are the very same processes repeated upon a wider stage" (Freud 1925, p. 72). Foulkes put it this way: "The individual is as much compelled by these colossal forces as by his own id and defends himself against their recognition without being aware of it" (1964, p. 258). But the social system is more than a context or matrix that shapes the individual. The social system is reciprocally affected by the force of individual impulses, needs, wishes, and defensive actions. As Freud (1915) put it, "Each individual somehow recapitulates in an abbreviated form the entire development of the human race" (p. 199).

THE SOCIAL UNCONSCIOUS

The term social unconscious was introduced in Europe by S. H. Foulkes to refer to the mental representation of the colossal forces of history and culture and their impact on individuals (Foulkes 1964). This concept expands on Pichon Rivière's idea of the horizontal link connecting individual, couple, and family to the wider culture. Elaborating on Foulkes's idea, Hopper (1996) presented the social unconscious arising from experience in the social matrix as the foundation for human development. The social unconscious is a constellation of social, cultural and communicational arrangements which are governed by laws of functioning, just as the individual unconscious is. These laws of functioning protect the individual from recognizing the impact of social forces, just as repression protects the individual psyche from remembering impulses and experiences that were too painful to handle. Similarly people may not want to know about the social force-field in which they live, may not admit to what they know, or may not accept its impact in order to avoid feeling helpless in the face of influences too sweeping to control. Even when their impact is noted, there may be no way to reflect on the influences and respond to them while the person remains in the same culture. Cultural forces remain unacknowledged in thought, but they are registered unconsciously and persist as unease and fear. So the social unconscious supplies a defensive system to protect individuals and families from these shared unconscious fears. Institutions have defenses to protect their members against social anxiety in the institution (Jacques 1951). For instance, anxiety about illness is defended against in hospitals by hierarchical staffing structures that substitute recognition of authority based on skill and seniority for helplessness in the face of death (Menzies-Lyth 1959). With the social unconscious functioning to keep social forces out of awareness, some people may accept their circumstances, some develop symptoms of mental or physical stress that they cannot explain properly, and some experience relationship difficulties. The dynamic forces that the social unconscious tries to contain nevertheless continue to seek expression, and drive the re-creation of past social situations in the social world. The social unconscious connects each person to the wider culture and is the vehicle for the transmission of experience to the next generation, and it operates through what Foulkes and other group analysts have termed the foundation matrix (Hopper 2003). We think that Foulkes's concept comes close to the Latin American concept of the link operating along horizontal and vertical axes.

How do individuals respond to the influence of culture? They take in identifications with the large group or culture in the same way that they take in the relationship with parental figures or others. In each individual, this process of identification with the values or opinions of the large group leads to the formation of an internal object in the mind of that person. This is called the social object (Aviram 2005, 2009). Like other internal objects, it can be good or bad, satisfying, exciting, or persecuting. For instance, in the example that follows, we will see that the husband carries a powerfully motivating idealized internal social object—the value of having a son. His wife's refusal to gratify the wish stemming from this internalized value torments him, and she becomes a persecuting object attacking his idealized internal social object.

We will now review some of the social, cultural and communicational arrangements that comprise the social force field in China over the centuries.

SOCIO-DYNAMIC UNDERSTANDING OF HUSBAND-WIFE RELATIONSHIPS IN CHINA

Before 1911

Before 1911, before the collapse of the Qing dynasty, the last royal dynasty, the relationship between husband and wife, defined by social convention, was built on personal loyalty, goodness, intelligence, and above all, on ritual. Ritual was important in ancient China because the people knew less about science in those days. They believed that the world was ordered by the sky, a natural god of comfort and discipline with whom ritual could connect them. Concrete, complex rituals allowed them to express their respect, usually in the form of religious belief. In this social order, elderly men enjoyed the greatest privilege of respect, while women and children were devalued. Until she was married, a woman could not go about freely but must stay home reading and doing the housework. She was not even allowed to have visitors. When it was time to get married, she accepted the man selected for her as her fate, and she married him without getting to know him, without even knowing what he looked like. Confucius emphasized social authority, and relegated the marital couple to a position of less importance than the relationship between king and subject, or father and son. The couple was always less important than the extended family, a big family governed by authorities, all of them male, although women as grandmothers did exercise greater power than they had as mothers.

Looking ahead to her marriage, a woman hoped that her husband would be handsome, well-educated, and rich. She hoped that she would quickly bear him a child, preferably a son. She prayed that her mother-in-law and her sisters-in-law would be kind because she knew that a good relationship with them was more important than how she got along with her husband. She and her husband and any child they might have would belong to and depend on the extended family. The marriage would probably not be exclusive, and she must accept her husband's concubines and share him with them.

A man wanted a wife who would have an easy pregnancy and be kind to his mother. A wife from a good family should be well educated in poetry, chess, handwriting, and painting. She should be sympathetic and uncomplaining about his late nights and his concubines. He would do as he pleased with his time and his sexuality, although it should be added that the man would go to concubines more for the purpose of getting extra sons than for the pleasure of sex. Gu Hongming in the later Qing dynasty described this type of relationship as "one teapot filling many cups." The man wanted to be accepted and indulged by his wife, but he did not expect to show her affection in front of family members. He wanted her to bear him a child, preferably a boy. As a man himself and therefore the acknowledged authority, he would be a good son to his parents, and he would take full responsibility for the family and its lifestyle.

Men, and therefore sons, were given great importance. They carried the family name, they provided the work force, and they provided financial support and insurance against hard times. The man's name, his work, and his sons carried his legacy. The man was in the contradictory situation of holding authority and being a symbol of psychological maturity while at the same time having no autonomy since he belonged to his family. Meanwhile women were seen as having little importance beyond child-bearing. They were perceived as dependent, useless, and less well-educated than men. Their feet were bound to prevent them being active and self-determining. All they could do was to serve as a decorative ritual object.

In summary, the woman was a devalued, dependent figure who projected her wishes for fulfillment on her relationships with her father, husband, and son. The man was an aggrandized figure who sought fulfillment by getting a high social position through his level of learning achieved by reading and through the number of concubines he could support.

From 1911–1980

With the decline of the Qing dynasty at the turn of the twentieth century, the culture began to change. Chinese intellectuals spear-headed the New Culture Movement of May 4 to promote changes from 1915–1919. Feet-binding of girls was eliminated, women were allowed to get an education, and they could choose whether to marry. They could decide when to separate from their family of origin, whom to marry, whether to get pregnant, and when to have a child. The women's liberation movement had begun. After 1949, the People's Republic of China was established, and the lot of women continued to improve despite the economic travails of the Great Leap Forward and the Cultural Revolution that sent intellectuals to work in the fields. No longer controlled by men, women worked as hard as men, sometimes at two jobs, regardless of whether they were menstruating or pregnant, in defiance of the limits of their physiology. And as women do, they formed community associations, professional associations, and women's groups for support. The slogan used at that time to capture the changes was: "Woman holds half the sky."

The elevated status of women brought advantages. They had the right to their own identity in the family and in society. Their new status and earning power blew away the narcissistic fantasy of the Chinese being poor and gave China a right to respect in the world. This was a hard time for China who saw itself separated from Europe and the United States, threatened by its former ally, the Soviet Union, facing possible war with India and Taiwan, actually engaged in war with Korea, and confronting the usual natural catastrophes and political conflicts. Yet China under Chairman Mao remained optimistic, maybe even manic. The slogan for China at this stage was: "Human Being could make everything, could overcome even god!" Against a background of enormous change and widespread catastrophe, we see changes in the wife and husband's ideas about themselves, their beliefs, their relationship, and their families.

The wife now expected a husband to be egalitarian and independent, and to come preferably from a family of peasants or workers from the church, the military, or the government. She expected a modest life-style, partly supported by her earnings. She wanted to feel free to come and go as she pleased, and to be respected at work. She wanted to marry one man who would be faithful to her. The man wanted his wife to be a modern woman, not materialistic, not disabled, and to come from a respected military or peasant family. As for the husband, he wanted to be a good parent, to be respectful of others' feelings, to be faithful to his wife, and to be authoritarian with the child.

Men felt that women developed an inflated idea of themselves and their importance. Women identified with the independent masculine role but, previously confused by the male social role, now they were confused by their own interpretation of it. They argued with their men and with their society, and the children were more neglected than they had been in former times. Men were upset by their wives' argumentativeness because to the men, conflict was shameful and maintaining harmony was their responsibility, and therefore any domestic strife was their fault. Men were pretending to be good men rather than being good husbands.

From 1980–Present

When the Gang of Four (comprising Mao Zedong's last wife and her close associates) fell in a coup d'état on October 6, 1976, a mere month after Mao's death, a turbulent political era in China ended and gave way to a period of economic and social reform. In the 1970s, the one-child policy was introduced into China and was adopted as law in 1992. It applied to everyone in principle but it was more successful in the cities than in the rural areas where farm hands were always needed. Urban Chinese people got used to having only one child in the family. By the 1980s, society had recognized the value of knowledge, and intellectuals who had been relegated to manual work in the countryside during the Cultural Revolution were respected once more. Marriage to a spouse with a bachelor's degree became the new dream. At the beginning of the 1990s, business was devalued while students and intellectuals were highly valued. China, increasingly affected by globalization, changed and kept changing. With women more independent and men sharing their values of autonomy and fidelity, the actuality of the big extended family collapsed and the new small families became increasingly isolated.

We describe these phases of development in the last three eras in Chinese society and culture in terms drawn from social science as "ideal types"—accentuation of certain elements of the infinite variety of diffuse and complex social processes distilled into an abstract and unified analytical construct (Weber 1949). Our descriptions do not aspire to be historically detailed and comprehensive portraits of the social reality of China during these phases of socio-economic and political development. We are using them simply to explain the essential features of social processes over time in relation to the marital difficulties of Chinese couples for the purpose of understanding marital tensions in the cultural context. The phases described are similar to those detected in all countries that have developed from an agrarian to an urbanized, industrialized society. In China, the processes are implemented with astonishing speed because of the power of the dictatorial style of government. Social factors continue to change rapidly, and interact with personal dynamic factors in increasingly complex combinations. Since the mid-1990s, the country has been gradually opening its doors to psychoanalytic investigation (D. Scarff in press).

The following example demonstrates intercultural conflict resulting from rapid social change in China, the one child law, the differing expectations found in distinctly different Chinese sub-cultures, and changes in male-female expectations. It also illustrates the type of marital problem and couple therapy being offered in China for treating the symptoms from a perspective that is socio-culturally and psychoanalytically informed (Shi et al. 2006). We will comment on the unconscious constraints exerted by various features of social and cultural arrangements upon the societal context of the family and its effect on the family members. Even when a family is made aware of the social, economic, cultural and political constraints, they may not feel empowered to release themselves. This is similar to the family that becomes aware of neurotic defenses against development, and yet cannot move forward. Insight alone does not lead to change. But offering paths toward insight, we can begin a process of understanding and working through in the context of a healing relationship.

CLINICAL EXAMPLE: INTERCULTURAL CONFLICT

Mr. Wang and Mrs. Ayi (in Chinese culture the wife keeps her family name) met with a Chinese-trained medical psychotherapist who is introducing into the treatment psychoanalytic ideas from his training in

Western Europe (Shi and J. Scharff 2008). The vignettes are drawn from a therapy session with the husband as an individual and from a session with husband and wife as a couple. Our comments on the social and personal dynamic features are dispersed among the vignettes.

Wang Minxing is a 39-year-old man, married with one daughter. He is the owner of a private company. He is short and of medium build. He is warm, fluent, and cooperative, but his mood is angry and depressed and his speech loud—and louder when angry. In the assessment interview, his therapist felt that, although Mr. Wang Minxing looked relaxed sitting in the chair, he might stand up and confront him at any moment.

Mr. Wang told his therapist that since the spring festival of 2007, he had had discomfort in his throat but no difficulty in swallowing, and that chronic laryngitis had been diagnosed. When medical treatment produced no improvement, he had undergone bilateral tonsillectomy in hospital. One week after surgery, he had felt back to normal again but discomfort and swelling in the throat soon started up again. He experienced difficulty in falling asleep and staying deeply asleep, because of nightmares and early awakening. When the throat discomfort and insomnia became worse, he started seeking various treatments including herbal medicine, but without much improvement in his symptoms. Having experienced discomfort and swelling in the throat for 6 months and insomnia for 3 months, Mr. Wang still had no identifiable organic cause for his symptoms and no relief from a variety of medical approaches. He was referred by the outpatient clinic in a general University hospital for in-patient psychiatric treatment over a month-long stay (quite rare in the United States these days, but offered in China to accommodate patients from rural areas with no psychiatric services). Mr. Wang had 10 sessions of twice weekly individual therapy and 2 of individual therapy with a male psychiatrist over the course of a month in the psychotherapy hospital under the direction of Dr. Shi. In his individual therapy Mr. Wang revealed that he wished he had more time with his wife and he longed for her to be more caring of him. Ultimately, he acknowledged a deep fear of death. We will present material gathered during his individual therapy and follow with vignettes from individual and from couple therapy.

Mr. Wang was born in the countryside to peasant parents, now aged 70. Mr. Wang is the fourth of six children of this family. He has two older brothers, one older sister, and two younger brothers. Among the five boys, the second son did the best academically, followed by his elder brother and Mr. Wang, all three of whom finished college education. Mr. Wang was a graduate from the Department of Law of the local university. Two younger brothers graduated from middle school with 9 years of education.

The cost of education is a big concern for Chinese students from the countryside. If they do well up to middle school in the rural school, they have the opportunity to enter a high school in the town, but that can strain the already limited resources of the family. If they go to college, the tuition fee is $800 (a huge increase from $200 ten years ago). Some families are able to afford for one child to go to college, but it is difficult to support several college tuitions. Even though education loans and scholarships are available now, girls in the family often lose the opportunity to go to college in favor of the son. Mr. Wang was proud of his educational level and his eligibility for marriage.

In 1998, Mr. Wang opened his own furniture manufacturing business in Shenzhen where he had worked since 1993. In the early 1990s, Shenzhen became a city many people rushed to for job opportunities. The population of the new city became younger, more sensitive to social change, and fiercely competitive. Once Mr. Wang was successful, he began to look for a wife.

History of the Marriage

Mr. Wang met Ayi Guli, a woman from Xin Jiang Autonomous Region, through match-making services. Ayi Guli is of the Uyghur people, an ethnic minority in Xin Jiang (where some of the film *The Kite Runner* was filmed) in North Western China, which accounts for one sixth of China. Among the ethnic minority groups in Xin Jiang, the majority are Uyghur, mostly Muslim, and others that follow various religions. These minority groups have customs and life styles quite distinct from the Han Chinese who comprise more than 90% of the population in most areas of China and over 40% in Xin Jiang Autonomous Region. Ayi Guli was taller than Wang Minxing and she was very pretty, decisive, and adventurous. They moved in together and were constantly moving their home from one place to another in Shenzhen. Living together, but not married, she got pregnant twice and had two abortions.

In 1999, they married. Mr. Wang's mother-in-law did not like him, stating that he and his life situation in Shenzhen were not appropriate for her daughter. When he called her "Mother," she cried, leaving him at a loss for words. Later on, she explained that she cried because she missed her daughter too much after such a long separation, but he felt that she cried at losing her daughter to someone she regarded as unworthy. He appeased his mother-in-law by agreeing to give his wife 30% of the company. Holding 60% of the company, Mr. Wang was still the major owner but his wife was the legal representative and manager.

Now married, Mrs. Ayi became pregnant, and this time she did not choose abortion. However, she promptly had a suicidal reaction to her pregnancy. Terrified by her symptom of wanting to jump from a great height, she considered abortion again, but was dissuaded from it by the family. After the baby was born a girl, Mr. Wang tried to convince his wife to have a second child hoping to have a son, but she refused to go through the ordeal of another pregnancy.

In the history of the Han people, only the son of the family can inherit property and carry on the family name, an idea that is especially prevalent in the countryside where males also constitute the labor force. Unlike Han people, minority couples can still have more than one child. So, Mr. Wang, married to a Uyghur woman, would have been entitled to try again, but his wife was adamant in her refusal. This caused enormous conflict between them.

Ayi Guli was the only child of a textile factory worker in Xin Jiang. Her parents had good positions at work and loved and indulged their daughter. Not until she married, had her child, and ran the business, did she feel that she really matured from an irresponsible girl to a reliable, hardworking woman. Mrs. Ayi wanted to care more for her husband but she was too preoccupied with their business. Anyway, she felt that he was a hypochondriac.

Symptoms and Individual Interpretation

The Chinese psychotherapist operates within the link, the foundational matrix, of theories embedded in centuries of Chinese medicine. On this vertical axis, he carries with him the idea that the throat symbolizes a critical pathway, which if obstructed will cause great danger, as when a fishbone is stuck in the throat. He guesses that the discomfort in Mr. Wang's throat equates to a fear of loss of control and death anxiety. He hypothesizes that Mr. Wang is suffering from a constricted feeling that his fate is now in the control of his wife and her family, rather than looking for causes within Mr. Wang's experiences in his own family of origin. Mr. Wang grew up in a poor family and, by hard work was a self-made man with his own company, which was, however, gradually controlled by his wife's family. So, perhaps Mr. Wang worries that his company may eventually be taken over by his wife's family—a precarious situation like having a fish bone stuck in the throat.

The therapist has also been exposed on the horizontal axis to Western ideas of a symptom as the expression of an emotional discomfort, a block, a fear, or a feeling that has become separated from a disavowed thought, a symbol of unconscious conflict. He uses interpretation to make the unconscious wish or fear conscious so that it can be spoken about, addressed, relieved, and resolved.

The First Vignette, from an Individual Therapy Session

THERAPIST: Tonsillectomy is a minor operation and it has been almost a year since experts assured you there was no physical cause for your symptoms. Still, you are concerned about your health, and you are still feeling discomfort.

MR. WANG: Yes, I am still uncomfortable.

THERAPIST: I wonder if your throat problem might have to do with conflicts with your family and within yourself. How might conflict be connected to a problem in the tonsil area?

MR. WANG: I thought my discomfort was due to chronic laryngitis, but after the tonsillectomy I still had it, and so I thought it was an after-effect of the surgery. I have no idea what the scientific explanation is, and I don't know the way doctors think. I try my best not to believe that my discomfort is caused by psychological factors and family conflicts. I'd rather believe it was due to my tonsils. This is what I prefer to think.

THERAPIST: I see that you are reluctant to associate your discomfort with family and psychological factors, but there is no indication that there is anything wrong with your tonsils. You told me that before your wife came into your life, you were not ill, and that nothing was wrong with you. You told me that you need to be more cared for by her. You say that you'd rather be physically ill, not psychologically ill. However, what you suffer from is the need to be cared for. Your restlessness and insecurity, the need to be cared for, could all be attributed to psychological factors, rather than physical illnesses. Is there anything that could link all these together?

MR. WANG: During treatment, I expect the best of everything. I bought quite a few books, I spent 800 RMB on them ($117). All of them are on psychology, and all by the masters. For instance, I have one on Maslow's hierarchy of needs and one on neurosis written by a female American expert. I've been reading carefully, and now I think my throat symptoms are due to anxiety and depression. Is that right, Doctor? Yes, it must be. My illness must be a manifestation of psychological conflicts. This I no longer deny. Many things have contributed to my illness including my wife and mother-in-law's rather insensitive personalities, which is quite different from my own personality. I am a very cautious, sensitive person, maybe even a dependent personality.

Learning from Books or Professional Relationship

The therapist speaks to Mr. Wang from a theoretical perspective derived from his psychoanalytically oriented training. Like the therapist, Mr. Wang indicates the high value he places on education, intellect, and success. Interestingly he refers to Maslow, whose hierarchy of needs lists money as an important need—in Mr. Wang's life, a sign of his success as a businessman. He also mentions choosing a book on neurosis, which echoes his therapist's attempt to convince him of the dynamic source of his physical symptom. We feel a culture clash between Chinese and Western modes of expression. At first Mr. Wang rebuffs the therapist's interpretation, and then he swings over to accepting his idea rather quickly, as if shamed into it by the authority of knowledge. Trusting what he has read more than his therapist's interpretation, Mr. Wang goes on to interpret his own deepest anxiety.

MR. WANG: Through my reading, I got more understanding and realized a truth, a very simple truth: that is, I have been afraid of death all the time. Now I am still very afraid of death. Death has bothered me for quite a while since I started to read Schopenhauer and Nietzsche. This fear has been hidden in a certain dark corner of my heart and has controlled my emotions.

When I was sick this time, I worried it was something really serious, like cancer. However, I dared not tell my wife my worries. I once told her, "Wife, I would like to have a whole-body check-up, blood tests, laryngoscopy, a complete check-up. I would feel relieved if don't really have any organic illnesses, and my sleep would improve." But after I had the laryngoscopy, I thought, could it be the esophagus? I wasn't reassured. The worry about some severe illness exacerbated my anxiety and depression. I would like to tell my true feelings to my wife and ask her to care about me, but she is very busy with her work, and she is not good at expressing tenderness and care. She won't say, "How are you feeling, Husband? How have you been?" I've never got that from her. Even when she was on a business trip, she seldom called me. I really take that to heart. I said, "Wife, however busy you might be, you should be able to give me a call." On the days when she called, I slept better. When she did not call, I just felt uncomfortable.

Aggression and Longing

Mr. Wang's aggression is turned against himself in various ways. In his physical ailments, anger against others is hidden and turned against his throat. Discomfort in his throat gives him a reason not to shout out and perhaps not to say anything at all about his emotional distress, and so he fails to assert himself. In giving up control of his company, he attacked his success and independence. He longs for comfort and care from his wife who he feels does not wish to mother him. In his sadness over this deprivation, instead of crying about it, he develops symptoms of having a lump in his throat. Here we see a conversion symptom in which his throat expresses his grief, his fear, his aggression, his longing, and his humiliation that his masculine authority is no longer given pride of place. So his throat is an individual symptom, a symptom of the couple dynamics, and a reaction to cultural change.

The Second Vignette, from a Couple Therapy Session

In couple therapy, Mr. Wang and Mrs. Ayi sat at a distance and did not make direct eye contact. Mrs. Ayi did not talk much in the beginning, but when she did, she spoke eloquently and dominated the interview. Mr. Wang and Mrs. Ayi are each highly rational, emotionally distant, and blunt. The therapist is struck by her harsh tone towards Mr. Wang, and asks him how he feels about her manner of addressing him.

THERAPIST: (Speaking to Mr. Wang) Do you feel your wife treats you as a husband, or as a servant?

MR. WANG: I feel sometimes as a husband, sometimes, as a servant, sometimes both. (Turning toward his wife who is looking angry) This is how I feel. Wife, please don't be upset that I feel this way. (Turning toward the therapist) She is just so demanding. If it was an occasional thing, I would be very happy to do what she wants me to, but it is always like this, and it makes me feel oppressed. I am a man, right? It should be me who has the say, but it is the opposite.

Mr. Wang's humiliation as a disempowered man is a personal effect of his sensitive nature, and it is rooted in the cultural link.

THERAPIST: You mean that the man should take charge?

MR. WANG: The man should have the say at home, should take the lead. For instance, last night, I drove back home in my jeep following my younger brother's car. From Wu Jiang Mountain to Qing Shan Boulevard, my brother drove really fast. I followed him closely. Maybe I was driving too fast and too close to his car, but there was no traffic and it was close to 10 at night, but she had to pick a fight about it. She said, "Get out of the jeep. Let me drive." My second oldest brother was sitting on my right hand without saying anything. She was sitting in the back trying to get me to stop and get out of the jeep.

THERAPIST: Was your daughter on board?

MR. WANG: Yes. Our daughter was on board.

MRS. AYI: Our daughter was in the jeep with other two kids. So there were THREE kids sitting in the back besides me! He drove so fast, and would not slow down . . .

MR. WANG: The car in front of us was driving even faster.

MRS. AYI: I don't care about the car ahead of us, but we had three kids on board! My daughter was so scared that she covered her eyes. She was holding on to me tightly, panicking, and telling me she was scared. Right?

MR. WANG: But actually . . .

MRS. AYI: So I said, "Why don't you get out of that seat? Let me drive!" I don't think what I did was wrong. We argue a lot about this. He likes to speed as if this is what a man should do. As far as I am concerned, as a man he is irresponsible. For instance, he bought insurance, but what he bought is not enough. I told him that as a man, he should have a sense of responsibility. When there are elders and children on board, you should not drive as fast as you always do because all their lives are in your hands. When he is alone, he drives like crazy. I asked him if he ever thought about our family. Does he ever think about us?

THERAPIST: You have a point there, but when you didn't like his driving, you got nasty. Would it have gone better if you would have said it nicely, like saying softly, "Honey, can I drive?"

The therapist is speaking from his identification with Mr. Wang as a man who is bossed around and victimized by a woman's harshness.

MR. WANG: She was giving orders.

MRS. AYI: Yes I was! I feel it is quite reasonable, given that he was driving so fast. You are not supposed to speed like that.

MR. WANG: The therapist is asking about the tone of your voice, the tone!

THERAPIST: How would it be if she talked to you in a different tone?

MR. WANG: Exactly. I was not happy about the tone in her voice. If she said, "Husband, please don't drive so quickly, it is not safe to drive like this," I would have listened. Yet, she was so angry and demanding, which made me lose face in front of my older brother. If I was not sick and in treatment like now, I would have been so pissed I would have driven even faster. Do you understand what I mean, Doctor? Because when I am driving fast, I forget about my pain and my illness. It is therapeutic for my illness. If you told me to speed on the highway, I would do it now, because, it is good for my illness. I forget all the pain, all the worries. Even the depression disappears.

Feelings of Powerlessness, Lack of Confidence, and Humiliation

Now we learn about another symptom—fast, reckless driving. The Chinese therapist formulates his understanding in terms of his identification with the man. Mr. Wang's biggest wish is to have a son, who will inherit the family business. In China, especially, in rural areas, not having a son to continue the family line and fill the labor force is considered the worst offense against the concept of filial piety. In driving fast, Mr. Wang is using aggressive driving to feel powerful so as to cover the pain of longing for an obedient wife to love him and give him a son to carry his legacy.

It seems to us that the therapist is encouraging sympathy for the humiliated man, promoting the idea of placating him, and supporting male authority and dignity. From a Western point of view, we see the symptom of fast driving as a triumphant discharge in which his expression of phallic aggression and defiance of his wife relieve his humiliation and subordination. But the Chinese therapist is closer to what is on Mr. Wang's mind.

MR. WANG: The reality is I want a son. I talked to her so many times, yet she still doesn't want to. She said she is not ready to accept a child, she won't get pregnant, she won't have a child. Then . . .

THERAPIST: But she hasn't refused 100%, right?

MR. WANG: About 70%.

THERAPIST: What she said in the last session was that she wasn't ready psychologically, not that . . .

MR. WANG: She said only when she could accept a child psychologically, would she be able to get pregnant. But she is past 35, too old already! Besides, my oldest brother had a son just last month when he was 46. His daughter is 13 years old, and now he has a 1–month-old son. My second older brother has two sons. My two younger brothers both have two daughters, but they are preparing to have more children. I believe in Buddhism. If you don't have a son, you disappear from the family tree. I am working on my family tree, the Wang family's genogram. My family name is Wang, you know. I looked at the previous generations. Where you only have daughters and no sons, the family line is discontinued on that branch. I am afraid that after I die, my gravesite would be very lonely. No one would come to mourn me. I only have a daughter, and when she is married, she will belong to another family. She won't be able to come back often to worship me. Believe it or not, I feel I would be so lonely without a son. I would be a lonely soul and a wild ghost. While I am still alive, I want to plan for the future when I am dead. However, she does not understand.

She scoffs at my idea and at my pain: "Want another child? A child is only a toy. One child is fine." Financially we can afford a second child, but she just won't even consider it. I guess it means first of all she does not love me much; secondly, she cares too much about how she looks; third, to be fair, she is busy working. But I still feel, however busy she is, getting pregnant and having another child only takes a year. In fact, her mother also supports her having a second child. But she just refuses to.

THERAPIST: (To Mrs. Ayi) Do you think you can still have another child?

MR. WANG: (Answering before she can say a word) We should be able to.

MRS. AYI: But, I am not ready psychologically. I can not accept another child for now, because my last pregnancy was not an easy one. I vomited from the beginning to the last minute. This whole process was so painful. When I was pregnant, I cried everyday. I told him I did not want to live. I did not. It felt horrible.

MR. WANG: It is true that she had a difficult pregnancy.

MRS. AYI: So I am always terrified of having a child. Terribly afraid.

MR. WANG: Once we went on a business trip to Zhangzhou. We were driving on the highway. At first, we were talking pleasantly about something. (Turning to Mrs. Ayi) Do you remember, wife? (Turning to the therapist) All of a sudden, she said, "Husband, please do not expect me to give you a son in this life." That moment, my heart sank to the bottom. I felt so bad that I would rather crash on the highway and die. (Turning to Mrs. Ayi) Let us die. There is nothing worth living for. You and I might as well die together. (Turning back to the therapist) This is how I felt. I wanted to die. But she was not aware of my feelings. I wanted to crash our car into the curb and die. We would have died instantly at a speed of 130 km per hour. (Turning toward Mrs. Ayi) You know, that's how I felt.

Now we see that both members of the couple are expressing death anxiety: Mr. Wang is frightened of dying by not having a son and Mrs. Ayi by being forced to have a pregnancy that could make her suicidal again. His individual symptom is speaking for the couple. The conflict over the personal and cultural future has become a life or death matter for both of them. Mr. Wang feels unconsciously that his loss of control over his wife and her procreativity will kill his future and Mrs. Ayi feels that his attempts at seizing control will kill her now. When Mr. Wang put into words the death anxiety that his Chinese therapist had suspected from the beginning, it could be worked with and detoxified for him and for the couple. The Chinese therapist reported that the pressure on the couple diminished and their adjustment improved. After his discharge from hospital psychotherapy treatment, Mr. Wang went home, rededicated himself to his goals, and opened a new company, not managed by his wife. Mrs. Ayi agreed to consider having another child in three years, and she sent her mother back to Xinjiang.

Couple Transference and Countertransference

Mrs. Ayi who is determined, young, beautiful, and confident, feels that her husband is not her equal, but she is vulnerable and needs to be cared for by him. She has a transference towards him as a parent she longs for, but defends against it by thinking of him as a child. She projects her hated neediness into him and denigrates him for his weakness. Mr. Wang longs for a wife who will look up to him and bolster his authority. He wants her to make him feel worthy as the father of a son, and without an actual son, the husband remains in the son role himself, looking for a nurturing mother in his wife, but experiencing his wife as a bony fish that sticks in his throat. He projects his masculine strength into her as a strong person who can run his company and take care of him. Then the loss of control leaves him feeling emasculated, for which he compensates by fast driving. The couple is filled with seething resentment, distrust, and rebellion, voiced also by Mrs. Ayi's mother.

Countertransference develops as a reaction in the therapist to the way that the couple behaves in the here-and-now during the session as the partners talk about what has happened and how they feel about each other. Both members of the couple, and the two of them as a pair, evoke a response. In this session, the husband recruited the therapist to form alliances against his strong-willed wife. The therapist felt as if there were a three-member family with the therapist and the wife both being the adults, and the husband being the dependent child in need of care. Monitoring this response leads to an understanding from inside the therapist's own experience. As a Han Chinese man himself, the therapist is living in a similar link as the man in the couple. This helps him be empathic, but it is also a constraint against seeing beyond the cultural imperatives. This can be a stumbling block if it remains a blind spot, but when the therapist understands the social forces upon the family and therapist system, he can use his experience to empathize with the patients and and analyze the nature of his engagement with them.

Social Interpretation

The pressures facing this couple are typical in this time of rapid economic change in China. Most families who seek counseling are among the newly rich who have become wealthy through their own hard work, not from inherited family money. This couple is from Shenzhen—a rapidly growing coastal city in the frontier of economic reform in Southern China. In the early stage of the reform, the ideologies in Shenzhen were often in conflict with that of the more reserved inland China. The couple's structure, however, is unique: the Han Chinese husband is from rural central China where more conservative traditions still prevail while the Uyghur wife is from Xinjiang Uyghur Autonomous Region, a diverse region with a number of religions and minorities not dominated by Han Chinese assumptions about male dominance and respect of elders. The main conflict over the lack of male offspring in the family also serves as the location for the conflict in the couple over meeting dependent needs and finding self esteem.

The Chinese Concept of Ruin after Good Fortune

For generations, Chinese have looked down on doing business as the way to wealth, however profitable business can be. Chinese people place great value on becoming a great learner first. After that, if you still have extra time, then you may consider becoming an official and serving the government. The Chinese also believe that frugality is the cornerstone of wealth. This began to change in Shenzhen in the late 1980s, when many people became wealthy by doing business, sometimes illegally when the rules and regulations were not yet clearly defined. Many became rich all of a sudden, and spent lavishly. There is a saying in "I Ching" (the Book of Changes) that extreme good fortune will eventually reverse. Becoming wealthy overnight and having too much good fortune could spell ruin. The excess of good fortune would make the loss of it more dramatic, more unbearable, and traumatic. This rule applies both to individuals and families. There are many memories to feed the fear of loss provoked by good fortune—natural catastrophes, sweeping agricultural policies that backfired, and the confiscation of land and property from people of wealth beginning in 1949.

There is a Chinese saying: A family won't be able to sustain its wealth over three generations. This aphorism could also be applied to the country of China itself: the past few years have been a time of great economic development in China. The stock market index jumped from 3000 to 6000 in less than 6 months. People could not help asking how much longer good days like this would last. Successful couples grew anxious, wondering whether they could get ahead financially without risking misfortune that would cut them down to size and punish them for their wealth and implied greed. They wanted to enjoy progress to live a comfortable life and provide for their parents, but without humiliating them. They wanted to embrace the new opportunity and yet maintain their Chinese family values, including honoring their parents.

Patricide versus Filial Piety

From a Western psychoanalytic point of view, a son from the countryside who finished college and made money could feel that he had defeated and emasculated his own father in a symbolic act of parricide. This formulation goes against Chinese culture. The Chinese version of the morality of the Oedipal conflict is that the son would kill himself before he would kill his father (Shi 2004, Zhang 2008). This hypothesis fits with Ming Dong Gu's assertion that "the Oedipus complex in Chinese culture has transformed into a related filial piety complex" (Gu 2006). Mr. Wang's symptoms result from aggression turned against the self, preventing healthy functioning of his body, his family life, and his business. Mr. Wang's decision to give up management of his company may have been due to an unconscious preference to lead an ordinary life as an expression of filial piety, leading him to project his masculine strength into his wife in unconscious deference to the authority of his internal father.

In ancient China, the concept of filial piety was used to maintain order in the family. In the traditional Chinese family to this day, children are indoctrinated with the value of filial piety from an early age. People of younger generations have to suppress their own needs and desires, which affects their personality development during the formative years. As adults, the sons must "have their own precious sons early" and "the more sons the merrier." Sons carry the family line and in an agrarian society sons maintain the labor force. This societal emphasis from a time when China was an agrarian society developed into a widespread admiration for the male and his phallic power. A daughter-in-law who can produce male offspring is well received by her in-laws; otherwise, she is discriminated against. In this way, the gene pool and the name of the family is preserved. In this ethic, it is more important for a man to bring a son to his parents than to earn more money. Without a son there is little reward in having money.

Understanding how thoroughly the value of sons imbues Chinese culture to this day helps us understand why Mr. Wang gave up on his business. His feelings of helplessness, his counterphobic reckless speeding on the highway, and his death anxiety, all relate to his lack of standing without a son.

Cultural Formulation in Terms of Traditional and Modern Ideology

The term "traditional, inland, and countryside attitudes" implies conservative, backward, and obsolete ways of thinking and behaving in which filial piety, patriarchy, and having male offspring top the list. These attitudes often mean living near one's parents, working for one employer, loyalty to the leaders, blind obedience to management, and proper behavior and appearance. Emerging attitudes in the last 25 years include freedom, geographical mobility, equality of respect for men and women, pursuit of new fashion, no longer obeying blindly, and not being controlled.

Although Mr. Wang is successful in the new economy, his attitudes are more traditional than Mrs. Ayi's. Coming from the Xinjiang Uyghur ethnic group, she has strong family values and is conservative, not unlike Mr. Wang's family, and yet, in taking action without reservation, she is like her own pioneering people who live in the vast, desolate Western region where there is an emphasis on self-reliance. Unwilling to be confined to the role of housewife assisting her husband and teaching the children, she wants to work and play to the full extent that modern life affords. She enjoys singing and disco, and she plays an important role in the management of their company. She is far from a traditional Chinese woman. Coming from the Uyghur culture, Mrs. Ayi is more adapted than Mr. Wang to the pioneering life in Shenzhen.

The conflict between Mr. Wang and Mrs. Ayi over the change of financial authority, her lack of concern for her husband and her unwillingness to have another child, is equally a conflict between traditional and modern ideology. The conflict arises from the fact that the husband who is not capable of individuation regresses in the face of changing demands, whereas his wife, unprepared to be bound by traditional constraints, is more able to adapt to the changing society.

An Object Relations Perspective: Projective Identification

Marital partners recreate versions of their internal object relationships in relation to their partners through an unconscious mental mechanism called projective identification in which they displace aspects of themselves into their intimate partner in order to communicate their experience to their partner, find relief from pain, struggle to deal with it by coming to terms with the partner, and so refind lost parts of themselves in each other.

Mr. Wang is suffering from a punishing and rejecting internal object relationship. If he cannot project this internal problem of his own into his wife and have it be modified by her love, he feels out of touch with her, and may need to turn an aspect of himself that he cannot find in her, back into himself.

Mr. Wang projects this painful object into his own body. There he identifies with it as a painful lump in his throat, which serves to get him the attention he is missing. This hysterical conversion of emotional pain to somatic symptom is a type of pathological expression, like those that Freud saw in sexually unliberated Europe in the nineteenth century, and that is now seen in sexually overstimulated areas, such as the United States in the twenty-first century where the incidence of anorexia is increasing as a defense against the sexual imperative of a fertile body. From the little we know of Mr. Wang's history, we cannot be sure of the origin of his rejecting internal object relationship. We know nothing of Mr. Wang's relationship with his mother. We do know that Mr. Wang has become more learned and economically successful than his father, a situation that may cause him Oedipal guilt, but we do not hear enough about his father to know how that fact has affected their relationship. Instead we hear about Mr. Wang's view of himself in relation to his brothers who are more like him.

Mr. Wang projects his persecutory object onto his brothers in relation to whom he feels likely to be shamed. He projects it into his wife by whom he feels rejected for needing her loving care and by whom he is denied the affirming joy of a male child. He creates a rejecting pair consisting of his brother and his wife, united in their disapproval of his desperation, a recreation in the real world of an internal couple in relation to which he feels unworthy. He also projects his rejecting object into the unborn son who is not there to give meaning to his existence. He projects it into (and receives it from) the cultural preoccupation with the lack of a son as the absence of affirmation and legacy of the father. There are ways in which he may perceive his wife as an exciting object too. The report tells us of her height and beauty, which could stimulate his desire for her and make her rejection the more painful, leaving him not just lonely but needy and craving for attention. As an Uyghur woman she has Government approval for having another child, a tantalizing opportunity to have the son for which he longs more desperately than if she were forbidden to conceive again.

For her part, Mrs. Ayi views Mr. Wang as an irresponsible father who dismisses her concerns for their daughter, their safety, and their future, causing her to attack him as her rejecting object. She sees him as a needy and demanding person, whose persistent longing for a son prompts him to ask her to endure the torture of another life-threatening pregnancy without concern for her. She experiences a prospective fetus as an equally demanding object with no concern for her. The case vignettes give little material about Mrs. Ayi's Uyghur parents except to say that they doted on their girl (which Han parents would probably not have done), so it is difficult to see whatever internal object valency drew her to find a rejecting and demanding object in Mr. Wang, but she does have the model of her mother rejecting her husband. However, in a situation where marriages are made as financial arrangements by the parents and not love matches by the young people, the matter of unconscious marital fit becomes relevant only after the couple is married. Perhaps as a self-made businesswoman she feels subordinated by her husband in being expected to be pregnant and by the demands of the Han culture for a son. The rights of her Uyghur culture to have more than one child exposes her to her husband's pressure. She experiences her husband (driven by personal and social needs) as a personally demanding object craving her love, and her mother as a controlling object, rejecting of her choice of husband, and yet paired with her husband in wanting her to bear another child. Did she perhaps wonder if Mr. Wang married her despite their cultural differences because, as a Uyghur, she could give him more than one chance at having a son? Mrs. Ayi in not wanting her pregnancy refutes aspects of the maternal role and identifies herself as a businesswoman, a role formerly enjoyed only by men. In this she identifies with the male privilege most valued in Chinese culture and so affirms Mr. Wang in valuing what is male while denying him access to it in terms that his culture requires.

Mr. Wang is unaware of the personal dynamics and social factors underpinning his somatic symptoms, but he is able to get some insight from reading and talking so as to move a bit beyond the hysterical somatic conversion of his emotional pain to formulate his depression as a failure to live up to his own ego ideal and to the cultural demands upon him. In terms of the social unconscious, Mr. Wang is not ignorant of the cultural forces at work in creating a desperate wish for a son but he is internally so much in their grip that he is unable to contemplate them in such a way as to formulate a more flexible response in keeping with his wife's wishes and capacity for maternity.

As a couple, the Wangs problems embody the conflicts between cultures in China, between generations, and between ancient and modern cultural values. China's economic and social movement under contemporary Western influences affects Chinese values and lifestyles. The vertical link to the ways of the previous generations is under pressure from the horizontal link to the ways of other countries in the global economy.

The Wangs project their individual intrapsychic conflicts born of the interaction between cultural experiences, family life, gender roles, and temperaments into each other and identify them there as if they were a part of the partner and not of the self. In this way, the conflict is out there, externalized in the partner where it can be seen and addressed. Each of them tries to control the conflict by badgering the other into submission. Unfortunately this means that the partner is diminished, or overvalued, in ways that reflect how the individual's ego attacked or cherished repressed objects prior to their projection into the couple relationship, and how, after the marriage, it continues to do so in the part of the self evacuated into the spouse. With help, the couple can observe and modify their projective identifications, recognize their cultural history and become aware of the impact of the social unconscious. Then they can mourn their personal, family, and cultural losses so that their marriage can become a healing environment for them and for their child.

SUMMARY

Unconscious thought, fantasies, and actions of individuals as a group give form to the social system, and the social system affects the unconscious of individuals in a cycle of mutual influence.

Chapter 6

The Social Link in Group Dreaming

When dreams are offered in group situations, they give the group access to the social link from the intrapsychic recesses of the individual who has the dream, through the shared space of the group link, to the wider culture. We have presented material on how couples relate unconsciously as illustrated in their dreams (D. Scharff and J. Scharff 1991, 2004) and we have previously written about the same process in families (D. Scharff 1992; D. Scharff and J. Scharff 1987). Here we want illustrate aspects of group and social links through work with dreams in three learning institutions.

SMALL GROUP TEACHING EXAMPLE: THE INDIVIDUAL DREAM AND THE GROUP EXPERIENCE

The first example shows the work of tying the meaning of a dream and the experience of the individual dreamer to shared group experience. Several years ago, we held a three-day conference on the theme of separation anxiety. The presenters, Jean-Michel and Danielle Quinodoz, discussed varieties of separation anxiety, and the emotional and psychosomatic reactions to it, including emotional vertigo (J-M. Quinodoz 1993; D. Quinodoz 1997). Over the course of the weekend, the conference members discussed the presentations in the large group and in small affective learning groups of five to nine members with one or two leaders, using our Group Affective Model for the teaching and learning of psychoanalytic concepts and their clinical application (J. Scharff and D. Scharff 2000). The small group is a field that incorporates the ideas being taught and the resulting group process. Group members have the integrative task of bringing together in discussion the intellectual appreciation of the concepts being taught and the individual and group-wide emotional reactions to them, so as to arrive at understanding in depth with internalization of the concepts.

In one of the small groups of the second day, a participant reported a dream: "Two people get in a car to begin a trip. I feel sad that they are leaving. I want to go with them, but that is not an option. It's hard to accept that relationships have to end."

The group discussed the dream as a group product, giving various associations. One woman thought of the loss of the guest presenters as a couple, who would be departing the next day. A man linked the image of them as a couple to the parents a child has to leave behind to grow and go his own way. Another woman thought of the couple as the group she would be leaving. The group leader noted that the group members were about to face separation because they would have to leave the conference and each other, whether or not they had made the trip into the areas to be explored, and that they had feelings of grief about the impending separation and loss—of each other and of opportunity—which was the subject of study for the weekend.

This brief example demonstrates the integration of themes at several levels. The dream expresses the theme being studied that weekend: separation anxiety. The person who has the dream is the dream-bearer for the group (Kaës 2007). The dream gives a personal, individual experience of that member's internal reaction, and provides a link to the group's here-and-now experience of coming together "to begin a trip," encountering losses during the educational process, and leaving it behind. From their integrated intellectual and emotional, individual and social appreciation of separation anxiety, the group members can then internalize the concept for use in their clinical work and enjoy an improved ability to manage separation and reunion in treatment.

Group Leader Training Example: Dream and Social Unconscious

The second, more detailed example shows the unconscious life of a training group and its connection to the social unconscious while learning group leadership skills. A group-leader training program designed for six participants met in the conference space at our house for two days. The design featured a seminar lecture-discussion by a faculty member, followed by a small group, and a consultation to the group—in all six lectures and 12 small groups. Each training group member twice in turn led the small group, and then received consultation on their group-leading from a faculty member who had observed the group. Five of the group members were assigned to lead the group alone. Two group members agreed to share paying one tuition for which they agreed to co-lead the group. Using the Group Affective Model, the small group had the task of integrating the theoretical ideas being studied, clinical experience to which these ideas apply, and personal experience as a group member learning the concepts (Scharff and Scharff 2000). In groups working on understanding the unconscious organization of shared experience, group analysis of shared dreams gives access to unconscious elements and provides a language for ongoing study.

Group Dream Seminar

I (DES) was assigned as faculty to the sixth and final seminar of the two-day program. My topic was the occurrence of dreams in groups and how to work with them. I asked the class if any members had had any dreams for us to work with. The group reported that two dreams had already been discussed in the small group (possibly a response to having read on the program that dreams were to be featured). A few group members said that they had had more dreams but did not elaborate, and one of them said that she did not want to go first.

The Dreams

Eugenia stepped in to say that she had had a dream fragment: "I remember an image of my mother. I was five years old. I was getting acquainted with the kindergarten school setting. My association was: I used to wonder about a boy I had in treatment, what kindergarten would be like for him because he was very attached to his mother."

Anna Maria told her dream: "I was back in San Francisco where I used to live. I was in a shop with familiar people including all the members of this group. I was intrigued by the chairs that were carved out of wood in strange, interesting shapes. I turned one chair to the back, where there were images on the back and on the seat. In the dream I thought this was a group of 'Grateful Dead' chairs, very old, classic. I woke up with the image of the Grateful Dead."

Ralph wanted to tell his dream, even though he had already told it in an earlier group: "The night before I had this dream, I had been deeply wounded at the end of the day. So then I had the dream: I was by myself in a crowded grocery store. I was annoyed by the long line and the slow cashiers, so I drove the cart of groceries out of the front of the store, took it somewhere else. It occurred to me that I had the cart of groceries and hadn't paid for them, so I abandoned the groceries. I felt extremely upset.

"Then I was walking in San Francisco to the Aids Health Project where I used to work. I needed somewhere to take my tears. Mary Beth was there, a friend who would listen, but I was obstructed by new employees whom I didn't know. I loved working there. It used to be an agency for gay men, a wonderful, cheerful place, but now I feel alien there. I felt like I had a wad of wet, bloody tissue in my heart, but I didn't want to burden Mary Beth with deep sadness in the workspace. I wandered on in a large place and met two social workers. One was writing the second of two thank-you cards. She showed me the cards that she had received. It said, 'The Aids Health Project is now a family place.' I think in this dream I was going back home and there was no place for me. I felt a kind of unrequited longing."

Deborah now told her dream. "There was chaos going on. There were elements I was trying to figure out. I don't know if I was on a plane or outside the plane while it was flying above the beach. I could see the ocean. Sometimes I was on the beach, and sometimes I was in the plane. The plane crashed, and I landed on the hard sand. I began to run. Something was catching me. My cell phone rang, and it was my mother-in-law saying something about getting hamburgers . . . was I going or should she? I said 'No, I will.' I tried to get back home. I was running, and then I'm in a car I used to drive before I was married. I picked up my mother-in-law. She gets in the car while she's talking to someone on the phone. I'm not sure if I was dead or not dead. I called the airline to ask about my plane. The woman said there was an accident, and I woke up."

Deborah continued, saying, "I had a second dream. Yesterday in our group Anita had said something about spiders, and that reminded me that I had had a dream about spiders the night before. I felt something on my head, shook my hair, and spiders fell out of it. The spiders had been taking something out of me."

Seminar Group Associations to the Dreams

With this collection of five dreams, the members of the group began to associate to them. Anita said, "There are similar themes: death, seeing people from the past, going someplace we've been before."

Ralph said, "We told a lot of dreams. It's amazing how many of us were dreaming and waiting to tell you them. Perhaps we think if we give you a lot, maybe we'll get a lot of good back. I was struck by Eugenia's image of the five-year-old going to kindergarten. It reminds me of us in the group here, in transition from being students to being group leaders."

I said, "So this is a kindergarten for group leaders!" The group burst into laughter!

Eugenia said. "I had a visceral reaction to the spider dream. I was frightened by the repetition of death in the dreams. And, in fact, we found a flyer on Deborah's car after lunch. The American Nazi Party invited us to join. It said what a toilet bowl America is today. But there it was on Deborah's car! How come it was only on Deborah's car, when she happens to be the only Jew in our group?"

I said, "So it's not only your dreams that deliver the social unconscious into the group."

Meg said, "This is about the fears of crashing and not knowing. The plane that crashed, and the question of being dead or not dead, is about the past and wanting to go back to the past. Some kind of regression is pulling at us. But we're also wondering if in the future, when we try to grow here, we might be heading for a crash."

Anita said, "I also had a thought about the plane on the beach. There's a potential for falling. The plane image says to me that our conscious and unconscious are on different planes, different dimensions. I also had a thought about the hamburger image—I don't know where that was from, but it was out of place and, to me, was the most interesting thing in Deborah's dream."

Wendy said, "It belongs with Ralph's dream about the groceries, too."

Anita, now associating freely to the image, said, "If we're making hamburgers, it would mean we're making mincemeat of something."

Meg said it reminded her of Hamburg, Germany, which took her back to the notice on Deborah's car from the American Nazi Party, and that carried an undercurrent of unease.

Eugenia said, "That association brings me to the time John Kennedy said 'Ich bin ein Berliner' which wasn't good modern German for saying, 'I am a Berliner.' It was as wrong as if a person from Hamburg had said, 'I am a hamburger.' There's a Pink Panther movie about somebody teaching someone English, and he can't say hamburger."

I now said, "Hamburgers are what I serve at the summer institute graduation cook-out."

The group members (all of whom have been to that annual party) mentioned that they had been talking about that party in the prior group and that they had noticed a tantalizing smell of cooking from my kitchen the day before.

Eugenia said, "About the Grateful Dead: there's something about grateful and dead that should make me think of the depressive position where gratitude can happen, but that band was stoned out of its mind on drugs in reaction to seeing the horrors of the Viet Nam war."

Anita said, "The Dead had all these groupies. That's a reference to us studying groups here."

I now began to pull things together in terms of our study of the role of the dreams. I began by mentioning the themes of food, feeding, and gratitude, and the vivid dreams about a mother and a mother-in-law. The hamburger reference referred to the need to learn a new language and tied the food theme to the transference via mention of the institutional graduation celebration and the smell of cooking the day before, and reflected a group-wide theme of whether the nourishment being offered by the leaders was adequate or not.

Ralph said, "Yesterday, the training program leaders, sat where you are now, and reviewed the day's teaching and learning experience. We observed and listened without talking. When the leader asked what was it all about, my bringing some food to the meeting when I know that you provide food, I was offended. She blindsided me without an opportunity to say something back. I was aware of the power differential and I thought, 'Pick on someone your own size.'"

I said to Ralph, "You were retaliating in your dream by stealing her food, but then you had to abandon it. Even though you were hurt, you might have been thinking about her question, because as co-leader you interpreted the group's unconscious fantasy that, 'if we give you a lot, maybe we'll get a lot of good back.'" To the group, I said, "But clearly Ralph's dream spoke for a more general group experience of ambivalence about the fare that we provide and how we may hurt you, as if we are perceived as the Nazi party providing food from Hamburg or making mincemeat of you.

"There have been so many dreams that it is impossible to connect them all up. And there are still a lot of loose strands waving around. We can see how some of these themes, as well as ones we have not focused on, offer the group a vocabulary for unconscious threads."

As we stopped, Anita said, "It's all so interesting. I thought about that image of a spider and all these threads not connecting—all these loose ends!"

The exercise's design offered an opportunity to see themes from the dreams woven into the fabric of the seminar.

Small Group Dialogue: Unconscious Themes from Dreams

Now it was time for me to observe the small group following the seminar. It was to be led by Eugenia and Ralph, and I was to consult to their group-leading while the rest of the group listened. I will not report my consultation to the co-leaders because here my focus is on the group process as an elaboration on the unconscious themes introduced by the dreams. So, I comment on the co-leading only to the extent that it relates to the unconscious group process arising from work with the dreams.

In this group, a number of dream themes became part of the dialogue. Eugenia allowed herself to get sucked into being a dependency leader, answering questions put to her by the group in an unconscious group-wide challenge to her leadership role. In this process, we could see the kindergarten theme, as the group symbolically regressed in their current development, where, however, her leadership style also fostered their play. In role as co-leader, Ralph (who had dreamed of the delay he experienced at the store) did tolerate delay in letting the group wait for knowledge to emerge, but he did not have the experience to confront the group's use of Eugenia and step up as her co-leader to work interpretively as a pair (a more advanced skill).

Just as Ralph's dream had introduced themes of waiting and frustration, about leaving and getting nothing, so the group now used this language to examine those fears in the pursuit of their own growth. For instance, the Nazi note on Deborah's car helped the group to confront what it wanted to avoid by using Deborah as the unconscious target of their disowned unconscious aggressive attack. Slipping momentarily out of his leadership role to give his personal input, Ralph said he had become aware of his own sadism when he encountered the Nazi sadism. Meg said that growing up in a family with unbridled aggression was extremely threatening, just as aggression was threatening here in this group of family size. Back in role as co-leader, Ralph connected this theme of internal group aggression to Deborah's dream in which she wasn't sure if the plane had crashed or not and whether she was alive or dead. The group wondered whether the most threatening aggression came from the outside or inside? A group could call itself names, but name-calling from outside felt unsafe. Was it safer to have a sadistic group member or a sadistic leader? Deborah said it was worse to have a sadistic group leader, because a good group leader can help work with a sadistic member. All of this discussion was connected with the dream question of whether they were inside or outside a crashing plane.

As the group drew to a close, Anna Maria asked, "Is this part of the group a dream, or is the dream the group?" This opened the question of whether they wanted to take responsibility as group-leaders in the institutional family, or would they prefer the safety of living in a dream. As the group closed, one member mentioned that the co-leader of the training course was about to take a flight. Perhaps the plane in the dream had to do with the fear that their transferential anger towards her would harm her.

In this small group, not all the themes latent in the dreams could be worked on, for instance, the issue of getting knowledge without paying fully for it, the unconscious chaos of shifting between levels of development and understanding, strange and interesting shapes, the obstruction of learning by having to share with new people, the price of learning, gay sexual identity versus family belonging, prejudice, foreignness, the longing for nurture and personal treatment, gratitude and rejection, and the predatory spider aspect of the mother. Nevertheless in the space of one and a half hours for the lecture, the small group and the consultation, many of the themes from the dreams and associations reported in the seminar on the shared unconscious meaning of dreams were imported into the group—aggression, being dead or not dead, the threads of the spider's web unraveling from their minds, the search for knowledge, the threat of falling and crashing, attachment to good or bad parents and their substitutes, and the fear of loss at the end of the training later that afternoon. In this way, the dreams and their group-wide associations spurred unconscious conflict to conscious exploration. Even those aspects of the dream that are not consciously addressed become part of the group's mentality. In an ongoing group they contribute to the evolution of the group as a link to the unconscious life of the individual group members and their social contexts, to the history of the group, and to other groups in the institution.

International Conference Example: Therapist Dream, Patient Dream, Large Group, and Culture

The third example connects a therapist's dream to a patient's dream, the experience of a large group of therapists, and the culture they share.

Recently, we interviewed a Chinese couple in Beijing for five successive days, observed by an audience of approximately 75 therapists from many places in China who were in a national training program we were asked to teach on analytic couple therapy. The husband and wife in the couple being interviewed were tied to their culture in complex ways, and were experiencing considerable tension over their relationship. The husband was older and educated to the PhD level, while the wife, from a rural family, had not been to college but had become a successful small businesswoman before marriage and motherhood (J. Scarff and D. Scarff in press). In the interview, the wife told of a repeated dream she had: "I dreamed of being in a river with big and little fish. I could only catch a little fish. All the fish were colorful and fat." She said that she had wondered why she caught only little fish, but had come to the conclusion that a big fish would be too much to eat, and said "A small fish is enough for me." The couple had rebuffed our attempts to work further with the dream.

The Individual's Dream

In the group discussion about the couple, we asked if anyone among the trainees had had a dream, with the idea that one or more dreams from the group might expand both our shared understanding of the couple and the overall shared training experience.

A woman volunteered her dream:

"I have been anxious being away from home to be here in this training, and I had a dream the day before yesterday. In the dream I was going home after some time away, to check on my husband and child. As I got home I saw that the neighborhood was being built up with walls. I went into my house and there were walls being built up inside it, too. My husband's brother came towards me with a large knife. I was frightened, but he threw the knife onto the ground, and it became much smaller, more like a small carving tool.

"Then there was an old woman with short hair who showed me the side of her head. She said this man had hurt her (perhaps this was before he threw the blade down), and I should be careful of him. When the blade became smaller I calmed down. I wondered if I should call '011' (the emergency number), and if so, should I ask for the hospital or the police. In the end I think I did call the police but I wondered why."

Individual and Group Associations to Her Dream

We asked for the dreamer's associations, but she had little to share. She said there was something about her own relationship to her husband and child that she did not want to elaborate in the public setting, a personal limit that we regard as quite appropriate.

We then asked for associations from the group:

A woman said that she thought the dream represented feeling beat up in her inner world.

Another woman said she had a tight feeling in her chest as she heard the dream.

A third woman connected the image of the old woman with short hair to Jill. When she imagined the knife being thrown at the side of the woman's head, she thought of Jill and felt worried because Jill seemed to her to be weak.

A fourth woman felt confused when the dream wavered between calling the police or the hospital. She connected her confusion to making a choice about staying here or going perhaps to America. She also felt scared of the husband's brother.

A fifth woman, whose image seemed to us to be particularly vivid, said the wall and the very high roof gave her the idea of a golden fish pool built in the new walls with beautiful fish inside. This echoed the wife's image of colorful, fat fish.

A man said that the inside structure of the house reminded him of collapse of the frame. He was scared for the couple that David and Jill were interviewing, because the husband and wife seemed unable to understand each other, even with help.

Another woman thought about the knife becoming smaller, which she thought represented aggression becoming less dangerous. She was followed by a woman who agreed, and added her thought that the knife, representing male aggression, became a carving tool, possibly a kitchen utensil, representing female aggression in the service of nurture.

A second man noted that in the dream, nothing changed on the outside but, in the dream, things became different inside. He said, "That's like what happens here in the training: People will leave looking the same on the outside, but many will be changed on the inside."

Another woman said, "I felt anxious when our group member started to tell the dream. And I thought that the organizer of the training here in Beijing, was also anxious. So it might say something about the anxiety in our training group."

Finally, a woman returned to the image of the old woman in the dream. She too connected her to Jill seeming older and weaker, while David seemed more powerful, more like the brother-in-law. She said that David seemed very sharp and aggressive in the couple interview, and Jill seemed softer and more protective of the couple during the interview and of the participants in the teaching sessions.

The dreamer spoke again. She said, "I couldn't understand the dream at first, but now I got to thinking. I've been upset about my self experience (this is the word that Chinese therapists use for their personal psychotherapy) because of something that happened between me and my therapist over an appointment change. What happened is that one of her other patients, who is my colleague, told my therapist that I would be willing to make a change in the time of my appointment in order to accommodate my colleague's need for a switch. When I saw my therapist, she mentioned the switch that she had arranged. I felt very uncomfortable with this because I had not even been told of the change or anything about it, and because the therapist had believed my colleague without asking me. I was hurt and I felt misunderstood by my therapist. Now, thinking about the dream and this discussion, I understand that my therapist was also hurt by what my colleague did."

Making Sense of the Dream and the Group's Work with It

A group's dream occurs in the space of the interpersonal unconscious and the link. In the process of being shared, it helps to illustrate group links both to the couple being studied and to the teachers. This space is opened for examination as each person shares the dream space with the dreamer.

The dream works first at the level of the dreamer's own inner world, and says things about her relationships to her family, husband, colleagues and therapist, but we did not pursue the individual meaning of the dream in this setting. That would have been too exposing, and should be a matter for therapy, not education. We gratefully accepted the sample of individual experience that she wanted to share, namely the association about being displaced and hurt in relationship to her therapist. That let us compare her personal experience with what the dream comes to mean for the group. In the group, we had the area of shared dreaming, teaching, and learning.

This dream includes many elements: There is an internal couple: a man and an older woman. He has a knife that in the dream is at first a lethal weapon, but changes into a small weapon that might be a tool for cooking or sculpting. Her head is hurt. We can see the attack on her as retaliation for the destructive aggression felt during our teaching and in our clinical interviewing of the couple, but the responsibility for being so aggressive was assigned more to David. The group characterizes us as a couple in which there is an aggressor and a victim, a threatening one and a protective one in relation to the group.

The dream describes the way things are changing inside and how the group unconsciously fears aggression. The dream graphically poses the question: When teachers demonstrate their clinical tools, are they tools for improving minds, or are they weapons for hurting heads? The dream speaks to what everybody is afraid of—new learning that threatens to destroy what is already known, just as patients are afraid of learning in therapy. Here, the group clearly appreciated knowledge that we brought, but the dream brings in conflicting unconscious elements: hate and fear of the teachers for expecting them to learn and therefore to build new walls. Would the new structure confine the learners, or would it give room for a beautiful pond full of gold fish, as appeared in the association of one member of the group?

In listening to the elaborations of the dream, we were struck with the theme of the reaction to the training. We have been aware of the foreignness of many of the Western concepts we and other analysts bring to China, where psychoanalysis and couple therapy are quite new, and jar with aspects of culture in China where it continues to be difficult to look at some of the damaging effects at a societal level of many events of the second half of the twentieth century. So it is not surprising that our whole teaching enterprise would be felt to be a knife aimed at the venerable Chinese culture, the structure of the family, and the kind of household our Chinese colleagues value. The associations of the dreamer to how she was unknowingly displaced by her colleague who coveted her therapy appointment time (and perhaps also her relationship with the therapist whose time and attention they shared) could equally apply to the group. Here are we as upstart trainers who displace our students from their places with their Chinese teachers, offering radical ideas from the outside that do not always respect Chinese culture with its own sense of time and place. What we bring can be felt as a weapon to attack the Chinese mind and cultural mentality.

Another association from the group offered the idea that after training like this, the outside seems the same, but the inside changes. The image of the husband's brother with a huge blade is a frightening image of training. The image of the pool with beautiful fish is a hopeful, benign version of its effects. We are experienced by the group as if we are the husband's brother—brought in by the seminar organizer as a brutal thug. Then in the dream, as indicated by other associations, the knife changed from something likely to be a weapon to something better designed for cooking or sculpting—an image of the teaching as nutritive and growth promoting. The inside is subject both to tearing down and building up.

We thought about the question of the call to the police or the hospital. Was the main issue the threatening man or the wounded woman? Was it a choice between Chinese and American methods for meeting needs? The hospital or the police offer vastly different kinds of help. It seemed to us that the ambiguity of the image in the dream also fit with training. Learning is always a frightening process: It beckons, but it also threatens to tear down existing knowledge under the impact of the new learning. Students put up walls against the pain of losing familiar structures before new walls can be built. Teachers are always, unconsciously, met with ambivalence about the likelihood that the tearing down necessary to new learning might be destructive. We bring a new link of *radical difference*, an *alienating other*, that is felt as destructive to the old order while spurring new creative structures (Berenstein 2010; Kaës 2005, 2007).

For a learning group, it is often difficult to hold the idea that teachers also must learn, and that our learning from students is central to any teaching task. So as teachers, especially when venturing into unfamiliar territory like China, we are even more aware than usual of our need to learn, both for the sake of the learning itself, and in order to be effective. But because learning is inherently threatening to existing structure and knowledge (the man with the knife, the woman's injured head, the hospital or the police), students fear and hate their teachers, and, in a reciprocal way, all teachers unconsciously fear and hate their students. There are grounds for teachers' hate: because if students take in what the teacher knows, they will make something different of it than the teacher does. The knowledge itself will change into something new. In any event, it will no longer be the exclusive property of the teacher. Teachers' envy of students is common, because they can so easily feel that students denude the teacher of her precious property, just as a baby drains a mother's body and energy. So the dream of the knife, the threat of attack on the older woman, can also be understood as an attack on Jill (on behalf of the teaching couple) by the students in whose house and country the teaching occurs. Just as our group's dreamer had to work to understand that her therapist must have felt hurt, and just as China and America have difficulty understanding each other's fear, so the group and we had to work to understand our mutual fears.

Despite these unconscious elements of fear and destructiveness, there is hope of a fruitful learning experience too. The image of small but colorful fat fish from the wife's dream connected her to us, to the group, to our learning project, and to Chinese culture, when we learned from the group that in the mythology from the wife's region of China, fish symbolize female fertility and potential. The cultural link to the social unconscious expresses a dimension of hope and generativity. In the newly structured house of learning, the association to a pond full of beautiful fish represents hope for shared teaching and learning, the fertility of ideas, and the development of richer understanding.

SUMMARY

Examples of dreams experienced in learning institutions in the United States and in China connect unconscious responses of the individual dreamer, the group, and the wider culture. The group has access to the social link via the individual dreamer and the group analytic work.

Chapter 7

Chaos Theory: Strange Attractors in Marriage

Chaos theory, the theory of dynamical systems, offers a new paradigm for understanding the dynamics of psychological, mental, and affective processes in the development, maintenance, and treatment of couple relationships (Briggs 1992; D. Scharff and J. Scharff 2007; Galatzer-Levy 2009; Van Eenwyck 1997). The couple relationship forms when two individual psychodynamic systems combine in unpredictable ways to develop a system that is essentially chaotic and inherently self-organizing. Couple therapy informed by chaos theory moves troubled couples out of their limit cycle functioning and encourages the development of new strange attractor patterns that confer enhanced flexibility of response in the paired oscillators of the couple system, bringing couples new adaptability and confidence to meet developmental challenges.

Every intimate couple relationship has a unique personality. This personality, described by Dicks (1967) as the joint marital personality, is evident on the surface through the observable interaction of the partners. It is constructed at the depths of the individual unconscious—a mysterious, unpredictable, and infinitely complex combination of brain interactions, attachment patterns, affective facial, bodily, and sexual signals, and verbal communication. And it forms at the crosshairs of the vertical and horizontal axes of the link, the vertical axis carrying the influence of earlier generations and the horizontal axis connecting the couple to the wider family and social world respectively. Any approach to understanding and treating the dynamics of the couple relationship must take account of this complexity. We look to *chaos theory* (also called the theory of non-random chaos, complexity theory, or dynamical systems theory) for another way of thinking about unconscious communication, the development of psychic structure, coupling, and therapeutic action in the analytic treatment of couples. Applying chaos theory augments our understanding of how individuals express the link in their choice of marital partner and how they develop links through complex interaction.

CHAOS THEORY: A PARADIGM FOR UNDERSTANDING COUPLE DYNAMICS

Iterated Operations

Chaos theory derives from the mathematical study of the action of complex dynamical systems governed by continuous feedback (Gleick 1987, Galatzer-Levy 1995, 2009; J. Scharff and D. Scharff 1998a). These systems *iterate* (repeat) their operations, each time beginning with a situation that is the sum of all previous experience. Chaos theory, which has been applied to the study of diverse unpredictable systems like weather, population dynamics, aesthetics, biological systems like heart rate and brain waves, applies to psychological systems as well. For instance, each of us uses our internal operating systems to proceed through life. At each moment, we are the sum of all our previous experience; and we use our internal systems to guide us through the next developmental stage.

Sensitive Dependence on Initial Conditions

In such complex systems, infinitely small differences in starting points affect the outcome profoundly. The processes of growth and development are iterations of life's operating equations, and they show *sensitive dependence on initial conditions*. Small and seemingly inconsequential variations in constitution, temperament, and parenting are magnified or minimized under various circumstances, leading to unpredictable results.

The couple relationship is a biological system repeatedly adjusting to feedback, both cementing the form of the marital joint personality and introducing slight variations that modify the spouses' personalities in the light of shared experience. Couple relationships, like those of all biological systems, are complex iterated equations with *sensitive dependence on initial conditions* as they apply their daily operating equations to the next set of life challenges. Small differences in the beginning of a day can affect the next weeks or even a life course in unpredictable ways, while something that seems to loom large at one moment may defy prediction and turn out to be relatively inconsequential.

Tuning Force for the Self-Organizing Potential

The current interactions of members of a couple and their family histories recorded in each partner's internal object relations affect the patterns of the couple. In chaos theory terms, interactions, affect states, and object relations separately and together exert a *tuning force* on the individual personality (J. M. Quinodoz 1997). A tuning force is the energy required to move a system from one state of organization to another, whether to shift from balance to disequilibrium or to stabilize a chaotic system. When a system is in a very stable state, it takes a large tuning force to disrupt it, but if it is near to disintegration—on the edge of chaos—it takes only a small amount of tuning force to effect a major change.

Interactions, affect states, and object relations act as a tuning variable affecting the marital joint personality and the family dynamics. Some family members have relatively greater effects than other family members, and their effect varies over time too. For instance, a mother's internal object relations exert a large tuning force on her infant's developing mind, while those of a child who has left home normally exert a relatively weak tuning force on the parental couple she has left behind. A therapist's affective atunement, conscious interventions, and receptivity to unconscious communication exert a tuning force on a couple dynamic.

The complex system of the couple relationship tends to enter periods of relative chaos (experienced as confusion, fragmentation, and tension that are disorganizing). The unhealthy system gets stuck there. The healthy system enters chaos temporarily, experiences some turbulence, and then *self-organizes* as a more functional interactive system, under the influence of the tuning force of the interacting partners' personalities, or of a more organized interactive system nearby such as the healthy marriage of friends or relatives, or the technique of an analysed therapist. When not hampered by histories of trauma or deprivation, a couple's self-organizing potential should lead to more complex and adaptive patterns over time.

Paired Oscillators

The concept of paired oscillators (Galatzer-Levy 2009) offers a model for therapeutic action in analytic therapy, and for the influence of one person on another in long-term relationships such as the couple or the parent and child relationship. When two oscillators such as pendulums or tuning forks are paired by operating in close proximity (a loose bond) or tied together electronically or mechanically (a strong bond), the rhythms of oscillation change to reflect mutual influence. Furthermore, new properties emerge that could not be attributed to either oscillator alone. For instance, one human leg can show the properties of motion in hopping, but walking is not possible without the other leg as the paired oscillator.

Galatzer-Levy shows that aspects of analysand-analyst pairing can be modeled on paired oscillators. Therapeutic action can be better explained in terms of the agreeable rhythm in the pairing of two minds in a long-term process than by correctness of interpretation. Changes in analytic process as described by the Boston Change Process Study Group (2005) is seen as suddenly discontinuous, as if the treatment is suddenly patterned by a totally different strange attractor. The process can perhaps be better seen as moments of sudden change of state or organization within a steady state, and understood as the shift from one part of a strange attractor to another, rather than as wholly discontinuous. Such shifts are characteristic of strange attractors which show very different patterns in one part of their range than in others. We are familiar with this in the pattern of personality of a person who is suddenly furious, but docile the rest of the time. The anger and the docility are both part of the emotional range of the same person, but not present at the same time.

Just as the therapeutic dyad can be understood as a paired oscillator, so can marriage, but here the relationship of mutual influence is more intense, of longer duration, and more emotionally significant. Here the interaction of emotional relating, the sharing of sexuality, the interaction with families of origin, and the interplay with the couple's children, all go together to magnify mutual influence to a degree that recalls the intensity of the early parent-child relationship. Patterns of influence that extend from the couple to their child, and from that child to the parental couple are inherently different from interactions with a single parent because the dynamic of three joined oscillators is radically different from the dynamic of two paired oscillators. When we expand our view of the life of a couple to include the wider family, the degree of complexity increases yet again. Individuals are tied together with life-long bonds of mutual influence than can produce something new that is not possible for each of them alone.

Fractals

At different levels of magnification of a system, patterns repeat, appearing not exactly the same but similar at each magnification. In chaos theory terms, each pattern is a *fractal* of the other patterns found at different levels of scale (Galatzer-Levy 1995). Each therapy hour contains themes that repeat in various iterations throughout a treatment, each session a fractal of the whole. Each moment in a person's life is a fractal of every other moment. "The present moment is an instantiation of a pre-existing more general pattern that (especially when it is unconscious or non-conscious) finds its exact form of expression as it is put into action in a particular setting. Its influence is expressed in all activities regardless of their size. This view is surprisingly close to the notion of fractals (Stern 2004, p. 138). [E]ach successive present moment in life is a different instantiation of the past acting in the present" (p. 139). As we listen to a single moment in a patient's report of their day, we find that it contains elements that repeat in every other moment past, present, and future, or to put it poetically, "the present moment (even as told) reveals a 'world in a grain of sand'" (p. 138).

A couple's sexual relationship, speech patterns, and relationship to extended families and children—all are fractals of their internal object relations and of their overall relationship (J. Scharff and D. Scharff 1998a). The transference-countertransference dialectic is also a fractal of all these elements of their relationship, a distillation and magnification that we experience and study together in therapy. All these elements both *organize* the system of the couple relationship, and at the same time are actually *produced by* the dynamic of the system. In chaos theory terms, the force that both organizes and is organized by the system is called an *attractor*. The attractor may be of one of three types: fixed, limit cycle, and strange.

Fixed, Limit-Cycle, and Strange Attractors

A *fixed attractor* appears to move a system through a predictable pattern toward rest at a single spot, like a gravity-powered pendulum that eventually comes to a stop at a fixed point. A *limit-cycle attractor* appears to move a system through a fixed pattern continuously, like an electrically powered pendulum that moves back and forth in an arc. A *strange attractor* appears to move a system through a complex, apparently random pattern, out of which an organized pattern gradually appears—like a whirlpool that seems to pull water into the whirl, although it is actually the flow of the water that produces the whirl. Similarly, a couple's fights appear to pull their relationship into an aggressive mode, even though it is the complex tension of their interacting needs and personalities that actually causes the fighting. None of the movements of the system are exactly the same, but contribute to a discernible overall complex pattern—the "whirl" of disagreement—that characterizes this couple's relationship. A strange attractor may exert an especially strong effect on the couple system and pull it, like a whirlpool pulls objects outside the whirl into the whirl, into its *basin of attraction*.

In the complex system of a couple with sensitive dependence on initial conditions, precise prediction of patterns of interaction is not possible. Like all self-organizing systems, we live life by looking forward and proceeding into the unknown, and can only understand when looking back. At times, life patterns shift under destabilizing conditions, like a whirlpool may be affected by a strong nearby current or a passing object. In the short term, more than one pattern may be evident consistently. For instance, a couple may have one pattern of fierce arguments over disciplining their children and another of co-operation and tenderness in love-making that is not predictable from the intensity of their arguments. Over the long term, general patterns of consistency and adaptive variation can be recognized.

Healthy couples, like healthy biological systems, move in and out of chaos in daily life, following the *self-similar patterns* of strange attractors—never exactly the same, but patterned enough to be recognizable as part of a dynamic system. Healthy chaotic patterns eventually self-organize and so have an enhanced capacity to adapt to new circumstances and needs. Healthy strange attractors have a capacity for flexibility and potential for adaptation and growth.

Dysfunctional couples get somewhat stuck doing the same ineffective thing over and over, following the *self-same pattern* of a limit-cycle attractor, and they get totally stuck following the rapid downward spiral of the fixed attractor ending up in a dead stop. The activity of a fixed attractor is characterized by a deadly repetition that stops forward movement, for instance totally predictable rage reflexes, violence followed by contrition and escalating violence, compulsive infidelity, or unshakeable paranoid beliefs. The activity of a limit cycle attractor also shows repetitive behaviours that keep on going, such as an enduring marital projective identificatory system that seems to be in balance until it no longer works, for instance a dominance-submission pattern that suits both parties until the dominant one is incapacitated or the submissive one gets empowered.

THE STRANGE ATTRACTOR OF THE COUPLE RELATIONSHIP

When two individuals form a couple, the patterns of each personality based on their histories behave as strange attractors, each of which interacts with the other and exerts a tuning force on it until the systems combine to form a new overarching strange attractor, namely the pattern of the joint marital personality. When that couple has a child, the strange attractors of the two parents' personalities and of their overall relationship pattern exert tuning forces, which create basins of attraction that interact with the inherent personality patterns of the child, pulling the child's self toward this or that system of organization. When we compare each parent's strange attractor pattern, the joint marital personality, the developing personality of the child, and the overall family interaction patterns, we notice that they show fractal similarity to one another.

Patterns of a couple's life appear to attract partners into repetitions of actions, and the couple will often report that they cannot resist the pattern. Or they might report that going to visit a set of in-laws, or dreaming about their family of origin, exposes them to a force they cannot resist. This is to say that the closer they get to the extended family's basin of attraction, the more they get swept up in the family's pattern.

A baby is a living embodiment of a couple's interpenetration, and gives life to their partnership. The child arises from, and is a representative of, the sexual and emotional coupling of the parents. In addition, the child is a person in his or her own right, therefore a new object of affection, interest, and hate for the couple. At the same time, the child is also a fractal of the parents' original objects and the internal objects based on early experience with them, and a reminder of their own parents, now grandparents. The parents respond to aspects of the grandparents that they imagine or actually detect in the child, and evoke them in the child unconsciously through projective identification. Experience with the child is installed as a complex internal object that is both old and new, and that in turn restructures the parents' selves and their couple relationship. Just as the sea shapes the edge of the land and the land shapes the edge of the sea, parents and child sculpt one another's interaction and personality. This happens every day as they iterate their family equations, each new day offering a new starting point with sensitive dependence on the day's initial conditions, resulting in an infinitely complex interaction of strange attractors and basins of attraction, perturbations, tuning variables, and self-organization at every fractal level.

Chaos Theory in Therapeutic Action

All this leads to the question of how we can promote change when couples seek help. By introducing *perturbations* into the operating system of the couple relationship, couple therapists disturb the relatively fixed, maladaptive, limit-cycle systems of fixed attractor patterns in which the couple is stuck. We use the tuning force of our own internal object relations organization honed by training, therapy, and supervision, to create a new basin of attraction, and to join with couples to structure a more flexible strange attractor system with better capacities for adaptation and self-organization.

According to the principle of fractal scaling and sensitive dependence on initial conditions, relatively small changes in therapy can have major effects. Theoretically, the flapping of a butterfly's wings in Brazil can create a hurricane in Texas (the so-called butterfly effect) (Gleick 1987). Similarly, an interpretation of the transference given at a propitious moment in a single session can produce a thunderstorm's worth of change in the couple's state of mind and way of interacting with the world. Then through the butterfly effect, a change in one partner can affect the couple or the whole family.

CLINICAL EXAMPLE FROM COUPLE THERAPY

Lucien and Dorothy are well into the mid-phase of couple therapy with David Scharff. They are now in their forties and have been married for 10 years. Both had been married previously to partners who betrayed and abandoned them, leaving them fearful of intimacy. They are slim, attractive, and in good shape but they have no sex life. They have no children, a decision reached by mutual agreement and without later regret. They stay in touch with their families in an occasional way. They experience Lucien's mother as a domineering woman and his father as a retiring man, emasculated by her and by Lucien's grandfather. They find Dorothy's mother to be a warm and friendly person, but her father is temperamental and not tuned in to Dorothy's wavelength.

Dorothy initiates sexual interaction but Lucien has no desire. His energy goes into fending off Dorothy, delaying the moments when intimacy might occur, and in general avoiding sex. If Lucien were to have sex wholeheartedly, he fears that Dorothy would take control of him. Dorothy tends to pressure Lucien, despite the fact that this tends to drive him away. Lucien blames her for pressuring him, but he invokes it by his avoidance.

Prior individual and couple therapy having been ineffective in releasing Lucien's sexual desire, the couple sought therapy. In marital and sex therapy, Lucien slowly became able to tolerate sex, find the idea exciting, and progress to pleasurable intercourse, but the couple still encountered a barrier in the approach phase of every exercise or encounter. Lucien repeatedly insisted that Dorothy shouldn't pressure him by scheduling times for sex. He wanted sex to occur spontaneously, but because he did not feel spontaneous desire, sex did not happen, and this fueled her need to pressure him for a schedule. Despite improvement, their sexual interaction remained a totally predictable, repetitively frustrating pattern, governed by limit cycle attractors.

Session 1: Dream, Associations, and Transference Show Fractal Similarity

In the first session of three that we will report, I (DES) worked on the husband's dream as a product of the couple. Lucien told his dream: "It was a dream of a man with salt and pepper hair, holding a dead baby in his lap. The man wasn't dressed as a physician, but he had been attending to the baby as a doctor. He asked me to understand and accept the fact that he had had to eviscerate the baby. I was horrified at the idea of what this man must have done. He wanted me to understand, but it wasn't my child, and I didn't have any feeling for it. I was just an observer."

Lucien associated to a business partner who might want to scuttle a new business venture that he refers to as "his baby," and to his aunt's late fourth husband, a gambler who wasted her money. Dorothy thought that the baby might be Lucien's self. I thought that the dead baby with no parents was the couple's sexual life for which I (a gray-haired physician who, however, does not wear a white coat) was responsible. Lucien said I was nothing like the physician in the dream. When he added that it was a hollow baby, I commented that he might be watching the sex therapy project die. He said that he was trying not to, and Dorothy objected that she had again been unable to persuade him to do a sex exercise.

Lucien's thoughts about the aunt's husband led to his feelings about his aunt. He said, "My aunt has come to be known as the 'black widow' because all her husbands have died. She tells my mother, who is quite overweight, that you can't be too thin or too rich. She is the horror show at our family Christmas. She dresses to kill and uses her money to lure men. She's not fit for society."

I said, "A lethal, predatory woman. Your association to your 'black widow aunt' tells me you feel at risk in this sex therapy project. The dead baby in the physician's lap represents the horror of what you might be doing right now, while acting as though you had no part in it. You cut yourself off from that feeling and put it into Dorothy, and then get mad at her when she expresses the anxiety and longing for a lively sexual life on behalf of you as a couple. You then feel as if she is luring you into her web, and you stay away from her and from your own desire. It is your own desire that is the spider's web you fear."

Lucien said, "I recognize that I cut myself off. I enjoy the absence of pressure. Each week, I try to buy as much time before sex as possible [*by not specifying when to do the exercises*] because if we put down a marker [*like a gambler*], the clock starts ticking, and I get anxious. I want sex to be something that is just normal, not special, and I don't know how to get to normalcy."

Dorothy said, "I think normalcy for you is not having sex, and we'd still be stuck with that."

The various elements of the dream and the couple's associations in the session (transference manifestations, family history, fantasies about women) reflect many facets of individual and couple organization. Each element is a fractal of the other, showing pattern similarity on different orders of scale.

Shifting my focus from the transference to the fractal of Lucien's self and his object relations, I then commented that I now saw the gray-haired man as Lucien himself in the future, still unable to protect the baby (both himself as an infant and the sexual life with Dorothy about which he was avoidant) and vulnerable to death at the hands of the black widow, which he sees in her but which is active in him, entrapping him and killing off his desire.

Lucien and Dorothy have no children and take no pleasure in sexuality. Lucien's dream shows that their procreativity and capacity for pleasure is being pulled into a basin of attraction dominated by limit cycle attractors governed by death anxiety and murderousness, in turn attributed to the destructive seductiveness of the sexual woman, from which both of them turn away to avoid the impact of their own desire.

Session 2: Deadly Limit Cycle Attractor Gives Way to Strange Attractor in Formation

At their session the next week, Lucien reported that he had had another dream. This time I was more clearly in it, and it was set in my waiting room at the end of a session. Lucien said, "In the dream, Dorothy left your office ahead of me. As I left, I reached what I thought was your front door until I realized that it was a beautiful, tall, gilded French armoire. When I opened it, I couldn't see anything inside. Next to it, a fourteen-year-old girl was admiring an iron sculpture of herself. You and your wife entered the vestibule. I admired the furniture, and your wife accepted the compliment. Then she showed me a spot on the lower right-hand corner of the armoire where the gilt had been rubbed off, and she repaired it with some gilt from the other side. It was like a magic armoire. You entered, reminded me that Dorothy was waiting for me, and I scurried off."

He continued, "You and your wife, you're keepers of the flame, healers. Gilt is like guilty. I might be guilty about my new business venture hurting my partner."

I said "That's quite an idealized image of my wife and me. What she does is put gold over the bare spot."

He said, "Right, healed by copy and paste, healed by a new reservoir of golden objects."

I said, "The dream also shows us a young woman admiring her lifeless statue. Who could that be? Then you focus on my wife quietly patching things up. Both are different images of women than your mother or your wife."

Ignoring my reference to the image of the young woman, he said, "I think of you and your wife as restorative figures, completely different than my mother, who is a destructive force of nature. She captured too much of me."

I said, "So you developed armor for your *amour*, and covered it in guilt."

He said, "The gilt is a protective adornment."

The dream presents the couple as split in time and space, as Dorothy goes ahead and Lucien gets lost in contemplating the magic armoire. Lucien's dominant image of a black widow in a deadly couple (a limit-cycle attractor) has given way to the pull of new female objects (strange attractors), in the form of the young girl looking at her own statue and the therapist's wife who deals with his guilty conscience by "a cut and paste operation" that gilds it over. These new strange attractors draw Lucien and the couple away from the limited attractor functioning most often seen in their sessions. Their pattern loosens in relation to the appearance of new objects in foreground of the dreams—the young girl in a self-examining, possibly admiring pose, the magically reparative woman, and the idealized generative therapist couple—and in the context of the therapy, new strange attractors in the form of the therapeutic relationship and the therapist's technique. New images of women as objects and as parts of Lucien's own identity lead the internal organization of a more complex internal couple with restorative potential.

In the meeting of the unconscious organizations of Lucien and the therapist seen both in Lucien's dreams and in the couple's analysis of them, the therapist's inner world acts as a tuning variable that causes a perturbation in Lucien's inner world, bringing to the surface latent, previously suppressed organizations that bring new possibilities for reworking the couple relationship. This is an example of a strange attractor in formation. In these two sessions, Lucien's part of the pattern is most apparent. We will show its fractal similarity to Dorothy's, as the couple works on her dream in the third session, to which we will return after the next section on concepts regarding neurological development and complex attachment.

Neuroscience, Attachment, and Affect Regulation Related to Chaos Theory

We have dealt more fully with the topics of findings from neuroscience in Chapter 1 and attachment research in Chapter 10. We will recap the major points in order to show how they relate to chaos theory.

There is now ample evidence from brain imaging and developmental research that the infant's brain grows best when the infant is nurtured in a warm, reciprocally responsive relationship with a well-attuned mother or devoted caregivers (Schore 1994). The right brain is built for the task of processing interaction with the mother quickly and repeatedly, and for receiving and reading the complex emotions of others. The left brain enables the development of linear and logical thinking, and fluid verbal communication. The baby's brain is organized by the mother's brain in a cycle of exchange determined by attractor patterns that move naturally from limit cycle to strange attractor patterns as the infant matures (Schore 2003a, 2003b).

We have referred to the presence of *mirror neurons*, which are activated when one monkey watches another monkey make movements (Cozolino 2002; Modell 2003; Rizzolatti and Craighero 2004; Rizzolatti, Fogassi, and Gallese 2006). Similar mirror neurons in the parts of the human brain record facial expressions and tone of voice, giving a neurological basis for the mental mechanisms of projective and introjective identification that convey emotional experience among intimate partners. In partnership, mother and infant read each other's minds at levels far beneath conscious awareness and far more quickly than two adults can understand one another's words.

At first, a mother mirrors her newborn's expressions exactly, and the infant feels understood emotionally. This is called *contingent marking* (Fonagy et al. 2003). Later, at about three months of age, infants want their mother's reaction to be nearly the same, but clearly not the same. This is called *non-contingent marking* (Fonagy et al. 2003). The mother makes an expression similar enough to convey that she has received the message but different enough to modify the original affect, for instance by tuning its volume up or down. Thus she not only marks the affect but begins to regulate it. Similarly in the intense intimacy of couple interaction over time, each partner's mind structures and restructures the other through continuous non-random chaotic interaction.

At birth, the baby's brain is already rich in neurons but not in the rich connective networks that experience builds. Attachment research has shown that secure attachment fosters the growth of connectedness between neurons and sub-units of the brain. Brain scan studies show that the brains of those who suffered severe neglect and trauma show more rigid, limit cycle patterns of brain function, less overall right brain growth, accentuation of fear centers, and less neural network interconnectivity (Cozolino 2002, Schore 2003a, 2003b).

In each member of a couple, the right orbitofrontal cortex processes reciprocal emotional interactions through projective and introjective communications in a continuous unconscious communication (Schore 2003a, 2003b; J. Scharff 1992, D. Scharff and J. Scharff 1991). In chaos theory terms, each individual intrapsychic organization exerts a tuning force on the other. The horizontal and vertical axes of the link also exert a tuning force on the couple and on the maturing adult mind of each partner. In couple interaction over time, each partner's mind structures and restructures the other through continuous non-random chaotic interaction.

The principal evolutionary importance of the mother–infant attachment relationship is to provide the platform from which to teach the infant to regulate affects and states of mind, thereby establishing both an autonomous self and a self-in-relation to others (Sutherland 1980). Autonomous people form healthy couples. In the process of forming their relationship, each couple forms a *complex attachment* in which partners depend on and support each other (Clulow 2001, 2006; Fisher and Crandall 1997, 2001). Healthy couples use their relationship to regulate affect, to support healthy individuated selves, and to enjoy the vitality of intimacy through multi-channel communication—verbally, affectively, and sexually, as parents, lovers, or friends. Their patterns of interaction, both on the large scale and moment-to-moment, have mainly a reassuring self-similarity in which patterns of reliable, accurate atunement are combined with small but crucial variations in response. For instance a wife might feel thrown into confusion by her husband's anger, but responds from the position of feeling sure of his commitment and love, and expects that they will work together to recover their equilibrium.

Couples come together in an infinite variety of combinations reflecting the complexity of two minds in interaction with multiple influences in childhood (Morrison et al. 1997a, 1997b). Secure partners whose relationship is organized by strange attractors enjoy reciprocity and flexibility in role differentiation, equality, and respect. Insecure partners take up rigid roles, defensive positions, and interact by limited attractors such as patterns of domination and submission. Traumatized partners have the most predictably repetitive and suddenly chaotic patterns. Governed by fear and reactivity, their mental states follow fixed attractor patterns that suddenly devolve into cascades of unorganized chaos (J. Scharff and D. Scharff 1994).

Trauma and deprivation limit maturation at every level, narrowing the brain and mind's repertoire of responses to those most basic for survival, and depriving an individual and couple of the quality of vitality that depends on freer ranging interactions. The right amygdala is the seat of the first alarm response to new experience, when fear and avoidance of danger may be the safest option. Trauma and deprivation leave the developing child with a propensity to insecure attachments characterized by fixed- and limit-cycle attractor patterns. Mutually persistently fearful couples like Lucien and Dorothy are haunted by ingrained, amygdala-driven limit cycle responses (Schore 2003a, 2003b). Returning to the third session, we see Lucien and Dorothy work to increase the range of motion in their relationship by gaining access to unconscious patterns.

Session 3: The Strange Attractor of the Therapist's Mind

At the next session, Dorothy described a dream of her own. She said, "I only remember the end, and I awakened screaming. We were in Paris, my favorite place in the world, looking for a selection of good cheeses, and we got separated by crowds. When I saw Lucien again he was on an old street, carrying a thin, young French woman who was feeding Lucien his favorite cheese. I started yelling at him that he'd been lying, and that being with some other woman *did* make a difference."

Dorothy said that the dream relieved her guilt about the sexual relationship going wrong. It showed her Lucien's attachment to another woman, his carrying her and receiving nurturance from her the way Dorothy would like him to carry their sexual life and its repair and to receive nurture from her in sex. Lucien asked whether the French woman could be his mother who had been thin before his birth.

Both dreamers referred to guilt, and to a thin young woman. Lucien had ignored the image of the thin, young, self-absorbed woman in the dream he reported in the previous session, and now Dorothy was picking it up, feeling anguish at being excluded by Lucien's pleasure in being fed by the young woman. Dorothy's dream was marking Lucien's concern but doing so non-contingently, upregulating the volume of distress with an infusion of her own alarm. The limit cycle attractors of their paired amygdala-driven fears magnify the dread of their relationship.

I talked about the overlap in the two dreams. In Dorothy's dream, Lucien is searching for something, and he finds it with a thin woman in his arms, feeding him. In Lucien's dream, a thin woman is self-involved. Lucien is opening the door looking for something, not seeing anything, and closing it again. Then, another woman connected to me marks the gilt/guilt on the armoire/armor in a contingent way and down regulates it by magic repair, the way that a mother's kiss can make it better. What did this mean for them as a couple?

Lucien said, "She fixed it so easily. I wanted to look inside, but it was blank."

Dorothy said, "I see you caught up in the emptiness of your relationship to your mother and the damage it does to us."

Lucien's mother is quite overweight, but Dorothy is thin. Dorothy had seen a thin woman in his arms. Yet when Dorothy asks for sexual intimacy, Lucien sees her as the intrusive, enveloping mother that he must fend off. Lucien is afraid of searching for her in case he finds nothing inside. Dorothy is sad that she can not compete with Lucien's fantasy of a nurturing mother and cannot dispel the image of one who will overpower him.

Now I said to Dorothy, "You have an image of a woman who has captured Lucien by feeding him his favorite food in your favorite place—that is, your sexual life—and frequently, you're furious at his mother."

Dorothy agreed, "Yes, I feel she is a rival for his affection even now."

I said, "Lucien carries inside a black widow mother who seduces his attention from you. But this is your dream. Who is the woman inside *you* who seduces the man you yearn for and keeps him from you?"

Dorothy said, "I love my mother. She's great. She keeps herself in great shape. We're good friends. My father was the difficult one for me. He wasn't as bad as Lucien's mother, and he really loved me, but he was temperamental and difficult, and arrived at some terrible misunderstandings of me. My mother put up with him, and she got the best of him. She kind of seduced him into a relationship that was much more loving than ever I could manage with him."

I said, "So although your father cared for you, there is a part of him you could never have, but your mother could. This is the thin, seductive mother that you see inside Lucien winning him over. His attachment to his black widow overlaps with your thin, attractive mother. And inside his overweight mother hides a thin attractive fourteen-year-old who could be self-involved or who could seduce him with food. Both your mothers seduced men: Dorothy, your mother seduced your father and left you out; Lucien, your mother seduced you into her web and left your father to die emotionally, and that also leaves you feeling left."

Dorothy's dream shows up the area of overlap in painful internal objects, which are psychic strange attractors. Both have organizations that trigger overlapping, amygdalae-driven fear responses. Their mirror neuron responses reinforce fear and rejection in each other. The result is the development and reinforcement of a limit cycle attractor in each of them individually and in their interactions, which colors their joint marital personality.

In this session, Dorothy follows Lucien in sharing a dream. The dreams are close together, resonate with the same theme, and move the work forward. The swirl of the attractor patterns in therapy both brings the image of a couple closer and shows that the block to Dorothy and Lucien establishing a sexual couple is their longing for a feeding couple and fear of emptiness. The strange attractor of the therapist's mind exerts a destabilizing tuning force that continues to bring previously hidden patterns to the surface, and then works to increase the range of motion in a new interactional strange attractor.

SUMMARY

A therapist's main influence comes through unconscious communication—right brain to right brain. The strange attractor of the therapist's endopsychic system exerts a tuning force on the couple relationship. The complex co-regulation of affect between couple and therapist leads to new self-regulation and self-growth. The couple therapist's verbal understanding helps the left frontal cortex to develop a capacity for self-reflection in each individual, and therefore in the couple, which reinforces unconscious right brain reflective function. The couple can learn to expand the use of mirroring from simply appraising the danger of the other to the complex function of actually understanding the other's interior experience.

Attachment theory, neuroscience, trauma theory, object relations theory, and chaos theory all affect the way we listen to couples, and how we interpret the transference. These theories are the link into which the couple therapist is born. Like a secure parent caring for a child, the couple therapist mentalizes, senses, imagines, understands, and verbalizes the couple's experience. This is the link into which the couple that seeks treatment is delivered. In supervision and personal therapy or analysis, as couple therapists we have learned about our own links and our object relations set and, in relation to the strange attractor of the mind of our own therapists, have tuned our mind as an instrument for receiving and modifying the fixed and limit cycle attractor patterns in the couples who present to us for treatment. The mind informed by theory and experienced in self-reflection is the tuning force we bring to couple therapy. We hope—but cannot predict for sure—that our tuning force will introduce perturbations in the most limited of the couple's attractor patterns, throwing them into destabilized, chaotic and confused states, and that from this edge of non-random chaos, new, more flexible strange attractor patterns will take over and bring a capacity for vitality to the newly autonomous self-organizing couple relationship.

Chapter 8

Strange Attractors in Individual Dreaming

Strange attractors, a concept from chaos theory, gives us an additional dynamic tool for studying the processes of organization and reorganization of personality and of therapeutic process (Spruiell 1993; Galatzer-Levy 1995).

CLINICAL EXAMPLE FROM INDIVIDUAL PSYCHOANALYSIS

Here we give an example of a patient's dreams to show the application of chaos theory to individual therapy, the evolution of the treatment, and the link of the therapeutic relationship.

The Constricting, Somatizing Effect of a Limit-Cycle Attractor

Celia King, a 38-year-old, highly functioning divorced mother and successful entrepreneur is in analysis with David Scharff. She came to analysis because of an inner sense of emptiness that led, over the first two years of work, to a sense that she did not really know who she was. Married at 19, she immediately had a son, then a daughter, and divorced at 23. Her children, now adolescent, did well academically, socially, and in sports, but they complained and whined at her a good deal. She had chest pain found to be a somatic expression of anxiety and depression when it proved to be neither cardiac nor esophageal in origin and disappeared on treatment with a small dose of SSRI anti-depressant. In analysis, Mrs. King regularly presented her family and colleagues as offering her mainly persecuting and rejecting experiences: Her live-in boyfriend was unreliable, her children refused to help, and her employees lacked initiative. She handled irritation by becoming obsequious, doing favors, failing to set limits, and other "too good" excited object behavior, thereby keeping her painful internal objects split off from central, satisfying experience.

Superficially, Mrs. King's pattern appeared to be a flexible adaptive strange attractor. Underneath, it resembled a limit cycle attractor designed to allow no conscious connection with painful affects, a stricture producing inner meaninglessness. Mrs. King's limit-cycle attractor pattern of self-organization was less adaptive than a more chaotic strange attractor pattern. It offered predictability and control at the expense of spontaneity and access to feelings. It led to somatization of her "heartache" into chest pain. In analysis, she regained contact with experience split-off by repressed anti-libidinal, limit-cycle attractors.

Friction of Interpretation as a Tuning Force

Analysis introduces destabilizing perturbations under the tuning force of the analyst's mind and the basin of attraction of the therapeutic relationship. Taking her complaints seriously, I (DES) began to challenge her affective disconnection by linking adult patterns and somatic pain to current and childhood disappointment. I came to realize that Mrs. King's idealizing transference and compliance produced a complementary countertransference in me as a good analyst who was, however, superfluous and empty of real function. In chaos theory terms, iterations of our interaction produced an excited countertransference pattern. With minor exceptions, she agreed with what I said. Her trust was too-good-to-be-true, an excited-object projective identification designed to keep me from becoming a persecuting object. Using my countertransference sense that her unquestioning trust made me feel less useful, I began to show her the transference pattern in which she used projective identification to keep me feeling good but untested to avoid friction between us. The friction of my interpretive comments introduced a tuning variable between us, a destabilizing force that could throw her personality and the equilibrium between us into or out of chaos and confusion.

As I interpreted the limit-cycle nature of her pattern, Mrs. King began to voice small annoyances towards me. These gentle criticisms represented the first excursions away from the limit-cycle attractor of her character defenses. Introducing small perturbations into the initial conditions of the iterations of our interactions had produced unpredictable changes in subsequent interaction because of sensitive dependence on these initial conditions. Slowly we moved away from the limit-cycle attractor in which both of us felt empty, and the analytic relationship and discourse began to oscillate across a wider and less comfortably predictable range. A new strange attractor was in creation, our link was in evolution, and our analytic third was developing.

Tolerating Increasing Chaos

Mrs. King now experienced a slowly increasing inner chaos, or a move to unintegration (Winnicott 1960) that she had previously foreclosed in childhood to stop the threat of disintegration in her family of origin when her alcoholic parents' weak attempts at control failed to provide safety. Her father had been dictatorial and alcoholic, and her mother alcoholic and ineffective. She complained about her parents and her current family, but soon denied any resentment. I pointed out her retreat from awareness of resentment to avoid the threat of being pulled back into the chaos of her original family. She was avoiding the infantile basin of attraction where family chaotic dysfunction was pooled (Palumbo 1999). Successive iterations of descriptions of her childhood, her current family experience, and my interpretations slowly produced new patterns. Where pain had been avoided by cutting off affect, there was now room. Just my saying to her that she was disappointed in people or that she resented them, created a perturbation in her fixed reactions, a new turbulence that moved her toward tolerating the chaos of ambivalence and futility, the pull of split-off and repressed gravitational bodies—inner painful objects she had kept out of her conscious universe until now. Having lived with rigid predictability, she was disconcerted to be less predictable to herself. Having lived in the realm of rigid limit cycle attractors, she could hardly dare to face life in the universe of strange attractors. Although these more flexible patterns offer opportunities for growth, they threaten emotional chaos for people like Mrs. King with unconsciously constricted personalities.

As the urgent pull of the compliant, excited object relations basin of attraction loosened, resentment, rejection, and longing appeared more openly. With more awareness of her resentment came her realization that she feared being like her parents, irresponsible, abandoning and damaging to children and partners. She had taken care of her sisters, and then of her children, boyfriend, and employees to avoid being like her negligent parents. Her denied unconscious identification with bad internal objects based on deprivation and impingement, led to her relentless need to repair old objects. Each of these isolated patterns had become limit-cycle attractors constrained from becoming adaptively chaotic. As I commented on the contrast between the way she presented herself and the way her unthinkable anxieties reached me through iterations of projective and introjective identification, the whole range of my input into our shared interaction produced repeated perturbations in her psyche. These disturbances to her inner organization were small at first, but grew over time. Mrs. King faced more affect than she had previously allowed, providing an inner tuning variable that began to move her from one attractor to another.

A Destabilizing Cascade

Dynamically, the situation worked like this: Each incident that might trigger resentment could either evoke a rejecting object constellation, or could quickly lead to an idealizing compliance—two regions in her limit-cycle attractor pattern that, although connected, look utterly different behaviorally. In terms of chaos theory, the points of connection are *saddle points.* Saddle points are branch points in a non-linear equation. At these saddle points in her treatment the *operating equation* of her personality split into two opposing solutions determined by contrasting affects. Before analysis, the resentful anti-libidinal attractor had been largely unconscious, subject to intense repression by the idealized excited object attractor. As analysis proceeded, Mrs. King was transported across one saddle point after another, each one a new branch point in her identifications and unconscious organization. The tuning variables that propelled her into chaotic anxiety-ridden experience came from previously repressed affects. The rapid unconscious crossing of the saddle points she now experienced in anxious situations became a destabilizing cascade of rapidly escalating emotional solutions for her internal operating formulas, until chaos ensued in the form of confusion about her sense of herself. Now Mrs. King could no longer maintain her previous dominant identity as "the good-natured fixer." She no longer knew who she was.

An Iterated Experience of New Strange Attractor Patterns

Influenced by the new attractor pattern formed within the analytic matrix, analyst and analysand form a new overarching shared pattern of unconscious strange attractors identified by Ogden (1994) as the analytic third, or as the link by which both participants are joined and influenced. Mrs. King interacted consciously and unconsciously with me as an external object with both environmental and object-related elements that were gradually internalized (Winnicott 1963a, 1963b). We interacted through continuous cycles of projective and introjective identification, forming a new pattern for the container/contained (Bion 1967b, 1970). In this process, the analyst's mind becomes a new region of "phase space" through which the analysand's anxieties travel repeatedly in each iteration. A phase space is the area in which equations are plotted or show their pattern. For our analytic purposes, we can think of this also as an enhanced potential space in the atmosphere of the analysis where new strange attractors pull the patient away from old attractors and basins of attraction.

Analysis is an iterated experience of new strange attractor patterns moving into and out of chaos. The repetition compulsion, in which patients repeatedly use limited behavioral and emotional formulas, is also an iterated experience, but in this case the repeated running of the same pattern is governed by fixed or limit-cycle attractors that do not move into chaos and cannot therefore re-organize. In general, each repetition is a fractal of the patient's personality and of her relationship to others, whether the iteration of behavior and relating is limited to self-same behavior, or shows more flexible and vital self-similar range.

Pathological repetitive transferential patterns are self-*same* rather than self-*similar*. Mrs. King used an outer shell of exaggerated depressive position functioning to maintain the repression of frightening aspects of paranoid / schizoid object relations (Klein 1946). Her intrapsychic situation showed blocked movement between the positions, rather than the chaotic fluctuation between positions characteristic of health (Bion 1962; Ogden 1989). She was in a static position or psychic retreat (Steiner 1993), a limit cycle attractor that protected her from a collapsing sense of self. Change was like pushing a ball uphill out of a deep basin of attraction. But each therapeutic repetition becomes subtly different because of sensitive dependence on initial conditions—because extremely small differences can potentially make disproportionate differences in fixed patterns. The fractal influence of the small changes inside the analysis influence change at larger orders of magnitude in daily life. Slowly Mrs. King became able to move out of these basins to experience the chaos of the unknown, and move slowly through the analysis of transference toward a more integrated experience. As she did so, the foreclosed analytic space began to open into a more functional transitional phase space. This space was characterized by some states of more adaptive chaotic irregularity in which new attractor patterns could develop.

Two Dreams: Fractal Similarity to Internal Object Relations and Transference

Two of Mrs. King's dreams which are like a film of her endopsychic situation can also be seen as fractals of her personality, and as iterations of the processes of dynamic endopsychic structure that combine cognitive and affective organization. They also represent her relationships including the transference relationship and illustrate new psychic strange attractors evolving in the transference-countertransference encounter. They show the evolution in interpersonal unconscious communication, the move towards new unconscious pattern, and evolution in the link that marks progress in her analysis.

Mrs. King said, "I had two dreams last night. In the first I was a teenager hiding from a strange boyfriend who was going to beat and rape me. I went into the library where you were reading. You didn't look up, so I went into the ladies' toilet. I felt trapped because the dangerous boyfriend was still outside. A woman said, 'We'll help.' Some women gave me a military uniform and snuck me out a window. I joined a military parade and marched away to some barracks and felt safe.

"The second dream upset me more. I was living in a one-level ranch house with a low roof. My actual boyfriend was there and said, 'The cats are out tonight.' There were tigers and panthers. He said he was going to look for our dog. I didn't want him to. He's in the jeep with the roof off. He drives into the carport without putting on the brakes and crashes. Then he comes into the house carrying my son's head. It's obvious it was the cats that got him. I dial 911. The person answers, 'Once the cats target you, there's no hope!' I go on the roof and shoot 11 of the cats, but I know there are always 12. I decide the 12th cat is in the house, and I don't know if it's going to go after my son, my boyfriend, or me."

Mrs. King's boyfriend had a jeep, but she said the dream car also seemed to represent my convertible car usually parked in the carport in front of my office, a low-roofed one-story building. This led her to an image of the car crashing into my office, driven now by me. In the first dream, I sat reading although she was in danger, and she had to hide in a toilet associated with the one off my waiting room. This reminds her of the time she and her mother hid in the bathroom when her father threatened to shoot them during a fight with her mother. The military women could defend her against armed men related to her father with the gun. The lions and tigers of the second dream reminded her of the color of bees buzzing in my garden she can see from the couch. She likes seeing them, but she is allergic to bee stings, and so they also represent danger. In the last few days, she has felt afraid of them. As Mrs. King gave these associations, I felt sadness at the threat she was feeling in our relationship, a loss of transference idealization. At the same time, because I knew the idealization had limited our work, I felt an inner quickening in response to her bringing the previously excluded danger into the room.

These dreams show the cracking of the projective identification of an excessively, too-good-to-be-true holding pattern (a *limit-cycle attractor pattern*) that had protected us from knowing the ways in which Mrs. King feels unsafe, a dawning awareness of an unconscious lack of safety, of the invasive, rapacious and even murderous persecuting objects previously excluded from our relationship. The murderous cats and the bees represent apparently benign forces that carry severe threat. They are *fractals* of Mrs. King's unconscious internal object relations, her developmental history, and the transference-countertransference interaction. The sense of danger that characterized her childhood has returned. In my chair, I sit in front of book shelves, and now, unconsciously, she feels that I will not look up from my books to protect her. I appear as myself ignoring her, as the dangerous boyfriend, as the current boyfriend who cannot protect her. She uses the toilet to hide from danger emerging in the transference. The military woman refers to her mother in that situation and also to my wife, whose office is across the waiting room, who she has often fantasized could help her. Only her militant women friends will defend against the marauding men. We can now see that there is an unconscious way in which all men constitute either direct danger or inadequate protection.

The second dream iterates the same problem with her boyfriend in a more helpful role. She has previously been unable to speak of unconscious fears, partly because my awareness of her inner fright has been blocked by idealization. Through projective and introjective identification, I have been participating in a pattern in which we both exploited an attitude of exaggerated trust to keep the marauding cats at bay; therefore her fear that they would never rest until they got her could not be acknowledged. I am now also the 12th cat that is still out to get her.

The dream fractals of Mrs. King's internal situation and of the transference-countertransference exchange locate the cats as the ever-present sense of threat. I, her analyst, fail to defend her, and then pounce on her with interpretations that attack her and her children. The dream communications to herself and to me are fractals of her overall psychic organization, self-similar to larger patterns in which she is on guard because no one understands. They are also fractals of her relationship to her primary objects, and of the aspect of the analytic relationship in which she feels I do not understand, and that only a longed-for but unknown woman could arm her against the night. However, the fact that Mrs. King could now dream these things and bring them to the analysis is evidence of evolution in our shared strange attractor. Using the dreams, we can see dimensions of her inner world that were previously deeply under water, and they become available for shared examination, for the kind of consideration at the edge of chaos where she is open to reorganization of her personality and operating equations.

The analysis with Mrs. King that operated in many ways on a relatively opaque surface, now has access to unconscious themes of fear and anger. I can begin to help her pry loose from the pull of the protective, rigid basin of attraction that has gripped much of our interaction. As I feel her fear, I see the splitting and repression of her encapsulated psychic retreat—that is, a fearful limit-cycle pattern. Sitting in my chair behind her, looking past her to the magnolia tree in my garden, I silently think about how she watched protectively lest its buds be frozen before they could bloom as happened in the previous year. I imagine a cat on a branch, stalking a bird in the tree. The bees buzz on the petals of early flowers. I feel the danger lurking everywhere for Mrs. King. There has been a perturbation in this session, in this iteration, a move away from the basin of attraction that has held therapeutic action at bay. Now she is able to convey fear in such a way that I have been able to take it in. And it connects, too, to the blossoms we can both see outside. The terror and the beauty are closer together. They do not have to be so rigidly held apart as they were until this session.

SUMMARY

In this clinical example, psychoanalysis can be viewed as a series of iterating equations in which the co-created transference-countertransference dialectic operates as a strange attractor, which moves limit cycle attractor patterns of rigid rejecting and exciting object constellations into chaos, and then into new patterns of organization characterized by de-repression, re-linking of thought and feeling, and re-integration of parts of the self.

Chapter 9

Sexuality, Dreams, and the Somatic Link

A couple's sexual life draws on the history of each partner's experience of holding and handling in the mother–infant relationship. In adulthood, the capacity for genital arousal and orgasm in the shared situation with the partner grows on the foundation of the psychosomatic partnership—the physical and emotional connection established in the mother–infant relationship (Scharff 1982). In the beginning, the psychosomatic partnership is weighted more towards the physical, marked by the mother's feeding, holding, and positioning of the infant, responding to physical needs, and generally providing a sense of well-being and safety (Winnicott 1960b). The emotional component develops in the mother's fantasy about her fetus, and it flourishes after birth in her attunement to her infant's rhythms, as they engage in highly affective vocal and visual "conversations," the right brains of mother and infant in direct communication (Schore 2002). Physical interdependence recedes as the infant becomes capable of feeding, walking, toileting, speaking, and eventually reading, all of these autonomous activities built on the foundation of parental care. All of this early parental care is encoded in implicit memory, so that the body and a background tone of emotion are the vehicles for expression of memory of this phase of psychosomatic partnership.

Similarly, adult sexuality inherits its riches from early psychosomatic development. In the committed adult sexual relationship, in-depth psychological and physical relating closely intertwine for the first time since infancy. Adolescent masturbation, sexual experiences, crushes, and first loves draw on the psychosomatic partnership too, but it is the sanctioned promise of being together over time as part of a family that creates the degree of interpenetration of mind and body that is most reminiscent of infancy. Falling in love, unconscious fit between the personalities, the fit between attachment styles, emotional attunement, and sexual compatibility are under the control of the communicating right brains of the adult partners, as was the bonding of mother and infant. Needs for safety, pleasure, reassurance, and self-confirmation are all factored and condensed into the final common pathway of sexual exchange, which looks back on each partner's developmental history of inner object relations, and forward to possibilities in and beyond the physical aspects of the relationship. In the healthy partnership, satisfying sex brings not only individual and shared physical pleasure, but also confidence in individual well-being and in the couple's overall emotional bond. Sexual relating is one major building block of marital or long-term partner security. A vital sexual relationship builds a marital link that in turn continues to nurture each partner. In the dysfunctional partnership, sexual difficulty is both sign and source of distress in the couple relationship, eroding their shared link and often having ramifications in the behavior of the couple's children (D. Scharff 1982; D. Scharff and J. Scharff 1991).

Emotional difficulty becomes sexual difficulty by a psychological process of somatic conversion (Breuer and Freud 1893–1895; Fairbairn 1954; Scharff 1982). In this process, complex emotional issues are reduced by symbolization and condensation, and are expressed in the body language of the sexual parts of the body in interaction. In the couple, the converted emotional conflict may be projected into a sexual body part of the partner. The partner is perceived in the light of that unexpressed conflict. Since the couple has chosen to be together for reasons of unconscious fit, one partner may well have a valency to identify with the perception and develop a sexual dysfunction on behalf of the couple.

Communion between the personalities of the partners through projective identification creates a marital joint personality (Dicks 1967). Their sexual relationship, in its conscious and unconscious aspects, creates a shared sexual pattern that is part of their marital personality. Each personality is a system of parts, some conscious and some unconscious (Fairbairn 1954). The central ego in relation to the satisfactory ideal object remains largely in consciousness, a source of satisfaction and curiosity for learning and interaction. When the ego is not constitutionally weak or weakened by overwhelmingly frustrating experience, stimulating and unavailable aspects of the object remain in consciousness enlivening and confirming the sense of the self and its capacity for autonomy and intimacy. This conscious part of the ego-system represses unsatisfactory parts of the object that are too exciting or too rejecting to bear, along with split-off libidinal and antilibidinal parts of the ego and the affects that connect them. In unconsciousness, the rejecting object relationship further represses the exciting object relationship. In the personality with a weak or weakened ego, the unconscious internal object relationships are severely repressed, leading to a central ego shorn of desire or self-control and threatened with the return of the repressed.

We have modified Fairbairn's basic structure to provide a model of the individual psyche built less on pathology, and more on normal function (J. Scharff and D. Scharff 1998c). In this model, the personality is motivated by the need for relationship. Under the sway of this overarching need, there are needs for closeness and for separateness or autonomy. These represent the pull towards the object and the push for distance, both within the overall need for relationship. The central self includes some of each tendency: the pull towards the object as a libidinal pull for love, attention and nurture and sexuality; the push away as a need for boundaries, limit setting and private space. It is the excesses of these that include relationships that are so painful they must be repressed as either too exciting of need or too rejecting of need and persecuting.

In the process of falling in love, the divisions between these parts of the self become more fluid than they normally are, and at the same time, the boundaries between the self and other become more permeable. The selves of two courting lovers are dominated by a shared link of excitement that draws them together with heightened expectations. The boundary shifts to exclude others beyond the pair, but to provide a space for psychic merger. Joining in the physical act of intercourse involves interpenetration of body parts, which, as it crosses those boundaries, introduces a corresponding feeling of emotional at-oneness. Two personalities, each conceived of as a dynamic system of internal object relationships, then join to become a larger system of interacting parts. A needy woman's libidinal ego may seek an exciting object, and find it in her fiancé. Later, when, as her husband, he can't stand her demands of him, she finds his rejecting object instead. A faithful gay man may hope to relate lovingly to his partner as an ideal object only to find an exciting object that evokes sexual craving without offering intimacy. Two women may fall in love on the basis of each being the other's ideal object but if sexual interaction stalls, they cannot then be each other's exciting object as well.

Emotional conflict between parts of the self and between the self and the partner is often projected onto the screen of the genitalia of self or other. For instance, a woman whose dependent longings have been rejected takes care of her husband with excessive devotion and yet feels revulsion, irritation, or pain at having her breasts touched. A man who was physically abused by his father uses aggression effectively to close his business deals but erectile dysfunction reveals his conflict over identifying with his father.

One of the most effective avenues to understanding emotional life is through dreams. Dream analysis reverses the process of conversion and projective identification, and makes the underlying conflict available for interpretation and understanding. In couple therapy, the *royal road to the unconscious* (Freud 1900) is a dual-carriageway to understanding the unconscious underpinnings of individual emotional organization, the affective structure of shared bonds, the expression of various parts of the self recovered in the couple's relationship, and the meaning of the shared symptom of sexual dysfunction (D. Scharff and J. Scharff 1991; Scharff 1982, 1992; Nicoló et al. 2006). When we work with dreams in couple therapy, we take the stance that the individual's dream is a product of the couple and their therapeutic relationship. The dream is the expression of the couple's link. In treatment, dreams represent the process of living in the link to each other and to the therapist. Clinically we hear the dream and accept the dreamer's associations as we would in individual therapy. We wait for, or ask for, the partner's associations, not to interpret the individual's dream, but to use it to arrive at shared insight about the couple and their relationship to the therapist. The therapist's associations also inform us, not only about the meaning of the dream but about how to work with it. In the two vignettes from couple therapy that follow, the first with David Scharff, the second with Jill Scharff, we show how dreams give access to sexual and emotional difficulty and give information about the nature of the transference.

SHARED FEAR OF INTIMACY AFTER INFIDELITY

Robert and Diane, in their mid-forties, had both been in individual therapies with some benefit to them as individuals, but their marriage remained emotionally distant. On the brink of divorce, they were sent to me (DES) for consultation and possibly for couple therapy. Robert traveled constantly for his job with a multinational corporation, while Diane stayed home to care for their children, manage their home and household staff, and enjoy her social life with friends. They had had a college romance that Diane broke off when she met another man, got engaged, and then became pregnant by him. When she realized that she did not respect her fiancé, she terminated the engagement and the pregnancy. She went back to Robert, who still adored her, and they soon married, but he remained hurt over the earlier break-up and over her becoming pregnant by another man.

Robert and Diane's sex was always more perfunctory than passionate. Diane seemed physically and emotionally uninvolved, and Robert had periodic difficulty with his erection. She doubted Robert's love; he doubted her love and his potency. She was not reassured by the persuasion of lavish gifts. He sought confirmation of his potency by visiting call girls when he was traveling, but he remained loyal to Diane in his mind, even though he felt worn down by Diane's sexual and emotional reserve. Nevertheless, his marriage still came first if Diane would join the effort. Diane said she, too, wanted to give the marriage every chance.

In individual meetings, each spouse told me about the affairs that they had not disclosed to each other. Early in the marriage, Diane had had an affair in which she enjoyed sex more than with Robert. Two years before the couple consulted me, she had another affair with a man she did not respect but with whom she enjoyed terrific sex including her first orgasm in intercourse. Six months before the consultation, Robert had begun a passionate affair where he felt loved as never before. With my support, Robert and Diane explored the meaning of these affairs and came to realize that the emptiness of their marriage was connected to the fullness in the affairs.

Both feeling that they had little left to lose and hoping to reverse the flow of emotional energy and reinvest it in their marriage, they warily told each other about their affairs. Each felt more sinned against than sinning. Fully expressing their hurt and outrage in couple sessions, they then opened up to each other emotionally and sexually with newfound passion, until, as usually happens, passion gradually faded in the ordinary light of day. The couple continued the slow process of rebuilding their relationship in couple therapy (D. Scharff 1982; D. Scharff and J. Scharff 1991).

Robert's Dream

A month after the revelation of the affairs, Robert brought the following dream to the couple's session.

> I'm in a restaurant with Diane and the man she was once engaged to. He said that he was lecturing at the university. Diane ate part of my roast beef sandwich, and then he started to eat it, too. Someone asked who brought the sandwich. I said it was our housekeeper. I turned around and there she was, but with horrible black spots on her face. We wound up in my old Mercedes, the fiancé was driving, and Diane rubbed his arm. I threw punches at him from the back seat, but I couldn't hit him hard because of the headrest. I also hit out at Diane but without power. He stopped the car, and said, "Hit me if you can. Perhaps I deserve it, but you're not strong enough to hurt me." I felt that it was really my penis that didn't have enough power.

Robert said that when Diane had angrily threatened divorce the previous week, he had remembered how devastated he was when she had left him 30 years earlier for that fiancé. He remembered how humiliated he felt during a time of extended impotence when she had no sympathy for him. Associating to the spots on the housekeeper's face, he said that the marriage seemed poisoned. Associating to Diane and the fiancé sharing his sandwich, he remembered how he had cringed last week when she yelled at him that he could eat his lover's vagina if that was what he wanted.

Diane associated to the restaurant as the place where she saw Robert's lover occasionally. The spots on the housekeeper's face made her think that Robert thought she, Diane, was ugly.

Robert had two more brief dreams:

> A big guy wanted to beat me up. I told another man I would give him $2500 to defend me, and he did.
>
> I was at a motel where people go with lovers. I was in the bathroom there with Diane and an Indian man. We were naked and measuring our penises. I had a strong erection, but his was stronger, and I thought he had a better angle.

Robert associated to a woman who had an affair with an Indian man. Afterward, her husband forgave her. Perhaps the dream meant that he could forgive Diane, too.

Diane said that the dreams reminded her that Robert had told her that his lover had once caressed his penis as they drove to a motel. Perhaps he was wondering if she, Diane, had done this to another man. She thought that Robert, being the youngest in his family, felt inferior to other men, and so had to make his affair less bad than hers. Robert thought that her affair was worse because she is a woman. She said that he could not forgive her for being with a sexually effective man because accepting that meant accepting weakness and inferiority.

Robert began to cry, and said, "We had so much to look forward to. We both did something terrible. Now I feel I've failed in the most important task in my life."

I said, "I noticed today, that you, Diane, were initially fairly silent, leaving Robert more exposed while you hid your feelings behind his, and then you stressed his weakness and humiliation—which you yourself may be feeling."

Robert said, "*I* feel humiliated and angry."

"What occurs to you about paying someone $2500 to defend you?" I asked.

Diane said, "$2500 is a lot to pay for defense."

Robert said, "It's to defend my inadequacy and buy my way out. I paid prostitutes to make me feel better, but I also pay my analyst."

I said, "How do you feel about paying me to defend your marriage?"

Robert said, "I want my marriage to work. So, I buy your help. You protect us from having more affairs."

Diane said to Robert, "Or maybe he'd protect you from disclosing an affair if you went back to that woman."

I said, "You each disclosed affairs with my encouragement, and you felt beat up having to do that, yet also protected and helped. Is there a fantasy that I am penetrating the emotional depths of your marriage at a more effective angle than you are used to or feel you can do yourselves? Do you feel humiliated by me?"

Robert said, "You made me reveal the affair when I didn't really want to, but you did it to turn our relationship onto a positive track, instead of staying in a race to see who could humiliate the other more."

I said, "Diane, you felt I beat you up too?"

Diane said, "I feel both that you beat me up, and also that you're helping me."

Robert said, "We feel that way with each other, too. We were in a friend's swimming pool Saturday, and Diane asked for a glass of wine. Even she thinks she drinks too much and that she should lose weight. So I stopped her. I said, 'You don't need to drink. You should lose weight.' She did stop, but she felt I was bullying her."

Diane said, "I *do* have to stop drinking to be thin and healthy. But it's so hard, and even if I do, his other woman will always look better than I do, so why give it up?"

How Dreams Help Therapy Progress

The couple had been bogged down in accusations and counteraccusations. Robert's dreams took them beyond the daily level of the concrete to reach underlying issues of envy, inadequacy, mutual resentment, and disappointment, and then link them to memories of hurt. Through their associations they show how envy breeds jealousy, and the resulting acting out inflicts further hurt.

Robert's dreams depict his hurt that Diane is sharing herself with someone else, and his need for a strong man to support him against a persecuting inner rival that shrivels his penis. Diane supplies the link to his sense of inferiority in his family but she does so in an accusatory way. She bolsters her own inferiority by blaming it on the other woman for being too attractive.

The couple's associations bring up many elements familiar to both of them, each supplying important connections concerning conscious and unconscious conflict. They can help each other widen understanding in this process, and they can hurt each other by using these associations in persecuting ways. Once the dreams are delivered, they are subject to the same forces that already bedevil the couple, but in giving access to the unconscious they also present opportunities for expanding the limit-cycle, self-same quality of their regressed interactions. The possibility for change is enhanced when the dream also involves the therapist who sees their link expand to include himself.

We see the transference to the therapist as both positive and negative, to him as the Indian man (a reference to his summer skin color) who might help him reach forgiveness but who might humiliate him with the success of it, as a male rival (teaching at the University), and as the paid bodyguard who defends them from assault (asking for revelation and supporting reparation). Their mixed feelings about their therapist echo their ambivalence towards each other. Robert can speak to the way that they feel mistreated by him in the therapy, much as they do by each other. But they are able to see the useful ambiguity of the treatment situation: when the therapist hurts them, it is for a good reason. This is a less polarized view of the treatment relationship than they have of each other. It helps to pull their couple link towards more flexibility and less persecution. The dream shows how the couple's shared contextual transference expresses their problem. Telling the dream in the session brings the multiple links alive, shows the process of the links evolving, and thereby work on the dreams becomes a vehicle for resolution.

Diane's Dream

Two weeks later, Diane reported a dream that began in a pool—a link to the confrontation in the pool discussed in the session on Robert's dreams and also to the pool near my office. It seemed to me that the image of the pool indicated that the themes from the previous dream session were back with us.

> I was swimming with other people in a gorgeous pool below a waterfall, wearing a white bikini that looked great. It was time to go home. A guy got out of the water with me. As we walked up a hill, over some rough spots, he placed his hand on my shoulder. I said he was abusing me, and he reacted like, "You're a stupid woman to think I did something wrong!" We got in the car. Another guy sat next to me. It was crowded, and his legs touching mine felt awful. Now the white bikini seemed more like underwear and I felt naked and exposed, but not vulgar. I had to tip the driver, so I looked for a dollar bill. I opened my purse. There was money from all over the world, large bills in various denominations of 500, 800, 1000, but no dollars. I said, "These other currencies are worthless." I didn't feel good. These men were taking advantage of me.

Diane said that she felt uncomfortable wearing clothes like underwear in the company of these men, and this reminded her of the discomfort of her affairs. The money reminded her of her husband's use of prostitutes all over the world. As soon as she said this, Robert countered that the dream suggested *she* felt like a prostitute. "I hate to think I feel like a prostitute," Diane said. "I never had sex for money. I looked better in the dream than I feel, but I felt vulnerable."

I said Diane felt exposed and undressed by the discussions in therapy, and she agreed. In the same vein, I asked about the threatening man who put his hand on her shoulder. She remembered a time when a man had called her repeatedly, and then denied sexual intentions. She said, "There's a sense of fear as I walked to the car, fear about the way the floor has fallen out from under my life."

Associating to the dream, Robert said, "The two guys stand for her two affairs. She is exposed, vulnerable and out of control. The money is cheap currency."

Diane said, "Yes, I feel cheap, and I wound up having affairs, acting like a prostitute. I'm so sorry."

Robert did not respond in kind. He added in an unempathic, self-serving way, "I feel like a good part of me has gone out of the window. I was bad to her by having my own affair, but I spent twenty-five years being good and begging her for love. I'm less willing to give to her now. Look what my love got me!"

I said, "The sexual woman alive in the affairs and in the pool feels uncomfortable in underwear with the men in the dream just as Diane feels reluctant to bare herself at home with Robert and to expose her feelings in therapy."

I also had the thought that, unlike a prostitute who takes money from a man for sex, Diane takes money from Robert while *not* having sex.

Then I asked, "What might it mean that you were searching for a dollar bill for the driver of the car?"

Diane said, "The car is therapy, which feels too close for comfort. You touch me uncomfortably when you remind me of unpleasant things. In the dream, I couldn't pay the driver. If we couldn't pay you, we couldn't see you. You only see us for money."

I began to see that I was also the prostitute, working intimately only for money. In this way I was joined in their degraded link.

I said, "Robert, you feel inappropriate when you approach Diane, and Diane, you feel accosted by Robert's sexual advances. Perhaps you feel like that about my comments. Do you think of using money to 'tip' me, to demean me like you demean each other, to lessen the pain of needing my help just as you try to lessen the pain of needing each other?"

Diane said, "Robert can't reach out to me, he's so busy flying around the world, making huge amounts of money that won't buy what we need most. That's why we need you. Partly I don't feel good about needing your help, although I also do feel good about coming here."

Mutual Dreaming

In this session, Diane's dream complements Robert's dreams from two weeks before, brings Diane's unconscious experience into the therapy on an equal footing with Robert's, and offers a route to further investigation in depth. It begins in the gorgeous pool, an image of the idyllic surface of their life-style, but also of the ideal that is refuted by coming to work near my pool where I see her exposed and my comments touch her uncomfortably. The men in her dream echo the rival men of Robert's dreams. Together, their dreams lead us to an understanding of the interplay of jealousy, rivalry, and envy that has come to characterize their joint marital link. Robert's finding his penis inferior to the penis of the other man (standing for the therapist) finds a parallel in Diane's projecting her feeling of lack into Robert. Both of them use the presence of other men to express their doubt and fear of intimacy. The mutual resentment they each express is ameliorated by remorse, but much remains to be done in tempering their inner persecuting objects and the resonating effect of these on their relationship.

Finally, this dream also expresses fear and hope in the shared contextual transference. This parallels the ambivalence that characterizes their marital relationship. They feel they need their therapist's help, but they also feel abused by the way he "touches" them in the therapy. This ambivalence is not yet resolved, but it is illustrated in the dream in a way that makes it available for work, for evolution in the link that couple and therapist share. In this way, the destructive aspects of Robert and Diana's link that had been converted into physical sexual distress have been relocated in verbal memories and expressions of feeling that are now, for the first time, available for understanding and work, offering to heal the polarizations and restore their more loving and admiring relationship.

Over the next months, this did in fact happen, and the couple resumed an active, although not vigorous sexual relationship. It was enough, however, to support a general renewal of their loving relationship that has persisted over many years.

SHARED FEAR OF ORAL AGGRESSION IN SEXUAL DYSFUNCTION

A couple had been in marital therapy with me (JSS) to save their marriage. The husband, Fred, complained that his wife was blocking his sexual initiatives and the wife, Kitty, complained that Fred took no initiative in their domestic life. Both had enjoyed fully satisfying sex together and with previous partners. They couldn't understand why their sex life was now a source of distress. The possibility of sexual pleasure was ruined because Kitty became aggressive as soon as she was aroused, which frightened both of them.

In marital therapy, Fred realized that he had been blaming Kitty for avoiding sex as if he, himself, had no fear of intercourse. Then he remembered his first failed intercourse during seduction as a teenager when he lost his erection because of fantasies of alligators in a nearby pool and fears of being found dead. He concluded that he was afraid of being eaten and killed upon entering the vagina. Kitty appreciated his sharing responsibility for their stalled sex life, and for co-operating more willingly and proactively in their domestic life. Together, Kitty and Fred built confidence in the value of their marriage, but sexual satisfaction continued to elude them.

I recommended a shift from marital therapy to sex therapy in which they would participate together in private in a series of exercises graded from non-genital pleasuring to full genital stimulation, from low arousal to high, containment of the penis holding still, and finally intercourse—and then discuss their experiences in their therapy session (Kaplan 1974; D. Scharff 1982; J. Scharff and D. Scharff 1998c). Kitty and Fred progressed slowly through the planned stages of non-sexual pleasuring and casual inclusion of breasts and genitals. When they arrived at the next level—focusing on the breasts and genitals with arousal limited to a low level—Kitty and Fred got stuck.

In the next session, we addressed the stalled sex therapy. Fred reported that they had once more been unable to do the exercise, this time because Kitty was sick. Beginning to touch his genitals, she had suddenly developed a sore throat.

Kitty said, "It was as if it had been scraped raw by an instant strep throat. I was scared. I had been able to let him touch me, but when I went to touch him, he had an erection, and I just couldn't. Then suddenly I had this sore throat!"

Fred said, "I sensed the sore throat was connected to her reluctance to touch my erection." He agreed with Kitty that he had tried to press on regardless, and then reacted angrily at the lack of sex, instead of being sympathetic about her discomfort.

Thinking back on his story of fear of the vagina connected to alligator mouths, I said that his comments connected the sight of his penis with an uncomfortable feeling in the throat.

Kitty immediately got my point and refuted it, saying, "I don't have memories of a penis being shoved in my throat."

At this moment, I, myself, started coughing and couldn't suppress the sensation in my throat. I said that I thought I was resonating with her wish to get rid of that idea and also with the underlying fantasy, as I tried to expel something from my throat, and at the same time pretend it wasn't bothering me.

Here is an instance of the interpersonal unconscious transmission of the couple's problem into the therapist. The transmission happens instantaneously, just as Kitty developed a somatic symptom instantaneously. The speed and strength of the communication go beyond the capacity of the therapist to process what is happening in her body. The communication is not only right-brain-to-right-brain, it is essentially a body-to-body enactment of unconscious conflict, an event that can only later be understood (Jacobs 1991). In this case, the enactment consists at first of a somatic expression of the link between the couple and therapist. In that moment, she does not speak from the experience because it requires time to digest and make sense of it.

Fred went on to say that this made him think of the time when Kitty was a teenager and woke up to find a guy in her bed doing oral sex on her.

Kitty shuddered, and said, "Well, that connects with the dream I had." She said:

> I dreamt I was in bed with our friend Alec who has a beard like that guy. In the dream, I was naked from the waist down. Alec had pulled off my pajama bottoms. I hear his wife May outside the room, about to come in. I try to cover myself but I can't. May thinks I've had sex with Alec. I have this awful feeling of having done something really wrong. I'm saying I don't want to lose May as a friend.

Kitty continued, "Alec and his wife May are actually good friends of ours. Being half-naked and trying to cover myself in the dream is like the way I am in bed with Fred. I feel vulnerable and naked and I prefer to have a towel handy to cover myself with."

Fred said, "That's how you felt when you were a teenager—that you had done something wrong when that guy did oral sex on you. That was horrible."

Fred is providing a needed sense of urgency to take up this memory that Kitty is avoiding.

I asked Kitty if she could tell me about it. She said, "We were in a hotel. My sister and her husband had a room, and they got a room for this guy and me. It had separate beds but he was thirty years old and my sister should have known better."

As Kitty said this, she made a biting movement with her jaw that struck me as both aggressive and frightened. It reminded me of the fantasy alligators Fred had been frightened of at a similar age, and perhaps it related to the unconscious assault on my throat.

Fred said to Kitty, "I noticed that your mouth opened and you clenched your jaw as if you felt like biting."

Kitty went on, "Well I hated him. I still do—he was so smarmy. It was dark in the room. I woke up murmuring, 'Lovely. I didn't know that sex was so . . . ,'" she trailed off, and then resumed. "What a repulsive character. I said to him, 'I don't want you to do that,' and he stopped."

Turning to Fred, she said, "You had a dream and it was about oral sex, too."

Fred said, "Yeah, Kitty was feeling better and we did the exercises again the next night. They went all right, and then I had this dream." He continued:

> I was in a room with another man and woman, and the woman was sexually aggressive with both of us. I started to take off my clothes and I thought, "Wait, this isn't right. What about Kitty?" Anyway, I was performing oral sex on this woman. I said, "I haven't done this in so long, I don't know if I'm doing it right." Again I thought, "This isn't right." I interrupted and left for a moment, and when I came back, the woman had left.

Kitty said, "That is so funny. Touching you the other night when you had the erection, I thought, 'I haven't touched your penis in a long time. Am I going to know how to do this?'"

I said, "You sound sad."

"Definitely," said Kitty. "It's been so long!"

Fred said, "When I woke up I thought of the strong images of oral sex I have. In college, I went into a garden with a woman at a party. In an instant, she was performing oral sex on me. Earlier than that, I was taken aback to see a couple on the beach where a woman was performing oral sex on a man and I remember staying to watch, totally voyeuristic, wondering if the alligators were around. It was very powerful. I'm so embarrassed."

When Kitty had unpleasant associations to the penis, Fred pushed forward to pass over the images bothering him, just he did in sex, as if the problem were only hers. Fred's had encouraged Kitty to talk about her trauma related to mouths and sex. Only thanks to his dream did he reach his own traumatic memories. Fred's and Kitty's dreams suggest that they experienced their therapist as orally encouraging sexual activity, and revealed their transference to me as a seducer, sexual object, voyeur, and judge of what is being done right. The therapist had experienced their unconscious revulsion to this inside her own body, giving her a sense of the degree of pain they were feeling as a couple in the therapy with her. Guilty about being the object of their attention and witness to their sexual life (as Fred had been to the couple on the beach) she tried to expel this projective identification. Given enough time to process the experience, she became able to use her countertransference to address this, and so arrive at a position from which to address the underlying fantasies revealed by the dreams.

Following the work done in this session, Kitty and Fred repeated the exercise. They moved on from the exercise "going all right" to its being a reliably pleasurable experience at a higher level of arousal, and they became eager to proceed to the next therapeutic step of containment of the penis in the vagina.

Discussion

In this example, the marital partners shared anxiety about the dangers of overstimulation, seduction, and coercion. Both had projected oral aggression into the mouth and the vagina. Fred had carried his combined fear and fascination of the orally castrating mother into the marital relationship. Kitty had brought to the marriage her combined excitement and fear in response to adolescent neglect and trauma. These were heightened by Fred's unconscious denial and projection of his own reluctance into Kitty, and his then berating her for the lack of passion in the marriage.

The couple's transference to the therapist also demonstrated these features. She experienced a psychosomatic countertransference enactment when their shared projection of aggression and sexual arousal got right into her and disabled her oral vehicle for communicating with them. The oral aggression they both shared and feared also characterized their attitude towards her: They seemed cooperative on the surface, only to resist the therapeutic process and the instructions and interpretations they feared would be "pushed down their throats." Experiencing the "instant strep throat" of their anxiously ambivalent sexuality, she felt their embarrassment, their efforts to hide their ineptitude, and their guilt. But she felt it in an immediate way that gave her a first-hand experience of how frightening it was for them. Tolerating that and speaking from inside her own experience allowed her to contain and hold the situation, and facilitate their progress.

Kitty's dream expresses on behalf of the couple their shared fear embodied in oral sex trauma and the lack of contextual safety. Fred's dream expresses sexual curiosity and voyeurism, which took him as an adolescent into sexually aggressive situations that he craved and feared. Now he is filled with unrequited sexual longing and he craves Kitty's sexual expressiveness but cannot evoke it. By projective identification, he puts aggression into her and fears her as much as he feared the alligators. As much as he feared what he witnessed and imagined on the beach, it also fascinated him. Fred's associating to Kitty's oral sex trauma, even before she had told her dream, is a clue to his use of her anxiety to both hide and express his own. Both dreams express the intense sexual pleasure that each of them longs for and each fears that it "just isn't right" and that they are inept as a couple. The dreams both enabled and signaled a new understanding for the couple. Because the dreams were delivered into the therapeutic setting, and in this case literally into the body of the therapist, they became part of the evolving link that moved them and the whole therapeutic project from transference resistance in the beginning phase to cooperative work in this mid-phase session.

The work went on through the containment of the therapist's mind. Two factors contributed to the enactment passing through the body of the therapist. First, because of the raw and unsymbolized quality of the material, it came to her in an unmentalized form that gave her the experience of how her mind could not, at least at first, serve as an adequate container for the somatic representations. Secondly, the work of sex therapy itself focuses on somatic expressions of emotional issues. So it is not surprising when the couple, asked to represent these issues emotionally through dreams, bring them to the therapist's bodily experience through projective identification. When the therapist used her training to metabolize the experience, the couple in turn took in that capacity from her, and then were able to move to the next step of therapy. These are "dreams that turn over a page" (J-M. Quinodoz 2002). The sex therapy exercises accelerated the emergence of anxiety located in the sex organs and the dreams illuminated the depth of the anxiety and gave us a lane through the transference obstacle.

SUMMARY

Dreams in couple therapy provide opportunities analogous to those in individual therapy, providing a royal road to understanding the couple's relationship, including both their individual and shared unconscious. Dream analysis in couple therapy has the advantage of using not only the dreamer's associations, but also those of the partner who shares in the dreamer's life and unconscious processes. The therapist's associations, including somatic reception of the couple's unconscious experience, form another pillar of the work, expanding and illuminating the therapeutic link. Dreams may be part of the ordinary working matrix, or at times of change, they may mark new directions and emergent maturation. Like the symptomatic sexual dysfunctions the couples bring to therapy, dreams draw on right mind organization of the highly affective and somatic representations of desire, relatedness, aggression, and sexuality. When the dreams feature sexual concerns, they can be particularly helpful in decoding the source of sexual difficulties and revealing their connection to marital discord and to the therapeutic process.

Chapter 10

Attachment Theory as Link and Context

Attachment research has yielded attachment theory which is of value in measuring relationship interaction. It also has a clinical application. Some analysts, however, find attachment theory incompatible with psychoanalysis in that it fails to address the pivotal role attributed to internal structural conflict, the dynamic unconscious, and the role of defense against drives in establishing compromise formations (Zepf 2006). Others find that it is compatible, but insufficient for dynamic understanding and therapeutic effectiveness. Object relations psychoanalysts agree that attachment theory cannot measure the dynamic unconscious, but they find it helpful in many ways, and more so as the concepts move toward measures of internal processes in the parent and their effect on the child. As clinically based theorists, we need to collaborate with researchers who will test hypotheses with various diagnostic groups and normal populations. Otherwise, we tend to elicit clinical material that conforms only to our own theory and supports our views. We have to get over our idea that clinical work is independent of experimental verification. Psychoanalytic concepts really can be stripped down to measurable core concepts to allow testing. Marcia (1994) acknowledged that such simplification is impoverishing to the concept, but maintained that the results of the process in turn allow new ways of looking at old ideas which enriches them.

Attachment theory is helpful in reminding us of the need for a secure context for the growth of a child and the devastating effects of its lack. Within that context, infants go on being, interacting with individuals and groups, and out of those relational experiences they build internal working models of relationships as secure or insecure and mental structure (Sroufe and Fleeson 1986). They build internal objects that capture the rhythm and tempo, the color and texture of those experiences. When parts of the ego interact with those objects, there is an affective connection of a particular color—for instance, satisfaction with good experience, anger at rejection, or longing for more excitement—and then internal object relationships form, mainly reflecting satisfactory experience and openness to learning in the conscious area, and mainly reflecting unsatisfactory experience of either a painfully rejecting or an unbearably exciting kind in the unconscious layer of the mind. In this way, experience in the attachment context gives rise to psychic structures.

Attachment theory emphasizes the developmental need for a secure base. Providing a secure base is essential for psychoanalytic practice. But it is not sufficient in and of itself to help us understand the internal object relationships that form in the infant. It does not address the internal modification of external experience. It does not explain how the object relationships are modified at various developmental stages as the constitution and temperament of the infant (and later the child and the adult) interact with the various attachment styles of the parents, grandparents, other children in the family and then spouses and children, as they all face unpredictable challenges along the path of life. However, by addressing the importance of affect regulation and empathic maternal attunement, the concept of mentalization (Fonagy and Target 1997) and elaborations on it (Luyten 2010) go some way toward connecting attachment theory not only to future attachment styles but also to the creation of psychic structure.

The quality of the relationship built by patient and therapist is the main determinant of the effectiveness of therapy. So, research that develops ways of measuring relational tendencies and visualizing the neural basis of psychic structure is highly relevant to grounding our work, elaborating new theory, applying it to technique in clinical work, and conceptualizing therapeutic action. The clinician wants to evaluate strengths and weaknesses in the capacity to relate during assessment so as to get an idea of the likely durability of the therapeutic relationship and an overview of the defensive characteristics of the relational capacities which will become the major focus of therapeutic work in object relations individual therapy. We look to current research studies to develop new ways of looking at personality variables, and to narrow our focus on particularly relevant items for observation in assessment and in therapy. We need research help to validate the effectiveness of analytic treatment. We want to modify therapeutic technique in the light of research findings.

Attachment research test instruments are valid only for research. Nevertheless, the categories that they have identified can usefully be used in refining our clinical assessment of the quality of attachment relationships in clinical practice. There we look for a picture of the patients' capacities for relating (an external measure of their internal object relationships) and their likely expression in close relationships in the realms of love, family, work, and social life—and in psychoanalytic therapy or psychoanalysis.

ORIGINS OF ATTACHMENT THEORY

Bowlby (1969) proposed that infants' behavior is motivated by the need for proximity to the primary figure during infancy and early childhood—true for all primates, mammals, and many other species, such as birds. Bowlby (1977) alerted society to the fact that environmental trauma in the form of loss or parental neglect is the main contributor to pathological growth and development. Initially, Bowlby described three types of behaviors—anxiously attached, compulsively care-taking, and compulsively self-reliant—as attempts to secure relationship to inadequate parents. These three types have been replaced by the present attachment classification system developed by Ainsworth et al. (1978) and elaborated by Main and Solomon (1990). As object relations therapists, we found Bowlby's original categories quite useful, because they fit with Fairbairn's description of the endopsychic situation, not surprisingly since Bowlby found Fairbairn's work to be complementary to his theory (Personal Communication, 1973), and with Winnicott's description of the false self (Winnicott 1960b). The category *anxiously attached* corresponds with Fairbairn's *exciting object relationship, compulsively self-reliant* fits with the *rejecting object relationship,* and *compulsively care-taking* fits with Winnicott's *false self.*

Infant Attachment Categories and Resonance with Object Relations

Ainsworth applied Bowlby's ideas in the Strange Situation Test of reunion behavior after separation from the mother. From her study of infants' patterns of behavior in seeking comfort when stressed by separation, she developed her own categories of securely attached (those who use the mother as a secure base) and insecurely attached (those who cannot use the mother as a secure base). Within the insecure category, she found two types: those who cling and those who dismiss the mother.

Secure

The securely attached infant finds comfort and safety in his mother's presence and keeps that security in mind during her absence so that he is able to leave her for periods of exploration of the wider world, knowing that when he returns, he will reunite with a calm, nurturing mother.

In Fairbairn's terms, this infant internalizes a satisfactory object in the conscious part of the self. Having not had more rejecting and exciting object experience than he can stand, he has less need to split off and repress persecutory internal objects of the rejecting or exciting type.

Insecure/Avoidant

The infant with insecure/avoidant attachment turns away when upset to avoid the inevitable rejection of his distress. He restricts his affect and becomes pseudo-independent (Cassidy and Kobak 1988).

In Fairbairn's terms, the infant internalizes a rejecting object, and if the mother's refusal of closeness has been extreme, further splitting and repression of this rejecting object leads to a state of schizoid withdrawal of part of the self.

Insecure/Resistant

The infant with an insecure/resistant attachment style resists separation and is angry upon reunion, sometimes clinging and other times rejecting the mother who is alternately too involved and unengaged with her infant (Cassidy and Berlin 1994).

In Fairbairn's terms, the infant identifies with an exciting object that stimulates feelings of painful longing that gives rise to hysterical behaviors.

Disorganized/Disoriented

The infant with disorganized/disoriented attachment shows frozen responses, confused or bizarre behaviors on reunion with the dysregulated, frightened or frightening mother who frequently has unresolved childhood traumas, such as physical and sexual abuse (Main and Solomon 1990).

In Fairbairn's terms, this is the mixed exciting and rejecting external object experienced as an internal exciting and rejecting object couple of terrifying proportions.

The attachment style is characteristic of the fit with a particular parent and may be quite different with another parent. So, in the clinical situation, the infant pattern re-invoked in the transference is specific to the particular internal object relationship dominant in the therapeutic relationship at that time, and other patterns will emerge at other times as treatment proceeds. When adults enter treatment, they show their attachment style in how they relate to the therapist as a secure base to be relied on or as an insecure one to be avoided and managed.

Adult Attachment Categories

Main and Goldwyn (1994) established a way of measuring parents' attachment styles, not by studying their separation and reunion behavior but by studying their behavior during an interview about their childhood. They found that adult attachment styles run the gamut from secure to highly insecure, and these correspond with characteristic attachment styles in their children, as shown in table 10.1 (Main and Goldwyn 1994). These correlations are observed in over 76 percent of mother–infant pairs, even if the parent is tested before the first baby is born (Fonagy, et al. 1991).

Autonomous/Secure

Autonomous / secure adults can speak coherently, recall their childhood experiences, report clearly on their parents' good and bad qualities, express their feelings, and recall their memories of separation and loss. They are healthy, independent, self-determining people who do not need clinical services but seek it freely in time of crisis.

Avoidant/Dismissive

Avoidant / dismissive adults have poor recall, and little range of emotional expression. They cover gaps in their memory and the distance they felt from their parents by giving bland idealizations of their childhood. They need therapy but avoid it or reduce its effectiveness because of fear of rejection by the therapist (Dozier 1990; Dozier, Lomax, and Tyrrell 1996).

Resistant/Preoccupied

Resistant / preoccupied adults give incoherent, desperately emotional, negative accounts of their childhoods. They blur self and other and establish enmeshed relationships in family life and in therapy to ensure that they are held in mind—even if negatively. The therapist will need a firm frame and a steady presence to tolerate the intense needs expressed in frequent phone calls, emergencies, outbursts, and calls for extra time.

Table 10.1 Correspondence of Adult Attachment Types to Infant Types

Adult Attachment Style	Infant Attachment Style
autonomous/secure	secure
avoidant/dismissive	insecure/avoidant
resistant/preoccupied	insecure/resistant
disorganized/unresolved	disorganized

Disorganized/Unresolved

Disorganized/unresolved adults are traumatized, disoriented, confused, dissociated, and sometimes suicidal. In therapy, they have trouble remembering events, do not have access to their dreams, and are afraid of the therapist as a repeat abuser. They dwell on everyday experience to fill in the blanks and help them feel that they are coping and avoiding falling into their denied affects and memories. The therapist needs to accept the need for conversation of this kind without interpreting it as resistance. It is a kind of going-on-being that enables survival and that maintains the therapeutic relationship at a tolerable level of exploration (J. Scharff and D. Scharff 1994).

Hesse's Cannot Classify and Slade's Continuum

Many of the adults that we meet as patients have mixed attachment strategies. They show patterns of attachment that vary from one to another family member, with each family member over time, with changing circumstances, and with the therapist as treatment progresses. We are therefore interested in the Cannot Classify category into which 25% of adults fall (Hesse 1996). As clinicians interested in chaos theory, we await further research in this category with interest, because we tend to think that study of areas of transition and chaos yield useful information. As a researcher who is also a clinician, Slade (1996) is well aware of the overlap between categories. She views the categories of attachment style, not in a list concerning security or insecurity, but lying along a continuum of affect regulation and structure characterizing the qualities of adult/child attachment, the regulation of affect being the important element in maintaining the infant's tie to the parent. On the middle of the continuum lie autonomous/secure parents and their secure children, whose affects and structures exist in balance. At the far left, are the avoidant/dismissive parents and their insecure/avoidant children have rigid structures for affect regulation. At the right, are the resistant/preoccupied parents and their insecure/resistant children with poorly made structures overwhelmed by affect, and at the far right lie the disorganized/unresolved personalities and their disorganized children which show even less coherence of structure due to areas of dissociation.

Mentalizing and Transmission of Attachment Patterns

How does the parent's attachment history shape the attachment style of a child? In object relations theory we find the explanation in unconscious communication via projective and introjective identification. In the field of attachment research, Fonagy and his colleagues (Fonagy et al. 1991, Fonagy and Target 1997) find the explanation in the parent's capacity for mentalizing (reflecting on, thinking about, and understanding) the infant's experience. Parents with a good sense of themselves and their history and a well-developed capacity for reflecting about their child's experiences, thoughts, and feelings, and for entering imaginatively into the mind of the child tend to raise a secure child. Those who are insecure themselves with restricted affect or flooding affect and who cannot reflect on the child's experience and imagine what the child might think and feel tend to raise children who are insecure to various degrees. The attachment theory concept of mentalization provides the main link to object relations theory, and is the advance that makes attachment theory more relevant to object relations therapists.

How Does Attachment Theory Fit with Object Relations Theory?

Attachment theory provides the relational context in which focused relating by mother and infant occurs. Winnicott's awareness of the attachment needs of his pediatric patients is expressed in his concept of adequate holding and handling in the physical sense (Winnicott 1945, 1958, 1960b, 1965). Within that sufficient context for going-on-being the infant can then do what needs doing to feed, to play, to engage with the mother and beyond her with the outside world.

In Fairbairn's theory, the infant is born with the capacity to form a relationship with the mother who is needed to respond to the infant's need for relating (Fairbairn 1952). While negotiating the vicissitudes of infantile dependence in that relationship with the mother, the infant has satisfying and unsatisfying experience, and sometimes intolerably frustrating experience. Fairbairn thought that the infant proceeds by taking in satisfying and frustrating versions of the experience with the mother. Fairbairn concentrates on the impact of bad experience that overwhelms the ego, highlighting the role of affect. He describes the need for psychic structure to cope with heightened fear and need driven by the anxiety and frustration inherent in total dependence on others. The infant takes in the experience and splits off that which was felt to be bad and represses it along with the part of the ego that connects to that experience of the object. So, in consciousness we see an internal object relationship consisting of a central ego connected on balance to feelings of satisfaction with a good enough object. In the unconscious we see two types of internal object relationships—the rejecting and persecutory object constellation comprising a split-off part of the ego called the antilibidinal ego connected by feelings of anger and hurt to an experience of the object called the rejecting object, and a split-off part of the ego called the libidinal ego connected by feelings of excitement and craving to an experience of the object called the exciting object because it stimulates feelings of longing for more. This is the endopsychic situation that Fairbairn described as forming under the developmental push of the infant's need to be in relationship and to find meaning in belonging to a loved and loving mother.

Melanie Klein (1946) also thought about the structure of the ego in relation to the introjection of good and bad objects, but she thought that these objects were created good or bad by the force of the life and death instincts. Threatened by the force of the death instinct, the infant operates in an anxious paranoid-schizoid state in which objects are not perceived as whole, and the infant cannot remember that the mother who says hello is the same person as the mother who says good-bye. Fonagy (2001) likens this to insecure attachment. In order to deflect the destructive force of the death instinct, Klein said, the infant projects it into the mother and misidentifies it as originating in her, and so the mother feels like a persecutory object. The infant copes with this persecutory object by internalizing it and identifying with it in order to control it. Fortunately the infant-mother relationship is also under the control of the life instinct and so there is good object experience to enrich the ego as well. Projective identification defends the self from the threat of the death instinct and is the basis of unconscious communication between mother and infant, from which it builds psychic structure.

Klein thought that the infant begins to think of the mother as a whole object by about four months of age. This fits with the findings from neuroscience that by four months of age the left hemisphere has begun to develop, bringing an improved capacity for early forms of thinking (Moore 1996).

Bion (1967b, 1970) extended Klein's concept of projective identification to show that the mother actually introjects the baby's experience of distress, identifies with it, mulls it over unconsciously in what he called her *reverie,* and returns it to the baby in a more manageable form. He used the term *containment* for this process of identification, reflection, and processing of experience. The baby feels relieved of anxiety, identifies with the mother's containing function, and becomes able to use thinking to manage the affects of experience.

Dicks (1967) extended Klein's concept of projective identification in mother–infant interaction to apply to the unconscious communication between spouses who form a special kind of attachment by choice in adulthood. That marital (or partner-partner) bond is also influential in providing a secure base for any children of the union. The children take in an experience of the parents as a loving and hated, including and excluding, couple (Scharff and Scharff 1998c, 2006). We believe that attachment to the parental couple is as important as attachment to any one parent for the development of the oedipal conflict and the expansion of the child's mental and emotional potential.

Internal object relationships are encoded in multiple sensory modes and narratives and the quality of this internalization is motivated by the accompanying affect. In our clinical work, we find that the internal object relationship is stimulated to emerge when current relationship paradigms (including the therapeutic relationship) evoke a similar affect that spreads to trigger the original one. The defining idea of object relations theory is that self and object are connected by affects, that they are present in a series of internal relationships, all in dynamic relation to each other inside the self, deriving from the interactive dyad and the family group, and that internal object relationships are not simply represented: they are the elements of psychic structure.

The affective quality of the object world, the capacity to distinguish between self and other, and the ability to invest in self and other are shaped in the early pre-oedipal years, and the affective tone of the object world is set in interaction with the mother. Object relations are not finalized by the Oedipal stage, but continue to develop from immature dependency to mature respect and love until adolescence—and, we would add, continue to grow and change through adult life experience with work, friendships, relocation, marriage, raising children—and in therapy.

Mentalizing from a Neuroscience Perspective

Collaborating with Fonagy and others, Luyten (2010) elaborated various dimensions of mentalizing based on his studies of brain activity during tasks related to mentalizing activity. He sorts them into polarities tied to specific areas of the brain and to types of pathology in reaction to stress. These are polarities, not separate categories: they represent various angles from which to contemplate the process of mentalizing.

Automatic-Controlled Polarity

Some people respond to stress calmly and thoughtfully: others fragment or freeze. Controlled responses rely on newer brain circuits, linguistic and symbol information, and are inhibited by stress. Automatic responses using older brain circuits, relying on sensory information, are promoted by stress. Under stress, we see a regression to automatic functioning and rigid views of self states.

Internal/External Polarity

Some people scan external features for clues to read the situation and others look inward to sense form their own feelings about what the other person is feeling. The external focus on facial expression, posture, and action is more automatic and relies on a lateral fronto-parietal network. It is normally used in early life before the infant has speech and continues to be active throughout life. In adults it is especially highly developed in people with borderline personality where it persists as the principal way of reading others.

When relating to older children, parents employ an internal focus on thoughts, feelings, and wishes. This internal focus is slower, relies on the medial fronto-parietal network and provides for active controlled reflection. The parent's appreciation of the child's state of mind must be conveyed through exaggerated mirroring responses that mark it as the parent's understanding of the child, not as a communication of the parent's state of mind.

The task of development and of therapy is to build the capacity for reflecting based on sensitivity to both internal and external features.

Self/Other Orientation Polarity

The ability to mentalize the mental state of another is closely related to the ability to reflect on oneself, and the two forms of understanding share two distinct neural networks. The first system involves the body-based, fast-acting fronto-parietal mirror neuron system (more about that later), and uses the face and body recognition referred to above for knowing what one feels and for understanding the feelings of others. The second system lies in the cortical midline, and processes information more slowly in abstract and symbolic ways.

Problems occur from falsely attributing one's own state to another (projection), from taking in another's state as if it were one's own (introjection), and from expecting full understanding by another. Some people are more other-directed: some are more self-centered. Some tend mainly to project painful unacceptable unpleasant material: others mainly introject it. But both types use both mechanisms in relation to unpleasantness: It is the balance that determines their style and their pathology. The person with antisocial personality disorder reads the mind of the other but cannot reflect on self, while the paranoid personality is preoccupied with self and not other.

These findings resonate with Fairbairn's (1941) description of transitional techniques for locating accepted and rejected objects. In Fairbairn's theory, the baby is caught between the developmental push toward autonomy and the need for dependency on and identification with those objects, and is conflicted by the urge to expel or retain objects. To lower the tension, the baby internalizes or externalizes satisfying and rejecting objects in specific ways (Fairbairn 1952, pp. 42–46). These ways may be hysterical, phobic, obsessional, or paranoid depending on whether the baby solves conflicts by internalizing or externalizing good and bad objects.

- In *phobia*, the accepted object is externalized and clung to; the rejected object is also externalized and feared.
- In *hysteria*, the accepted object is externalized and longed for; the rejected object is internalized and bodily function is attacked. The hysterical personality overvalues attachment to idealized good objects and denigrates the sexual self.
- In *paranoia*, the rejected object is externalized and returns to attack; the accepted object is internalized. The paranoid person overvalues his or her own perceptions and fears persecution by idealized bad objects.
- In *Obsessionality*, the rejected object is internalized and so is the accepted object; so the bad object is being appeased by careful attention and the person feels reassured only when achieving a sense of perfection.

The choice of techniques determines how the child relates to the caregiving figures. When these techniques persist in adulthood, they govern strategies for relating to others.

Cognitive/Affective; Visceral/Reasoned Polarity

There are two ways of knowing oneself—from gut feelings or from thinking it through. Luyten (2010) calls these visceral (automatic, emotional) and reasoned (controlled, perceived) forms of mentalization. Controlled mentalization can regulate automatic functioning and integrate cognition and affect. This is the effect we aim for in psychotherapy in an interpersonal setting. What begins as consciously reasoned mentalization over time with practice becomes more automatic, requiring less conscious input and effort.

Mentalizing and Containment

We think that Fonagy and Target's concept of mentalizing is similar to Bion's concept of containment, that process of bearing and metabolizing anxiety and then giving it back to the infant in a more manageable form. We think that the Fonagy-Target team's research has provided a way of measuring containment. We also suggest that their research in infant attachment and adult mentalizing together confirm that the containing function of the mother (Bion 1967b, 1970) is as important as her provision of a secure holding environment (Winnicott 1945, 1963a, 1963b). Slade (1996) reflects our view that "the mother's capacity to enter the child's mind, and give reality to his internal experience, is as vital an aspect of empathic mothering as maternal sensitivity, and is central to the intergenerational transmission of security" (Slade, p. 14). To this, we would add that it is essential to the formation of the child's psychic structure.

The concept of mentalization builds a bridge from attachment theory to object relations theory, much as projective and introjective identification built a bridge between Fairbairn and Klein (J. Scharff 1992). Like a secure parent who senses, imagines, and understands the patient's experience, the therapist mentalizes the patient's experience. When that patient pauses and slips, the therapist may get a feeling about his primitive anxiety or he may think about the research findings that point to speech hesitation as a sign of lapses in maternal mentalizing. From either cognitive or affective route, the therapist aims at mentalizing the patient's current and early experience. In object relations therapy, the style of the narrative, its content or lack of content, and the impact it has on the therapist are all important as a display of the internal object relationships. As therapists, we cannot stop at mentalizing the patient's experience. We cannot be effective as a purely reflecting object. We may need to be experienced as non-reflecting objects if those were prevalent in childhood. We must be willing to be an object to be used ruthlessly as the patient requires. In terms of attachment theory, we will hope to modify anxiety by new behavior in the mentalizing dimension, or in the terms of object relation theory, by our engagement in, and interpretation of, the transference-countertransference dialectic.

Commonality of Attachment Theory and British Object Relations

British object relations theory and attachment theory have in common the belief that human beings are motivated by the need to be in relationships, and their inner sense of security derives from the experience of early care. The person is not motivated by instinctual pressure and cannot be understood apart from the social context. Both theories see the connection between inner and outer worlds. Attachment theory deals with internal reality as a collection of internal working models; object relations theory deals with a self as a system of internal object relationships in dynamic relationship. Both theories are based on empirical observation, object relations theory using the freeform clinical situation and attachment theory the controlled research setting. Attachment theory narrows its focus to the observable units that can be subjected to research methodology, in the early years focusing on separation and reunion behavior that can be classified, while object relations focused on naturalistic, impressionistic infant observation in the at-home situation (Bick 1964). Object relations uses intuition and interaction to study and interpret complex, subtle shifts in behavior in the therapeutic relationship. Both theories focus on observable behavior and take account of defense, anxiety, and motivation. Object relations theory, first and foremost a clinical theory, crucially adds the concept of unconscious fantasy and unconscious communication by projective and introjective identification to elaborate on the connection between internal and external reality experienced in development and revived in the transference. Attachment theory, primarily a research paradigm, is now moving into this area of exploration by showing that the mother's capacity for mentalizing influences the child's attachment style.

Many psychoanalysts have rejected attachment theory as anti-analytic in that it diverted attention from the power of unconscious fantasy and instinctual drive during development and refocused it on the observable external reality of child-rearing experiences (Zepf 2006). These analysts may have been reacting to Bowlby's early rejection of the concept of unconscious processes because they were beyond direct observation and could not be measured or validated (John Sutherland, personal communication). But object relations analysts accepted Bowlby's findings from research because they fit with ideas emerging from clinical practice about how the infant took in experience to build the structures of the self.

Infant Brain Research

Schore (1994, 2003a, 2003b) was among the first to summarize neuroscience research in language that clinicians could comprehend. Advances in neuroscience gave an added dimension to attachment research and provided evidence of a biological basis for behavior in the mother–infant interaction. Analysts have always recognized that the quality of the early mother–infant relationship affects emotional health in adulthood. Now there is research to provide the underpinning for this impression. Interaction with the caregiver/mother is essential for the development and organization of the brain which is growing at an unprecedented rate in the first two years. The interaction occurs via affective signaling at a neurochemical level and by firing of mirror neurons that promote the growth of brain tissue.

Affect Signaling

Affective signals release autonomic nervous system activity and neurochemical substances that promote the growth of brain tissue, all of which are the basis for the infant's automatic ability to signal affect and gradually to experience and communicate more complex emotions, predominantly a right brain function. At first, the child's brain is capable only of thought that emerges as a fused, unpartitioned whole, and of communication in the form of single words like "no" and "up" (Vygotsky 1988).

This suggests a right brain form of early thinking that sorts experience into fused categories such as good and bad and accounts for the black-or-white quality of primitive object relations. Right brain memory stores early experience in an iconic form before there is speech for verbal narrative memory storage, a function of the left brain.

The proliferation of connections between the right brain and especially the orbitofrontal cortex and areas of the sub-cortex, especially to those parts of the brain that comprise the limbic system and the reticular formation is needed for the expression, communication and regulation of affect and for arousal and motivation. But this proliferation occurs only if the mothering person consistently and continuously provides an adequate environment of comfort and stimulation.

Affect is signaled through the smile and the gaze. The sight, sound and smell of her child brings out a gleam in the mother's eye, as her pupils dilate in response to sympathetic nervous system activity. The child receives a rush of endorphins and responds to this with dilated pupils too which further stimulates their mothers' maternal behavior. Here is a neurochemical basis for the eye-to-eye (I-to-I) relationship. The mother's regulation of affect not only modulates the infant's internal state but permanently shapes the emerging self's capacity for organization (Schore 1994). Through arousal sequences and regulation of affect, mothers mirror their babies' normal states of elation, build in healthy narcissism, and reinforce their interactions with the wider world.

An important proliferation of connectedness is the one that creates a visuo-limbic pathway that permits the identification of familiar faces, the child's emotional response to them, and the brain structure to retain a schema of the face that can be held in the mind when the mother is absent. This internal affect-associated image is the basis of attachment, object constancy, the formation of internal object relationships, and ultimately the self and its relation to the other. The left brain with its verbal capacity supports the self's narrative sense and its emerging autonomy, but the effectiveness of verbal thought always rests on the foundation of affective right brain development.

Mirror Neurons and Intersubjectivity

We have known that emotion is transferred from one mind to another, from seeing facial and postural expressions and from feeling a similar emotion. We feel the pain of others: we join in their laughter. The perception of emotion creates a resonant psychological state instantly (Tronick 1989). Neuroscience researchers working with ethologists to study various parts of the cortex have given us a neurological basis that supports these findings (Ferrari et al. 2003). They have isolated single neurons called mirror neurons in the fronto-parietal area (Rizollati et al. 2006). Mirror neurons fire off automatically as soon as the person whose brain is under study makes an action. They also fire off when that person watches or simply hears another person making the same action. These mirror neurons are not confined to the motor realm. In the visuomotor centers, they fire off when a person sees an obvious emotional action, such as laughing, raging, or crying, or more subtle affects like shame or disgust. Mirror neurons create a mirror image inside the self that echoes the inside of the other. They are the neurological basis for a shared manifold of intersubjectivity (Gallese 2003a, 2003b; Ferrari 2009). There is another midline cortical system that does not function automatically but requires the slower process of abstract, symbolic thinking and it develops over time in interpersonal relationships (Fonagy and Luyten 2009). Together the two systems offer a capacity for empathy and an ability to distinguish self from other.

Attachment Research in Non-Human Primates

Bowlby was aware of the similarity of attachment behaviors across species, and of the instinctual behaviors that support them—crying, clinging, rooting, sucking, smiling. Studies by Suomi (1994) of non-human primates show that monkey and apes attach to their mothers, are encouraged to play and explore the world, but even securely attached, weaned monkeys get very agitated by forced separation from their mothers, especially when the mother goes into the woods to copulate with her new consorts. The abandoned monkey screams in protest, and tries to follow her. Most of them get over it, but 20% of them get depressed. These are the shy, inhibited, and reactive insecurely attached monkeys and when she returns they cling to her and play less for days or weeks. This emotional and physiological reactivity is still seen in the adult monkey (Suomi 1995).

Monkeys are not capable of symbolic thinking, and yet complex behavioral and physiological consequences and poor ability to relate occur after interference with attachment needs. This suggests that internal working models are held in the implicit, non-verbal memory system, not in the later developed verbally competent, explicit memory system, and that internal working models and implicit relational knowing installed so early and so thoroughly are not repressed. This is an important alternative view to psychoanalysis and object relations theories that have located relational disturbance only in the repressed unconscious.

Bowlby thought that infant attachment experiences became internalized as internal working models that determine the nature of future relationships with the family of origin and procreation, and with peers.

Direct Human Infant Observation

Brazelton observed that comforting contact with the caregiver transforms the distressed lap baby's jerky arm movements to smooth, circular ones that reach successfully toward the object of desire (Brazelton, Koslowski, and Main 1974). Trevarthen's (1989, 1990) films show two-month-old infants in complex interactive sequences with their mothers (J. Scharff and D. Scharff 1998c; Shuttleworth 1989). From his observations of infants, Bråten (1992, 1993) concluded that the infant is born with an "other" in mind. He observed that within a month of birth the infant can create sequences matched to the mother's. Through attunement and dialogue-like interplay, the infant engages in a duet with the mother and she fills the image of the virtual other that the baby is born to seek. We have observed an 11-day-old infant imitating an adult's tongue protrusion in a sustained motor dialogue, a capacity also shown by a newborn monkey (Ferrari 2009). Direct observation of the infant's use of the mother supports Klein and Fairbairn's belief that the human infant is wired to be object-related from birth.

Qualitative research into the relationship of infants and their mothers gives texture and depth to the scientific research by including the impact of unconscious communication. This research is conducted by an infant observation seminar that focuses on its participants' reports of observable processes in the naturalistic setting of ordinary life. Using their countertransference, seminar members tap into unconscious fantasy to develop an imaginative construction of that infant's experience (Bick 1964). They see the infant in states of transition, their shifting bodily and emotional states being given meaning by the mother. Having expressed anxiety while held in the mother's mind, the infant finds his anxious mental contents transformed by her reverie and identifies with her containing function itself. This identification with holding and containment generates a sense of self competent to regulate affect and differentiate self and other.

Mother–Infant Interaction: Blank Face Studies

Lynn Murray (1988) studied stressors on mother–infant relationships using video replay. Babies look for responses and recognition, and if they do not get it, they become depressed. Murray found that when a usually lively mother is asked to give her baby a blank stare, the normal baby ramps up efforts to get her to respond. Eventually the baby looks upset, gives up, looks away, and physically slumps. Babies who get used to depressed mothers do not continue to protest like that. They take in a version of the experience with the mother as a rejecting object and identify with it. The baby's personality is a highly motivated, competent, proactive contributor to the mother–infant dyad, which in turn is memorialized in the baby's internal working models located in the implicit memory system.

Object experience is internalized as an object relationship, a structure based on a dynamic interactive process over many iterations, colored by the child's wishes, fears and fantasies of each developmental stage. The interactions include the actions of the significant other, the actions of the self, affect regulation by both, and the rhythm and pattern of their relationship (Beebe and Lachman 1988, Beebe, Jaffe, and Lachman 1993). These early interactions are the stuff out of which unconscious organizing structures as well as unconscious memory banks are made (Zelnick and Bucholz 1990).

Applications of Attachment Theory

Individual Therapy

Applying the findings of research on the insecure attachments of infants and adults does enhance psychotherapists' technique. We know to listen for inconsistencies and breaks in the flow of the patient's narrative. We notice whether the patient's memories are given in words (stored in the left brain indicating explicit memory from a time after speech is acquired or memory that has been put into words by a sensitive parent) or in images (stored mainly in the right brain, indicating implicit memory of early experience or trauma that a parent could not detoxify). When the memories have neither words nor images they are conveyed in a way of relating in the transference that conveys the quality of early experience. Knowing that internal working models influence the way that patients relate to their therapists, we prepare ourselves to function as a secure base from which they can embark on exploration. The patient's need for safety and consistent proximity informs the way we design the frame of therapy with regular sessions of predictable length and helps us to detect and then interpret the contextual holding transference as we provide a therapeutic relationship that has echoes of early childhood caregiving.

Couple Relationships: Complex Attachment

Fisher and Crandell's (1997) Couple Attachment Joint Interview (CAJI) adapted from the Adult Attachment Interview (AAI) is a semi-structured clinical interview which each partner fills out, and then both respond in a clinical interview. Their ideal of a healthy couple relationship is that, unlike the mother–infant relationship, in which the infant depends totally on the mother, each partner in a couple is able to be dependent on the other, or be depended upon, their roles shifting flexibly and seamlessly. This bi-directionality leads them to describe the couple bond as a *complex attachment*. They believe that secure attachment in both partners promotes reciprocity and mutuality and interdependence in the couple, while insecure patterns lead the couple to adopt fixed positions and rigidly defensive patterns. Every possible combination of secure and insecure individual internal working models drawn from each of the adult attachment categories influences the couple's complex attachment.

The strongest, most stable bond occurs between two autonomous/ secure adults. Also stable is that between avoidant men with anxious/ ambivalent women, but anxious/ambivalent men and avoidant women do not create lasting relationships. Insecure partners take up rigid roles, defensive positions, and interact by domination and submission. Secure partners enjoy reciprocity, flexibility in role differentiation, equality and respect. In the ideal case, the partners recognize the couple relationship as an entity larger than either of them, a secure base to which they each contribute equally and from which they gain confidence (Clulow 2001, 2006). Fisher and Crandell's work on couples gives hope that attachment research will some day be applied to the system of the family in which there are additional complexities because of interlocking relationships across sibships and generations.

Bartholomew and Horowitz (1991) added to the four-category adult attachment typology a positive and negative aspect of the internal working model of self and other based on the affective quality of the relationship, and showed how partners in intimate relationships experience each other. Let's take the example of a woman with secure attachment: she views herself and her partner positively. Now, let's take the example of a woman classified as preoccupied and resistant to attachment. She views her partner positively but sees herself in a negative light. A woman who is avoidant/dismissive because she prefers to rely on herself views herself positively and her partner negatively, but if she is avoidant of intimacy because she feels afraid, she views herself negatively as well (Bartholomew and Horowitz 1991). Again we see the resonance with Fairbairn's theory of transitional techniques for externalizing or internalizing types of object and with Dicks's discussion of projective and introjective identification in marital interaction.

Attachment Theory and Object Relations

Attachment theory has many clinical implications (Belsky and Nezworski 1987; Slade 1996). In working with patients, we follow Bowlby's idea that the quality of parental care draws forth specific attachment behaviors and characteristic ways of thinking, feeling, and remembering so as to secure the object and the self in relation to it. This recalls Fairbairn's idea of symptoms as arising from techniques for relating to the object by locating it at a comfortable distance from the ego. We follow Main's (1995) idea that incoherent moments in the structure of the patient's narrative communicate unintegrated experience due to lapses in maternal preoccupation. Slips are not just the sneaking of id material past the censor: they are communications of unthinkable anxiety—including dread of what Bollas (1987) called the unthought known—and may signal the effect of early empathic breaks with the mother on psychic structure (Slade 1996).

Attachment theory changes the way we listen to patients' material, and how we interpret the transference. In addition to the content of the narrative, we listen to the structure of thought, we note the choice of iconic or verbal memory, and we process the effect of the communication on us. We listen for memories of attachments and we look for current secure and insecure attachment behaviors. Transference behavior may now be seen not just as a re-edition of past experience, but as a behavior geared to securing the therapist's commitment to providing a secure base. This ties in to Winnicott's concept of the safety-providing environmental mother. And we recognize that the patient is an attachment object for us, as we are for the patients who are committed to their therapy with us. If, in terms of attachment theory, we accept that the greatest fear that the therapist faces is abandonment by the patient, then we can correct for those technical errors that arise from failed attempts to secure the therapeutic relationship. Attachment theory has value in helping the clinician establish a context within which therapy can take place.

To make full use of attachment theory ideas, however, we have to integrate them with a psychoanalytic perspective on intrapsychic structure—not to say that psychic structure forms only from defenses against instinctual drives, but to give equal value to the constitution and early experience of the infant. Unconscious fantasy is stimulated as a response to the attachment situation, further fuels the behavior, and then further affects the object. Although the infant cannot be held as accountable for the maintenance of the relationship as the mature partner, the infant does contribute to the quality of the attachment relationship by its early responses that the mother responds to, including snuggling, vigorous sucking, settling, eye contact, and smiling behaviors. The same mother can do much better with one infant than with another, because of differences in constitutional factors such as temperament, cognitive ability, physiological maturity, resilience—and, we add, capacity for unconscious fantasy and unconscious communication. Similarly the same therapist does better with one patient than another. A secure therapist will do better with adults of the dismissive and preoccupied category than a therapist who is insecurely attached (Dozier, Cue, and Barnett 1994). Like mothers who have family and community support, therapists themselves need a professional relational context as a secure base from which to venture forth into the unknown of therapy.

Attachment classification contributes to the way we listen, observe, and process experience during assessment and referral for therapy. The literature on attachment is now our firmest research evidence of the importance of the quality of early relationships, the containing function of the mother, and the impact of intergenerational transmission of trauma, not only for early development, but for the passing on of behavioral and cultural patterns through the medium of the relationship with the next generation, and for the technique of co-creating healthy attachment patterns in a therapeutic relationship. The well-researched findings from attachment theory to the therapeutic relationship support the view that therapy will have to go on long enough for the patient to build a relationship in which to re-experience old attachment patterns and develop new ones. This length of time varies from patient to patient.

SUMMARY

Attachment theory is useful in research and to some extent in clinical work. Attachment provides a context in which therapy can occur. It is a link into which the therapist's relationship with an individual or with a couple or family is born. We conclude that a secure base is a minimum requirement in therapy. It is a necessary condition but it is not sufficient. The most effective therapist will provide a secure base, mentalize the patient's experience, contain the unthought known, *and* be available for use as the necessary type of object.

Chapter 11

The Interpersonal Unconscious in Practice

In this closing chapter, we aim to show the action of the interpersonal unconscious as it is communicated through links, attachments, intergenerational transmission, the social unconscious, symptoms, and the re-organization of a system thrown in chaos. We show how these ideas underpin theory for understanding family, couple, and individual dynamics and how they inform our technique. Valuing complexity and understanding in depth, we aim for change by organizing complex factors in human experience into comprehensible form. Our theory says that we do this by offering a setting in which individuals, couples and families can undo the limited patterns in which they are stuck and move into more chaotic states that hold the possibility of reintegration at more adaptive levels. We know this is far from easy, and often prospective patients fear therapy because they sense that we are asking so much of them.

CLINICAL EXAMPLE: A FAMILY ASSESSMENT SHOWS THEORY IN PRACTICE

To demonstrate the action of theory in practice, we bring the ideas together in a family assessment session. The family we will describe sought help from David Scharff and Jill Scharff as co-therapists for a conflict between the parents over the handling of their toddler daughter. Married for 8 years, Mrs. Wall, a teacher, is now mostly at home caring for their two girls, Margaret, 16 months, and Lizzie, 4 years. Captain Wall is in military service. As parents the Walls found the first pregnancy and raising the first child quite easy, but they are reeling from the strain of the second pregnancy and care of their toddler Margaret who is difficult to soothe. We use transcribed recorded dialogue to show the actual words spoken between the husband and father, Tom, and the wife and mother, Roberta, as they interact with their playing children and with the two of us.

A family assessment is a tiny sample of the life of a family and yet it gives in-depth access to the family link and its social unconscious. The clinical experience of the assessment operates as a fractal of the whole structure of the personality of the family and its individual members. The patterns we see in one clinical assessment hour have fractal similarity to patterns that occur by day and night at home. We do not expect much change in a single session, but we do expect to see a fractal of the therapeutic relationship that could develop over time. In assessment we are simply establishing the initial condition for establishing such a possibility for change and growth. In ongoing therapy, we rely on our therapeutic personality, honed by training and personal treatment, to be an effective tuning force to produce change in the couple and family link and in the psychic structure of the individual family member in ongoing therapy.

Let's begin with the perspective of the link: We said in Chapter 2 that each person in a family is a subject of the link and subjected by the link. The link exists in the space between the family members and in the space between the nuclear family and the other generations. Tension between the child's drives for love, nurture, and safety, and the capacity of the outer world to meet and regulate those needs, creates the link and determines the structure of the child's psyche. The child's psyche is molded by the legacy of the previous generations and current experiences of the family and social world, or to put that in link theory terms, it lives in the links on the vertical axis between the generations and the horizontal axis where the family is surrounded by its own extended family and the social world, relating to them while at the same time being influenced by them. We will see unconscious traces of both worlds in this interview.

Our clinical work uses natural language not theory to communicate, but as we look back on it, we can see the flow of speech and the interactive behaviors of talking and playing, all of which communicate both consciously and unconsciously, in direct verbal ways and more thoroughly through non-verbal vehicles. We can get to know something about the effect of the link into which this family unit was born, the effect that the link has had on the attachment patterns of the family, and the family's ways of entering into and warding off chaos. We will pause after each segment to say something about which ideas we see illustrated there.

Fussy Baby, Calm Sister

Mom: (Talking about her 16-month-old daughter) Margaret seems to be very, very clingy, if I just walk out of the room she cries a lot, and she's ok in my presence, but if I leave the room she cries. (Margaret cries) She is very, very sensitive, extremely sensitive, like, I'll just walk out to go to the bathroom, and she cries.

Jill: I was wondering, can you explain what made her cry just then? Did she hear what we were saying?

Mom: Um no. Tom, did you take the pen away from her?

Dad: Yeah I took the pen away from her because she was sticking it in her mouth.

Mom: And she cried about that, but even if I just go to the bathroom now, and even if the door is open, if she can't see me, she cries. And I shouldn't let the crying get on my nerves, but it does. It gets on my nerves. And when she was first born, I don't know . . . I took Tylenol with codeine my last month of pregnancy with her.

David: On a regular dose?

Mom: Regular, every 4 hours. I had severe migraines.

David: Did you have headaches through that whole period?

Mom: Yeah, they were so severe that unless I had taken them I couldn't even get out of bed. They were that severe. I could not function. I went to the neurologists and they prescribed a ton of codeine, so I felt that my options were just to cut me open and take the baby out, which I asked them to do, and they didn't want to do, or do something, because I just couldn't even get out of bed, the headaches were that bad. So I took them on a regular basis for a month. And after she was born they said that most likely it would go away after she was born. But the headaches did not go away.

David: Are they still there?

Mom: I have them periodically, every now and then, but not consistent like that. I mean I've never had a headache last as long as that headache lasted. If I had a headache, I'd take medication for it now.

David: What do you take?

Mom: Fiorinal with codeine. They didn't want to give me that (then) though because I was pregnant. But after I had her the headaches didn't go away so for 3 weeks I still took the Tylenol with codeine. She just cried all the time. I just—she just had me very nervous because she never was at peace. At least my other daughter—you expect a newborn to cry, but they have a few moments of peace. But, she (Margaret) never really had any moments of peace. . . When I brought her in they said she was going through bad withdrawal. They said it was almost like . . . a child whose mother had shot up on heroin or something, the withdrawal was that bad.

David: What was she doing?

Mom: She was just crying and super irritable. I mean even if I held her, that didn't relax her. You know like in my mind, I was up like every hour with her. You know, I fed her, I tried everything and nothing seemed to work with her. And I thought something's wrong with this child because she never has any moment of peace. So I stopped the Tylenol with codeine, after they told me that, right away. And they said it would take a while for it to wear off on her. She seemed to improve.

Dad: They gave her Phenobarbital.

(While we are talking, Margaret has just drawn on Lizzie's drawing)

David: (Turning to the girls) Let me just ask, Lizzie, does your sister spoil your drawings sometimes like that?

Lizzie: I don't think so.

David: No, that's not a big problem? Ok. How do you like having a sister?

Lizzie: Fine.

David: Is it ok?

Lizzie: (Not very convincingly) Yeah.

David: You don't let her get in your way, I see.

Dad: (Continuing) They did prescribe her Phenobarbital, but I think we only gave her a dose or two. You know they wanted to wean her off the codeine and give her Phenobarbital instead. But we never completely gave her all the Phenobarbital.

David: Did things change?

Mom: They did change but . . . if I leave the room, she still cries a lot. There was a long time—I don't know how old she was—before I even left her with a sitter. How old would you say she was?

Dad: At least 6–8 months old, before you left her. Even then the couple that we had babysitting said she would cry and cry and cry.

Mom: She seems to be ok now if we have a sitter and Lizzie is with her. She'll cry for about 10 minutes. But she seems to be ok if she's with Lizzie. You know cry a little bit, but . . . She's not clinging to me in here!

David: So this is unusual, you're saying.

Mom: Well usually she is clinging to me a lot, like even in the house at home, I don't know the situation, or whatever. If I'm at home you know cooking dinner, she's clinging to my leg and crying the whole time. Like if I try to read Lizzie a story she cries and pushes her out of my lap and things.

David: If you try to be with Lizzie?

Mom: If I try to read. I was trying to read Lizzie a story the other night and she came and just pushed her out. She pushed her out of my lap and started screaming and crying and got pretty hysterical about it because I was reading her a story. I thought well, what I have to do is read it to her when this one is down or something. But . . .

David: What's she saying?

Mom: Doll.

David: (To baby Margaret who is holding a tiny doll baby) Oh, you want the baby? Thank you. That's the baby?

Mom: See, usually I wouldn't say she goes to people that well as she's doing? Would you, honey?

Dad: No. I don't know. I'm not around. Probably not.

Jill: You're not around her as much as your wife.

Dad: Well, no because I work all day long. I have a tendency to think that she (meaning his wife) overreacts to the crying so I'll turn her off (meaning his daughter), because sometimes she'll push me to my limits. But, I can just as soon leave her in the room and let her cry for a couple of minutes. Then she notices that I'm not paying any attention to her and she stops.

Jill: Is that difficult?

Dad: I think it's difficult for my wife for either one of my kids to cry, other than the obvious if they fall down and hit their head or they're hungry or something.

Mom: But wouldn't you say that she cries more for me than she does for you?

Dad: Yeah, she (meaning his wife) can leave for a couple of hours and she (meaning his toddler) won't say boo. She walks in the door; she runs in the gate and starts crying.

David: You agree?

Mom: Yeah.

David: So, there's a way in which you don't find it a problem. If there is some of the kind of crying that you complain about, you just put her in her room.

Dad: I don't really put her in her room, I just ignore her, and she stops.

Mom: I've tried that. If I'm cooking dinner or something, she's actually clinging to my leg the whole time, and I'm just going on through it. But I've tried it, and it didn't work. So I just have to sit down and pick her up, because after 10 minutes or so it gets on my nerves. She's still not sleeping through the night; she gets up about 5 times. She was up 5 times last night.

Dad: Well, 2 or 3, I think is more like it. It may be that she's teething.

The Link, Chaos Theory and Attachment

We already see signs of the unconscious transmission of distress as the baby's cry gives voice to, and reflects, a level of tension in the couple. We hear from the beginning of the session that the pregnancy with the toddler was extremely stressful, but we don't know anything about why that might have been so. Mother and fetus were joined in an intolerable cycle of physical distress for a month before the birth and after delivery when mother still had headaches and the baby was in narcotic withdrawal. So we have to ask if the body was bearing aspects of the link that could not be tolerated mentally, and that carried over the next two years.

In the link, Baby Margaret is the symptom bearer. Mrs. Wall is the speechbearer who describes what is wrong. Mrs. Wall describes the difficulty repeatedly as if only hearing the same thing many times will get through to us. This speech pattern is a fractal of the limit-cycle attractor that is governing their stressed relationship. Captain Wall wants to minimize the problem and imagine that distress can be stamped out. He refers to his wife and his daughter interchangeably as "she" which makes us think that he is somehow aware that the baby's cry is also a cry from his wife that he does not want to hear. He is dismissive of distress from both of them, but he maintains that the baby takes his limit while his wife cannot.

The baby has been born into a link that carries tension in the couple from the strain of caring for a fussy baby. The family has delivered the symptoms into the clinical session where we can experience them. The baby cries in the session as she does at home, and cries when things are taken away from her. Lizzie, the four-year-old, does not cry but uses her words to complain when things are taken away from her. Margaret picks up a baby doll and tries to give it to her father as if she wants him to see what she has to offer, as if to give back something that has been taken away. We wonder what the family and especially Mrs. Wall has lost. In other words, into what kind of a link to grief has the baby been born?

We already get some clues about the attachment styles of each of the family members in these opening moments of the session. The 16-month-old has a clinging, anxious ambivalent attachment to her mother, and perhaps a less anxious or even secure one to her father. The four-year-old can play alone, and seems to be more securely attached to both, but becomes whiny and apparently insecurely ambivalently attached when her play is interfered with by the baby. When the children fight, the parents attachment style shifts to one that is insecure and ambivalent. The complex attachment between the parents already looks as though it is threaded with anxiety on mother's part, and with a dismissive style on father's side. She looks to him for holding, and feels he turns her away, leading her to become more anxious. He tells her to be more distant and calm as he is, but she feels rebuffed by that. Their attachment styles appear to have worked for the couple when life was calmer before the birth of this second child. In the current "snapshot" of the family organization, we see an anxious clinging mother seeking support from a dismissive father.

In terms of chaos theory, we see a family organization that has a complex limit-cycle attractor—frequent nightly awakenings by the toddler and anxious clinging by day produce an exhausted, beleaguered mother, a father who is frustrated when he fails to move the system to order, and a couple with a persistent anti-libidinal pattern of mutual criticism and disappointment that shapes their marital personality. We do not yet have an idea of why this basin of attraction is so powerful that they cannot extricate themselves from it and return to the level of functioning that they enjoyed formerly.

Parental Tensions over Housework and Child Care

Dad: I felt that sometimes when I was home on a Saturday and she went to the store that I could get a lot more done in 3 or 4 hours than she could all day long. And that's mainly because I didn't allow the kids to dictate what I was doing unless one of them fell down or got hurt or what have you. And I understand that I'm a perfectionist. I line things up and I organize, and she just does not think that way. She'll forget to deposit my paycheck. So like my uniform shirts, she thinks if she irons them that I should appreciate that even if they got crease marks. And I often told her to just take them to the cleaners and she doesn't want to do that, because she thinks it's a waste of money.

David: Yes?

Mom: I do. But if I take his pants to the cleaners, that's an errand that you have to run. You know, I balance the checkbook. That's why I'm frustrated. I feel I'm organized, and I don't think he feels I'm organized. And I think I'm very organized.

David: You don't think she's organized.

Dad: No, but she's gotten better, I'll tell you.

Mom: I've had a lot of people, though, say, "You're so organized" and things, and I thought I'd like to hear that from my husband.

Lizzie: (Complaining about Margaret's disruption of her play) She just knocked it down!

David: That's funny, Lizzie, that's just what your mom's saying your dad did, and your dad's saying your mom did.

Dad: Ok, Lizzie.

Jill: Disappointing isn't it? She thought she was just playing. Lizzie! Was that a house you were making (that Margaret knocked down)?

Lizzie: Yeah.

David: (To father): So you felt she had let you down.

Dad: Yes.

David: (To mother): And what did you feel?

Mom: I felt mad and upset about it because I didn't think he wanted the deposit to be done that day. I thought it was no big thing. We were just talking about it. So . . .

David: So you felt something. I'm trying to get at what you were mad about.

Mom: I was mad that he was upset with me, because I thought that it was something that we were just talking about. (To Lizzie) What sweetheart?

Lizzie: Keep Margaret away.

Dad: (To his wife): It bothers you that you think the kids are fighting . . . I won't step in until there is blood.

Mom: There's not actual blood.

Dad: Margaret's a very active kid. (To David) She just broke your doll.

David: Right, I think we'll retire it, so it doesn't hurt her. There's another one.

Lizzie: (To her sister) Don't you dare touch this!

David: Lizzie feels like she is having considerable trouble with Margaret.

Dad: Lizzie is the type that will sit there for hours. She'll sit there for an hour and draw or she'll play with her blocks—where Margaret's span of attention is not very long. If you don't keep your eye on her, it could be dangerous. She'll crawl up on the kitchen table, and stand. So we have to move all the chairs away from the kitchen table, and sometimes put them upside down because in a minute she's gone, or she'll go into a drawer, and we've got all the drawers in the house with kid latches.

David: (To father) It seems to me that generally you feel your wife hasn't done as good a job as could be done.

Mom: Or that I don't get enough accomplished. It's irritating for me to hear "God! I can do this and this in a weekend and get all this done, why do you have a problem?" That's irritating when you're sitting there trying to do it. It's irritating to hear that. Like he said about me, I think he's improved a lot, these 7 years, as far as having to be neat. I think he has loosened up on some things.

Children's Play as a Fractal of the Couple Dynamic

Captain and Mrs. Wall are disappointed in each other. He feels she is not meeting his standards, and proves that in the short term he is better at managing the household. She works hard and does not feel validated. The older child, Lizzie was born into a link in which the couple was functioning well and meeting expectations. As a highly controlled four-year-old she fits the ideal. We wonder what links in the parents' childhoods led to their expectations?

Now we see that the children's play contains a fractal of the parents' arguments. Each parent feels that they put up a structure that the other disparages and knocks verbally. As they discuss this, the children's play echoes their distress. Margaret knocks down Lizzie's play structure, Lizzie lashes out at her or complains, and then the parents renew their battle over the management of the children in a cycle of disappointment and interruption. The attractor patterns of the parents' argument and the children's play are resonant, building on each other to produce a family personality of discord and dissatisfaction.

The Family Culture Link

Dad: See, I came from a background I grew up in where every Saturday, in an old German type family, every Saturday you got up and cleaned the house from top to bottom.

David: The whole family?

Dad: Yeah, when we were old enough at least. My parents, myself, my sister, we'd get up and vacuum and clean the toilets.

Lizzie: I can't get to finish coloring my picture!

David: Did you forget to finish it? Or you weren't finished?

Lizzie: (Showing David) I tried to finish it but she [Margaret] put a line right there.

David: I see.

Mom: I never cleaned toilets until I got married, because my mother and my father were both working, so on the weekend my mother refused to spend her time cleaning because she had worked all week. So once a week she would have a cleaning lady come in and do those things, like the toilets and floors, and we would go off and go to the mountains and have something fun to do on the weekends. So I never really on the weekends did do the kinds of things he did. I mean I never sat and did chores or . . . toilets. I mean I didn't, I'm just telling you. So, when I got married, I thought, I'm making a big adjustment because I'm doing a lot of things I've never done before, and I'm really trying to do a good job at it.

Children's Play and the Vertical Link

The parents talk about the domestic life they knew as children, Captain Wall's helping keep house and Mrs. Wall keeping household help. Captain Wall feels that Mrs. Wall is messing up his system and Mrs. Wall feels that he is not willing to have fun. In resonance with this dynamic, the baby messes up her sister's drawing. Throughout the interview, through unconscious transmission, the children pick up the emotional atmosphere of their parents' interaction, and their own interplay forms a continuing dynamic fractal of their parents' relationship. Now we see that their play also contains the conflict in links that each parent brings. Father is from a compulsive family that required conforming to set patterns, mother from one that valued differentiation, flexibility, and fun. In her play, Lizzie tries to get her work done, and Margaret disrupts it, an echo of the way that father feels mother disrupts his workmanlike efforts. We are hearing about three generations of vertical links. In the next section, we hear about the horizontal link.

The Social Link

Dad: She's improved. You see, the thing is, when I was in graduate school I was also a commander of a reserve unit so I had to be so organized because I had such limited time, that everything had to be boom, boom, boom. And it's hard to break habits like that.

David: Well, what's so concerning about the habits is the feeling between you that develops which is that she has a long way to go. Is that right?

Dad: Not a long way, but I do think at times that she doesn't know how to prioritize tasks and that sometimes she allows what I consider trivial to occupy her time.

Mom: See I feel the same with him. (To David) Do you just understand what I'm saying? I feel if I leave a bottle out or something, that's not as critical as something else. You've got to have room in your life to be able to goof up.

David: To goof up, not goof off, but goofing up is ok.

Mom: To make a mistake, I guess that's what I'm trying to say. And I'm not saying that you do it on purpose.

David: You're saying he doesn't give you the room to goof up.

Mom: Sometimes I feel he doesn't, and I'm not saying that you do that on purpose. Do you see what I mean, there's a difference? I feel he thinks I do it directed.

David: Do you think she does it?

Dad: No, I don't think she does it deliberately. I think careless, is sometimes the word I think of when I find something goofed up because what she'll say is, "Well I tried." And I guess I've been in situations where you know trying is fine but sometimes making a mistake costs you a lot. Whether it's you goof up a bill or forget to do something, whatever, it may cost you. She'll say, "Well I tried," and I'll say, "Well that's fine, but now we've got this big problem." I was always concerned that if the military sent me away for a month or so, would my wife be able to take care of business at home. And she's getting better. When we were first married, she didn't know how to balance a checkbook, and wasn't quite sure how to take care of things. If there were problems, I more or less coerced her to have her do it, because the issue may come up where I'm not around.

Mom: If he's really pressured at work or whatever, then it comes home.

David: (To Lizzie who is upset with Margaret) What happened there?

Lizzie: She knocked the blocks and I was making a barn for these animals and Margaret knocked it off. There's nothing else you can play with.

(Margaret cries)

Mom: Margaret, why don't you play with these things over here?

David: Did you notice that they went at it just when you started to talk about this mild difficulty between you two?

Mom: Well, she just does that a lot, just when we're trying to talk.

In this section we are reminded that Captain Wall works for the military, and that this carries a possibility of mobilization. This is part of the social link into which the baby was born. As the discussion proceeds we realize that beneath the pressure he puts on Mrs. Wall to perform perfectly lies Captain Wall's anxiety to ensure that the family can function without him. He is aware of the reality of emergency deployment, and denies the death threat by perfection. As they talk about this defense against unpredictable separation and danger, Lizzie pushes Margaret away for spoiling the safe home she is trying to make for her animals. Margaret cries, and she and Lizzie fight as an identification with, and distraction from, the parents' argument and the anxiety about the uncertainties and risk of military assignments. Now we can also see that the insecure attachment between the parents, and between Margaret and her mother, has something to do with the risk of separation. We might conjecture that Mrs. Wall's somatic symptoms (the violent headaches) in her pregnancy conveyed these issues, and that Captain Wall's compulsive orderliness and the pressure he puts on her is a limit-cycle defense against his own fears about being an abandoning parental figure. In any event, it must be an identification with a persecuting and demanding internal object.

Competition for Love Splitting the Parental Couple

The session continues with the children squabbling. David refers back to the toddler's cry interrupting her parents' conversation.

Mom: Well, she just does that a lot, just when we're trying to talk.
David: Just if you're trying to talk?
Mom: Yeah.
Dad: Just plain talk, ordinary.
Mom: Margaret, come over here. Lizzie, don't punch her ok?
Dad: (To Margaret who is writing on Lizzie's drawing) All right, can I have the crayons? Thank you.
Mom: One of the things that I wanted to mention about Lizzie is that I know some sibling rivalry is, you know, normal. But I guess what I find frustrating is Tom and I, ever since Margaret was born, have made an extreme effort to be very, very sensitive to a new baby. Ever since Margaret's been born, he does things one-to-one with Lizzie to make her feel that this new child hasn't taken her place. I've even hired a babysitter on the weekend for Margaret and the two of us. We've taken Lizzie like to the Ice Capades and things. During the week when she has ballet, I sometimes swap with my girlfriend, and she'll take Margaret, and I'll take her 4-year-old. And after ballet I'll take her out for ice cream with her other friend, or we go to McDonald's. And Tom does a lot really with Lizzie on a one-to-one. . . . Yet she comes up to me and says things like, "All you care about is Margaret." And I don't know if it's because I hold her so much. I find it frustrating 'cause I feel like we've both been so sensitive to that area and yet I hear that a lot from her.
David: From Lizzie?
Mom: From Lizzie, you know, she says, "Margaret gets all the attention. You can't hug Margaret all the time. Margaret's not the only one that needs the love." And he's very affectionate to Lizzie when he comes home. And she draws pictures, and he tells her how great they are. He takes the pictures to work and hangs them up. I feel we're both very positive with her. I tell her that she's pretty or whatever. He gets on the floor and reads to her a lot. So I find it frustrating when she says that, no matter how hard we try.
David: (Turning his attention to Lizzie's play) What's Oscar doing with the horsey?

Lizzie: He's living in the barn, he's letting all the cages open and all the animals are coming out.

David: Why is Oscar doing that?

Lizzie: Because he wants to play with someone, and that's why he's letting all the animals out—to play with them.

David: Is Oscar lonely?

Lizzie: Uh humm.

David: He doesn't have anybody to play with?

Lizzie: Yeah, he went away from Sesame Street.

David: And he's all alone?

Lizzie: Yes.

David: Oh, my goodness!

Lizzie: And all the animals were locked up and he can't play with them if they're locked up.

David: Why did Oscar leave Sesame Street?

Lizzie: 'Cause he wanted to play with some animals and that would be better.

David: I see. So are the animals glad to play with him?

Lizzie: Um humm.

(Margaret gives a piece of paper to her father.)

Dad: Thank you. Why don't you draw Daddy a picture?

David: (To Mom): I think that Oscar was lonely, huh? That's what we're talking about I think. And of course in a way, although I may be stretching a point, but in a way you're saying Lizzie's a bit grouchy about it.

Mom: Grouchy about what? But yeah, I feel that we give her a lot as far as on a one-to-one. I mean we have hired babysitters on the weekend to do things as a couple just with Lizzie.

Jill: Well you've done everything for her as a child of the age that she's at. What you can't do is make her be the baby. Do you see what I mean?

Mom: So she's jealous of the fact that she's not the baby, is that what you're saying? Yeah, yeah!

Jill: Yeah.

Mom: Sometimes she'll say, "Wa, wa. Hold me!" or whatever.

Dad: Well one of the things that she wants—while we're talking in a normal conversation—she'll insist on being heard. She'll actually say that, "Daddy I want to talk." And we'll ask her nicely to hold on for a minute because we may be talking about something very important. She gets very frustrated with that.

David: You think that Margaret might have also have issues about . . .

Jill: (Completing his sentence) Having Mommy to herself. I notice that there is something about Margaret's cry that is troubling—

I don't know if it's because you're in the studio and you don't want to make the noise in the microphones—but you do feel she has to be quiet right away.

Mom: I feel that way? I do! I admit that! He tells me I do. And I do.

Jill: And there is something about her cry that is very urgent. Like, it's not that loud is it, but she looks so distressed.

Mom: Her cry I feel is always that way.

Jill: So she gets you to hear her, so she can get you to zero in on her anytime she opens her mouth and cries. She even feels (herself) that she needs to stop her cry. I noticed she'll take her pacifier and put it in her mouth and try to stop it—while reaching for you.

Mom: What's frustrating is, I can't, like . . . if I just want to take a shower in the morning! I can't be with her every minute. And this morning when I went to take a shower, I'll leave the two of them down in the kitchen area, propped up watching TV. And there's toys and everything down there. I can't put her in the playpen because she crawls out of it. But, you know as soon as I get out of the shower, I hear her crying. (Margaret now cries in the session.) Come here, Margaret. We never say you're a bad girl, because I don't believe in that. I don't believe that somebody is bad. I believe that she may do something that I don't like, but she's not "bad." We never use the words bad or hate. And yet she says a lot to me constantly during the day that I'm just so tired of hearing it. Like I'll go, "I really like the way you're eating lunch." Lizzie wasn't finishing it, so I complimented the other little girl. I said, "You're doing such a terrific job." And I said to Lizzie, "I'd like you to try." And she left the table and said, "You think I'm bad now because I'm not eating my lunch." I said, "I never said that, did I? All I said was that I really like the way Julie's eating her lunch." But I hear this a lot from her and I'm always telling her that she's good, "I think you're good." She said it to me just yesterday because I wouldn't let her go out with shorts on, three days ago when it was cold. I wouldn't let her go out with shorts on and her friends were waiting outside the door to play with her and I said, "You can go out there with your friends when you put your long pants on." Because it was the day I think it was, like, 50 [degrees]. So, she literally lay down and threw a temper tantrum on the floor. And I said, "I'm just going to close the front door." And it was unlocked, and I said, "And I'm going to close it and I'm going to wait outside on the porch. Your clothes are right there in the living room and we'll wait out here for you to change." So, I stood on the porch and I heard her and she cried for about 5 minutes and just throwing a bad temper tantrum. When I opened the door she came out and she said to me, "I hate you, I hate you, I hate my mother!" Now, I didn't . . . I don't know, I think probably in our whole lifetime maybe she's been spanked 4 times. We don't really spank the children. I probably should have done something, like maybe sit on the couch and say, "I want you to think about what you said." Or something. I just gave her a hug and said, "I know you really didn't mean that but you were really mad because I wouldn't let you wear the shorts." Or whatever. I said, "When you're ready to come out, you can put the pants on." I wanted to just let her know that she can't go out with shorts in cold weather. I said, "You're going to catch a cold." I guess what concerns me is—I don't know where she's coming from. We never use the word "hate" and we never ever say, "You are a bad girl." We never say that. And I don't know why she is using those terms.

David: Actually, Lizzie does know something about how you feel.

Mom: She would?

David: She knows something about how you feel. So you say to this other child, "I really like the way you're eating!" And Lizzie says, "You mean you don't like the way I'm not eating." Which is true! I think it's true that at the moment that she said that, that at least some of the time—maybe quite a lot of the time—you actually are disapproving of her. Is that true?

Mom: Well, yeah, when she wasn't eating her lunch and asked me for candy, I was unhappy.

David: With that example anyway you were unhappy with her.

Mom: I was unhappy with it.

David: So she was right?

Mom: When she comes in and takes Margaret's bottle and whacks her on the head, I'm unhappy with it.

Jill: In fact you were annoyed about it.

Mom: I am!

Jill: You don't hate her, but you are mad.

Mom: (Agreeing she's mad but doesn't hate her) No.

Jill: The reason you don't hate her is that you know that you can be both mad and still love her.

Mom: Right.

Jill: But she doesn't know that for sure. Does she? I'd say if Lizzie's mad then she hates at that moment. An hour later she might love again.

Mom: One thing I think that Tom's good about, if we do correct her we always follow with affection. I'll always, if I correct her, he'll always hug her and tell her he loves her or whatever. So she doesn't leave feeling, "they don't love me."

David: Ok, at the risk of asking questions that may make you feel bad, why do you do that? What's the rush?

Mom: Why do I do what?

David: Why do you follow with affection? I mean you make it sound like it's an automatic follow-up, that if you correct her you have to follow up with that.

Mom: 'Cause I feel bad. I don't want her to feel like what she said, I don't want her to feel . . .

David: What do you mean, you feel bad?

Mom: Ok, she said that Lizzie doesn't know that difference. She's just a child. She doesn't know that difference that—How did you say that?

Jill: I said once she hates you she doesn't remember that she loves you. She just hates you.

Mom: And she doesn't know the difference—like when you said I can discern the fact that, ok, if she does something it's the thing that she does that I don't like, not the person. I can reason that out, but she can't. So, I guess because she's a child I feel like I need to follow that with affection to . . .

David: Now, I want to cut under this just a little bit. I know I'm interrupting you, but you said that both of you follow with affection right away if you correct her.

Dad: No, I don't, not right away.

David: You don't?

Dad: No, I usually unless you know I really blew my top too much and I think I overreacted. I generally wait until I see the behavior. I want to let her know that after she's behaved herself that . . .

In this section we get a chance to see how the parents, as a pair and individually, relate to the children as they play. As we interact, listen, speak, and play, we are examining the questions of interpersonal unconscious transmission between parent and child, and the link that constitutes these cycles of transmission. The insecure attachments organize these patterns, between the parents and between the children and their parents, acting as limit-cycle attractors that reassert themselves at moments in which distress acts like a tuning force to pull the couple to this repetitive pattern. We also note that Mrs. Wall's speech becomes repetitive in these periods. She goes over and over the same point as if we would not get it the first time.

The sibling rivalry is demonstrated in the session, but it becomes clear that it is magnified during periods of parental upset, and, playing on parental guilt and overconcern, it produces some excessive excited object relating. We learn of times at home when Lizzie has accused her parents (mostly her mother as the more vulnerable parent) of not loving her, throws in the common "I hate you!" to elicit more excessive care, and attacks the parents' attempts at ordinary limit setting. In the generational link, this hits the target of mother's vulnerable guilt. Father, in his own way fairly immune, leaves the mother to adsorb these attacks that also have an Oedipal coloring due to Lizzie's developmental stage. She splits her parents so that she can hope to hate mother and get more love from her father in compensation.

Then Margaret is also upset and begins to cry and to attack Lizzie as the older and (to her mind) favored child. The parents feel they can't do anything right. This attractor pattern produces an increase in the anxious/ambivalent attachment that now characterizes the family, in a repetitive limit-cycle way, made more difficult by the baby's crying, which has a fixed-cycle deadly repetition to it since she has such a limited repertoire in her moments of distress. The girls' squabbling and the baby's cry in turn feed back into the system to produce an added increment of anger and frustration throughout the family and between the parents.

We learn that Lizzie, the apparently perfectly contained child, has hateful temper tantrums when not given her way or when she feels criticized. Lizzie's strange attractor pattern suddenly jumps to a different, more chaotic region. To the therapists it is a relief to hear about more range in Lizzie's affective expression, but we also know that she is feeling persecuted while responding to the vertical link in which she feels judged by her mother, and that without modification of this link she is at risk for developing a fixed-cycle attractor of hatred and self-attack.

Now we return to the family with a segment that gives an intergenerational understanding of part of this pattern.

Vertical Link: His Mother and Father

Dad: I don't carry a grudge, because of the way my own mother dealt with me. Seemed like it just went on and on and on. So . . .

David: Tell me a little bit more about that, Tom.

Dad: My mom was the kind that, you know, two weeks later she would bring up an incident that I thought was all buried. So what I try to do is to think, "Ok, you goofed up!" (Baby cries.) And then I want to make sure that, after the situation is over with, that she understands that, ok, she's behaving herself. Now the issue is over, let's not drag it out.

David: When your mom did that to you, she'd bring up the grudge. What would it be about, what kinds of things?

Dad: Just about anything you could think of. You know, "You didn't do this in school; you didn't hang your clothes up" or whatever.

David: What kind of thing would it be about in school? What didn't you do?

Dad: Oh, you know I didn't do as well as she expected you to do, even though you really gave it your best and it may not be good enough.

David: So then she would carry this grudge. (Baby cries.) Do you remember how you would feel in those moments?

Dad: Frustrated.

David: Frustrated? Well that sounds like a kind of understatement.

Dad: Angry, P.O.'d.

Mom: She would even bring up things maybe like a year later, wouldn't she, Honey?

Dad: She still does that now.

Mom: She still does that now. She'll bring up something that maybe happened a year ago and say . . . I don't know if you want me to say anything?

Dad: Sure, go ahead.

Mom: Well, like when his dad died, it was an extreme emergency and it wasn't as if we knew he was dying of cancer or something. We got a call that he went in for knee surgery one week and every thing was fine. And then a week later he took a turn for the worst and he was moved to ICU. Well, the day we got a call that he was moved to ICU, his mom said, "We don't know. They said he may not make it." Well, that night I got on the phone and made an airline reservation. The earliest I could get, I guess I don't know if it was at 9:00 in the morning, but it takes 5 hours to fly from here and another 3 hours to drive to where his parents were at. So by the time we got there and got to the hospital, he missed by 2 hours. He missed his dad being conscious. And then he would have lapsed into a coma like 2 hours. If we had been there 2 hours earlier . . . But my God, he stayed with him in the hospital for the next 8 hours until he died. So his mom will still say things like, "You know you didn't get there in time, you didn't get there before he lapsed into the coma. Why couldn't you have gotten there the night before?" Well, you know, we did the best we could, being 3000 miles away. So, I'm saying she'll bring up things.

David: How did you feel about this?

Dad: It has gotten to the point where, as I'm older, I just think: "That's her."

David: How did you feel then?

Dad: It's not that important. I don't let it bother me any more. I just sort of tune it out.

David: I'm really after the times it did bother you.
Dad: Yeah, well . . .
David: That's not so easy for you. Can you try, because I think it might be that important.
Dad: Frustrated, sort of like no matter what you can do, it's not right.
David: I think the words that you're avoiding are about how hurt you feel at being accused of doing something that is less than your best.
Dad: I think what makes me more sensitive to it is sometimes I feel that I do the same thing to my wife. (Margaret cries.) What's the matter? Your sister picking on you, huh?

The family links are now coming into focus and we have some information on father's rejecting internal objects. Captain Wall hated his mother's nagging, grudge-holding behavior, and he is upset to see that he is behaving in the same way toward his wife. He sees his wife's upset at being picked on more clearly in their baby's reaction to her sister's complaints. The organizing of the house to prevent collapse in case of death has its antecedent in the family link that includes a sudden death of a father, made traumatic by distance imposed because of having moved across the country to their present posting, and magnified greatly by his mother's continuing pressure on his already harsh judgment about himself. His mother is a persecutory object with which he has identified against his will.

In the interview, we also learned that the family's last move had been particularly stressful for Mrs. Wall. It happened 8 months earlier, when she was eight months pregnant with Margaret, and took her away from the area of the country that is her home. She had been very close to her mother and sister; they had supported her during her pregnancies, and it made sense to us that she was distressed during only the last part of her second pregnancy after leaving home and losing their support. Now we could understand that the move was when the extreme stress had set in requiring medication that had effectively medicated the fetus, too. Then after the birth, both mother and child had to be withdrawn from the effects of codeine dependency. Mrs. Wall still worried guiltily that her baby's brain had been permanently damaged.

Here we see the interaction of the social link and the physical symptom bearing the stress from the fractured social link. In attachment terms, the physical and emotional separation from the secure base Mrs. Wall found in her family strained her level of functioning and then her physical and emotional suffering physically and emotionally strained Captain Wall's style of distancing attachments. As she needed and asked for more, he grew more anxious and intolerant, thereby making her even more anxious. This played out with both children in a cycle that has now taken on a life of its own. Now we hope to learn more about Mrs. Wall's object relations history, to build a more complete picture of the family link.

Vertical Link: Mrs. Wall's Family

David: (To Mrs. Wall) Tell me about your relationship with your parents? Do you just have the one sister?

Mom: I have one sister, and we were 11 months apart. She was older. And so we did a lot of things together. I mean, one summer we took courses in Hawaii together, you know we did a lot of traveling together. See, I wouldn't have gone to Hawaii and done that unless I had my sister. And my mom and I got along real well. I mean I could tell her the things that I felt and we had, I still think we have, a good relationship. I never felt she put me down or anything. She was always very supportive of things I did. Even if I overloaded myself, she still supported me. Just kind of let me find out for myself. I love my father, but I didn't feel as close to him as my mother, only because I didn't do as many things with my father as my mother. I did more things with my mom. Like we would be the ones to go on the weekend and do things. He was a perfectionist in the sense that he had to have his yard perfect. And so every weekend he would spend his time in the yard until it was perfect. About once a year he would say, "You should keep the inside as neat as I keep the outside." But, we didn't, so he just seemed to take it. He loved the yard, so he didn't seem to mind if we went off on the weekend and did something fun. He was satisfied being in the yard. Even though we would invite him, he didn't want to come. He would just stay home and work in the yard.

David: So the 3 girls would go off together.

Mom: Yes we did.

David: Still sort of like that?

Dad: My feeling is that when her father died, when she was about 20 or 21 . . .

Mom: 19.

Dad: 19 . . . when her mother assumed both of the roles. She was a little protective, perhaps that's why maybe the girls. . . . Well, her sister is fairly aggressive, she may have done it on her own. But perhaps that's why Roberta relied so much on her mom when problems came up—or on her sister.

Mom: Because she would try to do her best, to do it all for you. I mean if you said you didn't want to go down and exchange something she'd do it for you or whatever. I mean she would. I mean maybe I was thinking more like that kind of perfectionism bothers me.

David: 'Cause of your dad.

Mom: Well, I noticed that my dad, I felt, he missed some things. I felt he literally had the most perfect yard on the block.

David: So this is kind of the debate the two of you carried on.

Mom: I mean he died! They told him before he died. The doctor said, "If you do not slow down the work that you do in the yard and do not give up the idea that you have to have it so perfect, you will die. Hire somebody to do this yard work." So my mother hired someone. She said, "Fine I'll hire someone to do the yard work because if you don't, in a year you'll be dead." So my mother hired someone to do the yard work. But what he did is, after the guy did the work, he would go out and do it over because it wasn't perfect enough. And in less than a year he died. So I guess what I felt when it happened, "Was it worth the price he paid?"

(David is taken with Lizzie's animal play and does not notice Margaret playing quietly by herself. Now she lies down in the doll bed, which does not quite fit her.)

David: Lizzie, what's that mean over here with these animals?

Lizzie: This one is laying over here to eat.

David: Who is this over here?

Lizzie: The horse.

David: Now the horse is all alone, I notice.

Lizzie: Yeah.

David: The horse is lonely?

Lizzie: Uh huh.

David: How about the two sheep?

Lizzie: They're not lonely at all.

David: 'Cause they've got each other.

Lizzie: Yeah, yeah.

Jill: (To Mrs. Wall) Were you mad at him for not taking better care of himself that last year?

Mom: I guess in some ways I didn't understand, I guess I was. I didn't understand. I thought, "He could've still been here today, if he would have just had the attitude that . . ." Well, that isn't that important.

David: What did he die of?

Mom: He died in his sleep, his heart just stopped.

David: How old were you?

Mom: I was 19.

David: And how old were you when you met?

Mom: I was 26 and then we only dated 3 months and he asked me to marry him. So, I think we were married in 7 or 8 months. Married at 27 and I think he was 31.

Lizzie: The cow is going into the horse's place.

David: How come?

Lizzie: Because the horse is all alone.

David: So the cows are going to keep the horse company.

Lizzie: And then in a few days they're going to go back to their house.

David: (To Mom) Lizzie's horse was pretty lonely, and the animals that had each other did fine. You and your Mom and your sister had fun while your Dad was perfecting his garden. It became important for you not to do things perfectly, to *not* do them perfectly because that is what took him away from you and the family. And then it killed him.

Attachment Relationships

In this section, Captain Wall uses his wife's first name for the first time. This comes at a moment when he becomes sympathetic to her plight, after admitting fearfully that he may treat his wife in the painful way that his mother treated him. There has been a loosening of the limited pattern of referring to her as "she" which had been an indicator of his defense of emotional distancing to avoid longing for love and care.

Lizzie's play picks up the thread of a singleton being lonely and a couple being happy to have each other. Margaret plays out the deaths by lying still in the crib. Their play is not at all disruptive because now the parents are dealing with their mourning about broken family links. As the parents begin to talk about their losses and disappointments in a straightforward way, their relationship calms and becomes tangibly more secure and mutually supportive. Their relationship shifts to another region of their marital personality's attractor pattern, and we see its softer, more directly loving and supportive aspects. As this happens, the children become able to play calmly and with interest. As Mrs. Wall describes her father's obsessive behavior in the garden, we hear a fractal echo of it in her obsessive form of speech, which presents a thought many times over as if to get it right or get it noticed. This somewhat fractured speech pattern contrasts with the narrative about her family. Her flow of memory and coherent ideas about her situation in words that make emotional sense presents a secure picture, but the rhythm of the words is not cohesive. She seemed to have, overall, a secure attachment within her family, but we have seen how her vulnerability can push her towards an anxious ambivalent state.

Links

In family therapy we see the link as the super-ordinate structure, fed by interpersonal interaction. The child's need for love, security and firm limits drives the interactions with the parents who respond within the parameters set by their links on the vertical and horizontal access. This is how the psyche is structured by the links.

In the space of this one interview we do not learn about the generation before the parents' parents, so we have limited understanding of the vertical axis of the link from the previous generations. But we do know a fair amount about the vertical axis from the immediately previous generation in terms of expectation of hard work and play, perfectionism and guilt, and we know about the vertical axis from mother to baby at the level of physiological transfer. We observe the vertical axis affecting parents and children in their current life. We see how that aspect of the vertical axis intersects with the social link. And we realize that this is a family with two daughters, two women grandparents and an aunt. There is a dearth of men in this generation, and in the previous generation there was a vulnerability to sudden death which aggravates Captain Wall's anxiety about being absent.

Based on the single assessment interview alone, we can see how Captain Wall and wife express links from the vertical and horizontal axes in their relationship as man and wife and as parents for their children, and at the same time their couple relationship is being structured in relationship to their children. The stress on this couple illustrates our finding that the couple's relationship is at the crosshairs of the generations on the vertical axis and of current family and society on the horizontal axis. The couple does all the work of conveying history in the vertical link and culture in the horizontal link as it prepares for transmission to the future generation. The link is a complex organization for living with and being shaped by others while also shaping them and their world.

Margaret's individual's psyche has been built on the twin pillars of the constitution of the internal world (in her situation affected by drugs during her gestation) and the influence of the social. The link refers to *both* internal object relations and external interactions simultaneously. She was born into and shaped by a field that has a vertical axis and a horizontal axis in both conscious and unconscious dimensions. The vertical axis links her to previous generations and to her history and culture. The horizontal axis links her to her family and wider current social groups, for instance the military base where she lives. Her needs for comfort acquire meaning in the light of her mother's guilt about possible damage to her, and her father's need for family self-sufficiency to protect him from guilt and worry. Margaret expresses the link in her crying symptoms, her way of acting toward her parents, her sister, and strangers, and her bodily experiences of needing to suck on her bottle or her pacifier. She cannot tell us her dreams, and indeed none of the family members spoke of their dreams.

The Interpersonal Unconscious

In this session, the parents share unconscious fears about death, especially about the premature death of men who drive themselves to perfection or are driven crazy by the lack of it. That perfectionism is a defense for Captain Wall against his own fear of death and inadequacy. It meets up with Mrs. Wall's fear that his perfectionism will kill him and that it will kill all pleasure for her. He puts his imperfection in her and attacks her for goofing up. She feels ashamed and resentful at not being appreciated, and also feels guilty that her mistakes cause him distress that pushes him to be more perfectionist. They share the idea that they do not do their best. Through mutual projective identification, they agree to blame her for "not doing her best" on behalf of the two of them, in the hopes that he can help her with that—or that at least it will leave his coping capacities intact. Underneath, we postulate that there is a shared fear that if he cannot cope, it is an even greater danger to the family than if she makes mistakes.

The family demonstrates to us how these anxieties are transmitted to the children, from the inadequate limit setting by the mother, the overly distant limit setting by dad, and the parental debate with occasional acrimony, to which the children are frequently exposed. With their immature egos, they are unable to confront the complexities of the situation in words. All they can do is enact the conflict through upset and sibling bickering that form fractals of the parental struggle.

Chaos Theory

Our monitoring of the session is done through a complex mixture of our countertransference analysis as we respond unconsciously to the session, our theoretical and technical training housed both consciously and unconsciously in our self, and our own personalities in interaction with the family. We do not expect to do justice to describing how all these factors play out at a given moment. The session gives us an experience that has pattern similarity to the couple and family's organization at all levels from their individual personalities to the interactive pattern of the family. All of this intersects with the therapists' personalities and, in this case of co-therapy, with our interactive pattern. We hope that therapists have sturdy but flexible psyches, and that when they work together, the flexibility and sturdiness extends to their interactive work pattern.

In such cases, the flux of the family from one attractor pattern to another during the flow of the session will resonate with the interpsychic pattern of the therapists in differing ways. We expect that resonance to inform therapists from inside their own experience, at both conscious and unconscious levels. In this way of thinking, we value interpretations therapists make as attempts at understanding. But interpretations are only one part of the therapist's technique. The therapist begins with an offer of secure therapeutic holding in a safe setting, with tolerance and understanding, listening that helps the couple to speak, questioning that develops an inquiring attitude, inquiry, steady responding and follow-up, all of which help them face difficult material and acknowledge each one's part in the dynamics of the session. The therapist offers the trained mind as a container for the couple's unconscious experience, and understanding that facilitates growth and maturation. Mainly we offer to be vessels for unconscious resonance and understanding.

In this session, we experienced the limit-cycle aspects of the parents' argument, a pattern closely aligned with the fixed-cycle attractors of the baby's cry and the sisters' scrapping. And suddenly, as the session focused on the vertical link, we saw the parents' organization briefly move to a different region of their attractor characterized by mutual support and understanding. This shift occurred when they were sympathetic to each other's family histories. Then Captain Wall could refer to his wife by name, and say with empathy and humility that he feared he was perpetrating on his wife the hateful imposition of impossible standards that his mother had so often done to him. This shift within the session was a discontinuous moment embedded in the wholeness of the work. Such a brief core moment of affective change is a fractal of the more mature aspects of the individual mental state and the marital joint personality. Then, the play of the girls settled down under the influence of the basin of attraction of the parents' empathic stance, and the family became a working one in which Lizzie could tell us, through her play, of the fear of being alone that lay underneath all the defenses we had seen played out until then. All of this gave us a sense of the possibility of fruitful work in future sessions. We also knew from the repetitive cycles of interaction that the sturdy limit cycle defensive patterns would reassert themselves for work at a later date. In resonance with the strange attractor effect of the therapists' empathy, the couple could in all likelihood work over time to develop their capacity for mutual understanding and support, and the family would have a good chance of moving to a pattern of more flexibility and adaptability.

SUMMARY

A fussy baby, having been addicted to codeine in utero, is born into a link filled with her parents' guilt and irritation at her crying, sadness and resentment at loss of family support. Both parents are carrying grief and guilt in relation to the traumatic deaths of parents. On the horizontal axis, the parents' link is full of the anxiety of relocation and mobilization in case of war. The parents are caught in a repetitive projective identificatory cycle of disagreement and blame in which one is made to feel guilty and inferior in comparison to a standard of perfection. One of them uses perfection to avoid death anxiety, and the other believes it to cause early death. The parents' interpersonal unconscious organizes around fear of death.

In a family consultation, the parents work with the therapists to undo the limit-cycle attractor patterns in which they are stuck and move into more chaotic states that hold the possibility of reintegration at more adaptive levels. Working from the baby's symptomatology to the family's links, the therapists help the parents reach an empathic position and give the chaotic family system the possibility of arriving at a new organization. In this final chapter, we have pulled together, in one clinical narrative, theories of attachment, object relations, the inter-generational transmission, the social unconscious, and chaos theory, all components of our concept of the interpersonal unconscious.

Epilogue

We are entering an epoch of change, international exchange, and integration in psychoanalysis. There has been a paradigm shift in psychoanalytic thinking over the last few years, a groundswell toward plurality of theoretical positions evolving alongside discoveries from other fields of thought. Looking back, we can see that the seeds for this shift were sewn within psychoanalysis by contributions of Fairbairn, Klein, Bion, Winnicott, and Bowlby, among others, between 1940 and 1980. Since then, the shift continued to evolve from an emphasis on early relationships to an awareness of the importance of significant relationships throughout life. Then, with a slowly emerging clarity, the gaze of psychoanalysis settled on the importance of the therapeutic relationship itself for therapeutic understanding and change.

Psychoanalysis itself was influencing, and influenced by, parallel evolutions in other fields—new models of information processing and chaos theory from mathematics and science; attachment theory and affect regulation from child development research; the study of early relationships and affective learning in young monkeys from the field of primatology; experiments on the action of mirror neurons from neuroscience; and studies of complex interactions of large systems in the field of group and family therapy. Now, not only can we use individual analytic theory, but we also have access to the insights of couple and family psychoanalysis to enrich theories of development and change.

We became interested in many of these currents over the past several years. Then in discovering the Spanish- and French-language literatures on the theories of the link and the field as they became available in English, and as our overseas colleagues generously shared them with us, we saw that many of the threads we had followed separately were beginning to come together into a broader, deeper, more complex pattern, an enriched multidimensional analytic understanding. A particular virtue of our expanded concept of psychoanalytic understanding is that it encompasses the dynamics of couples, families, and groups, as well as those of individuals in psychoanalysis.

How do growth and development occur? We prune existing ideas, unravel previously coherent patterns, enter into a temporary chaos and confusion—and then, realign in a new organization. As the chaos yields to new pattern recognition and deconstruction gives way to creativity, we arrive at a more integrated approach to psychoanalytic theory and its application to clinical work. We are led to our concept of the interpersonal unconscious.

References

Ainsworth, M. D. S., Blehar, M. C., Waters, E., and Wall, S. (1978). *Patterns of Attachment: A Psychological Study of the Strange Situation*. Hillsdale, NJ: Lawrence Erlbaum.

Ammaniti, M. and Trentini, C. (2009). How new knowledge about parenting reveals the neurobiological implications of intersubjectivity. *Psychoanalytic Dialogues* 19(5): 537–555.

Aviram, R. (2005). The social object and the pathology of prejudice. In *The Legacy of Fairbairn and Sutherland*, ed. J. and D. Scharff, pp. 227–236. London: Routledge.

Aviram, R. (2009). *The Relational Origins of Prejudice*. Lanham, MD: Jason Aronson.

Balint, M. (1968). *The Basic Fault: Therapeutic Aspects of Regression*. London: Tavistock.

Baranger, M. and Baranger, W. (2008) [1961–1962]. The analytic situation as a dynamic field. *International Journal of Psycho-Analysis* 89: 795–896.

Baranger, M. and Baranger, W. (2009). *The Work of Confluence: Listening and Interpreting in the Psychoanalytic Field*, ed. L. G. Fiorini. London: Karnac.

Bartholomew, K. and Horowitz, L. M. (1991). Attachment styles among young adults: A test of a four-category model. *Journal of Personality and Social Psychology* 61: 226–244.

Beebe, B. and Lachman, F. M. (1988). The contribution of mother–infant mutual influence to the origins of self- and object-representations. *Psychoanalytic Psychology* 5: 305–337.

Beebe, B. and Lachmann, F. (2002). *Infant Research and Adult Treatment: Co-Constructing Interactions*. Hillsdale, NJ: Analytic Press.

Beebe, B., Jaffe, J., and Lachman, F. (1993). A dyadic systems model of mother–infant mutual regulation: Implications for the origins of representations and therapeutic action. *Newsletter of the Division of Psycho-Analysis, American Psychological Association* Winter xiv (1): 27–33.

Belsky, J. and Nezworski, T. (1987). *Clinical Implications of Attachment Theory*. Hillsdale, NJ: Erlbaum.

Berenstein, I. (2009). "Commentary on the Link and Clinical Material." Presentation at the International Psychoanalytic Congress, Chicago, IL.

Berenstein, I. (2010). "Presentation on the Link." Meeting of the International Association of Couple and Family Psychoanalysis, Buenos Aires, July, 2010.

Bick, E. (1964). Notes on infant observation in psychoanalytic training. *International Journal of Psycho-Analysis* 45: 558–566.

Bion, W. R. (1961). *Experiences in Groups and Other Papers*. London: Tavistock.

Bion, W. R. (1962). *Learning from Experience*. London: Heinemann.

Bion, W. R. (1967a). Attacks on linking. In *Second Thoughts*, pp. 93–109. London: Heinemann.

Bion, W. R. (1967b). *Second Thoughts*. London: Heinemann. Reprinted London: Karnac, 1984.

Bion, W. R. (1970). *Attention and Interpretation*. London: Heinemann.

Bollas, C. (1987). *The Shadow of the Object*. New York: Columbia University Press.

Bolognini, S. (2010). *Secret Passages: Theory and Technique of the Interpsychic Dimension*. London: Routledge.

Boston Change Process Study Group (2005). The "something more" than interpretation revisited: Sloppiness and co-creativity in the psychoanalytic encounter. *Journal of the American Psychoanalytic Association* 53: 693–729.

Bowlby, J. (1969). *Attachment and Loss Vol. 1: Attachment*. London: Hogarth Press. New York: Basic Books.

Bowlby, J. (1973b). Personal Communication to David Scharff. Tavistock Centre, London.

Bowlby, J. (1977). The making and breaking of affectional bonds. *British Journal of Psychiatry* 130: 201–210 and 421–431. Reprinted in *The Making and Breaking of Affectional Bonds*, pp. 126–160. London: Tavistock, 1979.

Bråten, S. (1992). The newborn's virtual other: A model for human communication. *Yearbook of Sociology* 8: 101–118.

Bråten, S. (1993). Infant attachment and self-organization in light of this thesis: born with the other in mind. In *Making Links: How Children Learn*, ed. I. M. Gomnaes and E. Osborne, pp. 25–38. Oslo: Yrkeslitteratur.

Brazelton, T. B., Koslowski, B., and Main, M. (1974). The origins of reciprocity. The early mother–infant interaction. In *The Effect of the*

Infant on Its Caregiver, ed. M. Lewis and L Rosenblum, pp. 49–77. New York:Wiley.

Breuer, J. and Freud, S. (1893–1895). Studies in hysteria. *Standard Edition* 2: 1–305.

Briggs, J. (1992). *Fractals: The Patterns of Chaos*. New York: Touchstone.

Cairo, I. (2007). Review of "*Ser Humano*" by Julio Moreno. *Journal of the American Psychoanalytic Association* 55(3): 1066–1075.

Cassidy, J. and Berlin, L. J. (1994). The insecure/ambivalent pattern of attachment: Theory and research. *Child Development* 65: 971–992.

Cassidy and Kobak (1988). (1987). Avoidance and its relation to other defensive processes. In *Clinical Implications of Attachment Theory*, ed. J. Belsky and T. Nezworski, pp. 300–326. Hillsdale, NJ: Erlbaum.

Clulow, C. (Ed.) (2001). *Adult Attachment and Couple Psychotherapy: The "Secure Base" in Practice and Research*. London: Brunner/Routledge.

Clulow, C. (2006). Couple psychotherapy and attachment theory. In *New Paradigms for Treating Relationships*, ed. J. Scharff and D. Scharff, pp. 253–266. Lanham MD: Jason Aronson.

Cozolino, L. (2002). *The Neuroscience of Psychotherapy*. New York: Norton.

Dicks, H. V. (1967). *Marital Tensions: Clinical Studies Towards a Psychoanalytic Theory of Interaction*. London: Routledge and Kegan Paul.

Dozier, M. (1990). Attachment organization and treatment use for adults with serious psychopathological disorders. *Development and Psychopathology* 2: 47–60.

Dozier, M., Cue, K., and Barnett, L. (1994). Clinicians as caregivers: Role of attachment organization in treatment. *Journal of Consulting and Clinical Psychology* 62: 793–800.

Dozier, M., Lomax, L., and Tyrrell, C. (1996). "Psychotherapy's Challenge for Adults Using Deactivating Attachment Strategies." Unpublished manuscript, University of Delaware.

Emde, R. (2009). From ego to "we-go": Neurobiology and questions for psychoanalysis. *Psychoanalytic Dialogues* 19(5): 556–564.

Faimberg, H. (2005). *The Telescoping of Generations: Listening to the Narcissistic Links between Generations*. London and New York: Routledge.

Fairbairn, W. R. D. (1941). A revised psychopathology of the psychoses and neuroses. *Psychoanalytic Studies of the Personality*, pp. 28–58. London: Tavistock and Routledge, 1952.

Fairbairn, W. R. D. (1944). Endopsychic structure considered in terms of object relationships. In *Psychoanalytic Studies of the Personality*, pp. 82–135. London: Routledge and Kegan Paul, 1952.

Fairbairn, W. R. D. (1952). *Psychoanalytic Studies of the Personality*. London: Routledge.

Fairbairn, W. R. D. (1954). Observations on the nature of hysterical states. *British Journal of Medical Psychology* 27: 105–125 and in *From Instinct to*

Self Selected Papers of W. R. D. Fairbairn, Vol. 1, ed. D. E. Scharff and E. F. Birtles, pp. 13–40. Northvale, NJ: Jason Aronson.

Fairbairn, W. R. D. (1963). Synopsis of an object relations theory of the personality. *International Journal of Psycho-Analysis* 39: 374–385. Reprinted in *From Instinct to Self: Selected Papers of W. R. D. Fairbairn*, ed. D. Scharff and E. F. Birtles, Vo. 1, pp. 155–156. Northvale, NJ: Jason Aronson, 1996.

Ferrari, P. (2009). "Understanding Others Through Shared Representations: The Neural Underpinnings of Intersubjectivity." Presentation, International Psychotherapy Institute. Salt Lake City, March 2009.

Ferrari, P. F., Gallese, V., Rizzolatti, G., and Fogassi, L. (2003). Mirror neurons responding to the observation of ingestive and communicative mouth actions in the monkey ventral premotor cortex. *European Journal of Neuroscience* 17: 1703–1714.

Ferro, A. (1999). *The Bi-Personal Field*. London: Routledge.

Ferro, A. (2009). *Mind Works: Technique an Creativity in Psychoanalysis*. London and New York: Routledge.

Ferro, A. (2010). Book review essay: *The Work of Confluence: Listening and Interpreting in the Psychoanalytic Field* by Madeleine and Will Baranger. *International Journal of Psycho-Analysis* 91: 415–429.

Fisher, J. and Crandall, L. (1997). Complex attachment: Patterns of relating in the couple. *Sexual and Marital Therapy* 12(3): 211–223.

Fisher, J. and Crandall, L. (2001). Patterns of relating in the couple. In *Adult Attachment and Couple Psychotherapy*, ed. C. Clulow, pp. 15–27. London: Brunner/Routledge.

Fivaz-Depeursinge, E. and Corboz-Warnery, A. (1999). *The Primary Triangle: A Developmental System View of Mothers, Fathers, and Infants*. New York: Basic Books.

Fonagy, P. (2001a). *Attachment Theory and Psychoanalysis*. New York: Other Press.

Fonagy, P., Gergely, B., Jurist, F., and Target, M. (2003). *Affect Regulation, Mentalization, and the Development of the Self*. New York: Other Press.

Fonagy, P. and Luyten, P. (2009). A developmental, mentalization-based approach to the understanding and treatment of borderline personality disorder. *Development and Psychopathology* 21: 1355–1381.

Fonagy, P., Moran, G. S., Steele, H., and Higgitt, A. C. (1991). The capacity for understanding mental states: The reflective self in parent and child and its significance for security of attachment. *Infant Mental Health Journal* 13: 200–216.

Fonagy, P. and Target, M. (1997). Attachment and reflective function: Their role in self-organization. *Development and Psychopathology* 9: 679–700.

Fonagy, P. and Target, M. (2007). The rooting of the mind in the body: New links between attachment theory and psychoanalytic thought. *Journal of the American Psychoanalytic Association* 55(2): 411–456.

Foulkes, S. (1964). *Therapeutic Group Analysis*. London: Allen and Unwin.
Freeman, W. J. (2007). A biological theory of brain function and its relevance to psychoanalysis. In *Self-Organizing Complexity in Psychological Systems*, ed. C. Piers, J. P. Muller, and J. Brent, pp. 15–36. Lanham, MD: Jason Aronson.
Freud, S. (1900). The interpretation of dreams. *Standard Edition* 4: 1–338.
Freud, S. (1901). The psychopathology of everyday life. *Standard Edition* 6: 53–105.
Freud, S. (1905a). Fragment of an analysis of a case of hysteria. *Standard Edition* 7: 7–122.
Freud, S. (1905b). Three essays on the theory of sexuality. *Standard Edition* 7: 135–243.
Freud, S. (1911). Psycho-analytical notes on an autobiographical account of a case of paranoia. *Standard Edition* 12: 1–82.
Freud, S. (1912). Recommendations to physicians practicing psychoanalysis. *Standard Edition* 12: 111–120.
Freud, S. (1915). The archaic features and infantilism of dreams. *Standard Edition* 15: 199–212.
Freud, S. (1917). Mourning and melancholia. *Standard Edition* 14: 243–258.
Freud, S. (1923). The ego and the id. *Standard Edition* 19: 1–66.
Freud, S. (1925). An autobiographical study. *Standard Edition* 20: 1–74.
Freud, S. (1939). Moses and monotheism. *Standard Edition* 23: 1–138.
Freud, S. (1950). Extracts from the Fleiss papers. *Standard Edition* 1: 177–280.
Gabbard, G. and Westen, D. (2003). Rethinking therapeutic action. *International Journal of Psycho-Analysis* 84(4): 823–841.
Galatzer-Levy, R. (1995). Psychoanalysis and chaos theory. *Journal of the American Psychoanalytic Association* 43: 1095–1113.
Galatzer-Levy, R. (2009). Good vibrations: Analytic process as coupled oscillations. *International Journal of Psycho-Analysis* 90: 983–1007.
Gallese, V. (2003a). The manifold nature of interpersonal relations: The quest for a common mechanism. *Phil. Trans. Royal Soc. London* 358: 517–528.
Gallese, V. (2003b). The roots of empathy: The shared manifold hypothesis and the neural basis of intersubjectivity. *Psychopathology* 36(4): 171–180.
Gallese, V. (2009). Mirror neurons, embodied simulation, and the neural basis of social identification. *Psychoanalytic Dialogues* 19(5): 519–536.
Gleick, J. (1987). *Chaos*. New York: Viking Penguin.
Green, A. (1986). *On Private Madness*. London: Hogarth Press.
Green, A. (1999). *The Work of the Negative*. London: Free Association Books.
Grotstein, J. (2007). *A Beam of Intense Darkness*. London: Karnac.
Gu, M. D. (2006). The filial piety complex: A Chinese form of the Oedipus complex. *Psychoanalytic Quarterly* 75(1): 163–195.

Heimann, P. (1950). On counter-transference. *International Journal of Psycho-Analysis* 31: 81–84.

Hesse, E. (1996). Discourse, memory and the Adult Attachment Interview: A note with emphasis on the emerging Cannot Classify category. *Infant Mental Health Journal* 17: 4–11.

Hopper, E. (1996). The social unconscious in clinical work. *Group* 20(1): 7–42.

Hopper, E. (2003). *The Social Unconscious*. London: Jessica Kingsley.

Hopper, E. (Ed.) (2011 in press). *The Social Unconcious in Persons, Groups and Societies: Volume 1*. London: Karnac.

Jaques, E. (1951). *The Changing Culture of a Factory: A Study of Authority and Participation in an Industrial Setting*. London: Tavistock.

Jung, C. J. (1953–1979). *The Collected Works* (Bollinger Series XX). 20 vols. Trans. R. F. C. Hull, ed. H. Read, M. Fordham, G. Adler, and W. McGuire. Princeton: Princeton University Press.

Kaës, R. (2005). A hypothesis for a third topic regarding intersubjectivity and the subject in a common, shared psychic space. In the online journal, *Funzione Gamma*, #21, 2005. www.funzionegamma.edu/articolo.asp?id=220&id_numero=41. Last accessed, August 2011.

Kaës, R. (2007). *Linking, Alliances, and Shared Space*. London: The International Psychoanalytic Association.

Kaplan, H. S. (1974). *The New Sex Therapy: Active Treatment of Sexual Dysfunction*. New York: Brunner/Mazel.

Kirshner, L. (2006). The work of Rene Kaës: Intersubjective transmission in Families, groups, and culture. *Journal of the American Psychoanalytic Association* 54: 1005–1013.

Klein, M. (1928). Early stages of the Oedipus complex. In *Love, Guilt and Reparation and Other Works: 1921–1945*, pp. 186–198. London: Hogarth, 1975.

Klein, M. (1945). The Oedipus complex in the light of early anxieties. In *Love, Guilt and Reparation and Other Works: 1921–1945*, pp. 370–419. London: Hogarth, 1975.

Klein, M. (1946). Notes on some schizoid mechanisms. *International Journal of Psycho-Analysis* 27: 99–110, and in *Envy and Gratitude and Other Works* 1946–1963, pp. 1–24. London: Hogarth Press and the Institute of Psycho-Analysis (1975); New York: Delacorte Press, 1975; New York: Dell (1977).

Klein, M. (1975a). *Love, Guilt and Reparation and Other Works 1921–1945*. London: Hogarth Press.

Klein, M. (1975b). *Envy and Gratitude and Other Works 1946–1963*. London: Hogarth Press.

Lacan, J. (1977). *Ecrits: A Selection*. Trans. A. Sheridan. New York: Norton.

Losso, R. (2009). Discussion of David Scharff's paper "The Concept of the Link in Couple and Family Psychoanalysis." Presentation at the Family

Therapy Small Discussion Group, International Psychoanalytic Association Congress, Chicago, IL, July 30, 2009.

Losso, R. and Losso, A. (2006). Intrapsychic, interpsychic, and transpsychic communication. In *New Paradigms for Treating Relationships,* ed. J. Scharff and D. Scharff, pp. 33–42. Lanham, MD: Jason Aronson.

Lyons-Ruth, K. (1998). Implicit relational knowing: Its role in development and psychoanalytic treatment. *Infant Mental Health Journal* 12(3): 282–289.

Luyten, P. (2010). "Mentalization-Based Approach to Understanding and Treatment of Psychopathology." Unpublished paper. Consortium for Psychoanalytic Research Annual Conference, Washington, DC, February 21, 2010.

Main, M. (1995). Attachment: Overview, with implications for clinical work. In *Attachment Theory: Social, Developmental and Clinical Perspectiva,* ed. S. Goldberg, R. Muir, and J. Kerr, pp. 407–475. Hilllsdale, NJ: Analytic Press.

Main, M., and Goldwyn, R. (1994). "Adult Attachment Rating and Classification System, Manual in Draft, Version 6.0." Unpublished manuscript: University of California at Berkeley.

Main, M. and Solomon, J. (1990). Procedures for identifying infants as disorganized/disoriented during the Ainsworth Strange Situation. In *Attachment in Preschool Years: Theory, Research, and Intervention,* ed. M. Greenberg, D. Cichetti, and M. Cummings, pp. 95–124. Chicago: University of Chicago Press.

Marcia, J. E. (1994). Ego identity and object relations. In *Empirical Perspectives on Object Relations,* ed. J. M. Masling and R. F. Bornstein, pp. 59–103. Washington, DC: American Psychological Association.

McDougall, J. (1989). *Theaters of the Body: A Psychoanalytic Approach to Psychosomatic Illness.* New York and London: Norton.

Menzies-Lyth, I. (1959). The functioning of social systems as a defence against anxiety. *Human Relations* 13: 95–121.

Modell, A. H. (2003). *Imagination and the Meaningful Brain.* Cambridge, MA: The MIT Press.

Moore, M. S. (1996). Attachment Theory and Brain Research. Lecture at the International Institute of Object Relations Therapy. Chevy Chase, MD, July.

Moreno, J. (2002). *Ser Humano: La Inconsisgencia, Los Vinculos, La Crianza (To Be Human: Inconsistency, Links, Raising Children).* Buenos Aires: Libros del Zorzal. 2nd Edition, 2010.

Moreno, J. (2010). "The Theory of the Link: Association and Connection." Paper given during weekend conference "Being Human: Psychoanalytic Approaches to Children and Adults" at the International Psychotherapy Institute, Chevy Chase, MD. January 29–31, 2010.

Morrison, T., Urquiza, A. J., and Goodlin-Jones, B. (1997a). Attachment and the representation of intimate relationships in adulthood. *Journal of Psychology* 131: 57–71.

Morrison, T., Urquiza, A. J., and Goodlin-Jones, B. (1997b). Attachment, perceptions of interaction, and relationship adjustment. *Journal of Social and Personal Relationships* 14: 627–642.

Murray, L. (1988). Effects of postnatal depression on infant development: Direct studies of early mother–infant interactions. In *Motherhood and Mental Illness Vol. 2: Causes and Consequences*, ed. R. Kumar and I. F. Brockington. London: Wright.

Nicoló, A. M. (2009). Discussion of David Scharff's paper "The Concept of the Link in Couple and Family Psychoanalysis." Presentation at the Family Therapy Small Discussion Group, International Psychoanalytic Association Congress, Chicago, IL, July 30, 2009.

Nicoló, A. M., Norsa, D., and Carratelli, T. (2006). Dreams and the introduction of a third into the transference dynamic. In *New Paradigms for Treating Relationships*, ed. J. S. Scharff and D. E. Scharff, pp. 297–310. Lanham, MD: Jason Aronson.

Ogden, T. (1989). *The Primitive Edge of Experience*. Northvale, NJ: Jason Aronson.

Ogden, T. (1994). *Subjects of Analysis*. Northvale, NJ: Jason Aronson.

Ogden, T. (2009). *Rediscovering Psychoanalysis: Thinking and Dreaming, Learning and Forgetting*. London and New York: Routledge.

Palumbo, S. (1999). *The Emergent Ego: Complexity and Coevolution in the Psychoanalytic Process*. Madison, CT: International Universities Press.

Parsons, M. (2006). The analyst's countertransference to the psychoanalytic process. *International Journal of Psychoanalysis* 87: 1183–1198.

Parsons, M. (2007). Raiding the inarticulate: The internal analytic setting and listening beyond countertransference. *International Journal of Psychoanalysis* 88: 1441–1456.

Parsons, M. (2009). An independent theory of clinical technique. *Psychoanalytic Dialogues* 19(3): 221–236.

Quinodoz, D. (1997). *Emotional Vertigo: Between Anxiety and Pleasure*. London and New York: Routledge.

Quinodoz, J-M. (1993). *The Taming of Solitude: Separation Anxiety in Psychoanalysis*. London and New York: Routledge.

Quinodoz, J-M. (1997). Transitions in psychic structure in the light of deterministic chaos theory. *International Journal of Psycho-Analysis* 78(4): 699–718.

Quinodoz, J-M. (2002). *Dreams That Turn over a Page*. Hove, East Sussex: Brunner Routledge.

Racker, H. (1968). *Transference and Countertransference*. New York: International Universities Press.

Rizzolatti, G., and Craighero, L. (2004). The mirror-neuron system. *Annual Review of Neuroscience*, 27: 169–192.

Rizzolatti, G., Fogassi, L., and Gallese, V. (2006). Mirrors in the mind. *Scientific American*, November 2006, pp. 54–61.

Savege, J. M. (1973). Psychodynamic understanding in community psychiatry. Proceedings of the Ninth International Congress of Psychotherapy, Oslo. Reprinted in *Psychotherapy and Psychosomatics* 25: 272–278, 1975.

Scharff, D. E. (1982). *The Sexual Relationship: An Object Relations View of Sex and the Family*. London: Routledge and Kegan Paul. Reprinted with new introduction, Northvale, NJ: Jason Aronson, 1998.

Scharff, D. E. (1992). *Refinding the Object and Reclaiming the Self.* Northvale, NJ: Jason Aronson.

Scharff, D. E. (2011a). Book review essay on *The Work of Confluence: Listening and Interpreting in the Psychoanalytic Field* by W. Baranger and M. Baranger, London: Karnac. *Couple and Family Psychoanalysis* 1(1): 146–149.

Scharff, D. E. (2011b). The concept of the link in psychoanalytic therapy. *Couple and Family Psychoanalysis* 1(1): 34–48.

Scharff, D. E. (ed.) (in press). Issue on Psychoanalysis in China. International Journal of Applied Psychoanalytic Studies.

Scharff, D. E. and Birtles, D. E. (1994). *From Instinct to Self: Selected Papers of W. R. D. Fairbairn, Vol. 1.* Northvale, NJ: Jason Aronson.

Scharff, D. E. and Scharff, J. S. (1987). *Object Relations Family Therapy.* Northvale, NJ: Jason Aronson.

Scharff, D. E. and Scharff, J. S. (1991). *Object Relations Couple Therapy.* Northvale, NJ: Jason Aronson.

Scharff, D. E. and Scharff, J. S. (2004). Using dreams in treating couples' sexual issues. *Psychoanalytic Inquiry* 24(3): 468–482.

Scharff, D. E. and Scharff, J. S. (2005). The interpersonal unconscious. In the online journal, *Funzione Gamma*, #21, 2005. www.funzionegamma.edu/articolo.asp?id=221&id_numero=41. Last accessed, August 2011.

Scharff, D. E. and Scharff, J. S. (2007). Marriage is a strange attractor: Chaos Theory as a paradigm shift for couple therapy. In *Couple Attachments: Theoretical and Clinical Studies*, ed. M. Ludlam and V. Nyberg, pp. 189–206. London: Karnac, and also in the online journal *International Review of Couple and Family Psychoanalysis* Volume 1, 2007/1. http://www.aipcf.net/web/doc2007-1-francais_2009415102144_2010122010229.pdf

Scharff, J. S. (1992). *Projective and Introjective Identification and the Use of the Therapist's Self.* Northvale, NJ: Jason Aronson.

Scharff, J. S. (Ed.) (1996). *The Autonomous Self: The Work of John D. Sutherland*. Northvale, NJ: Jason Aronson.

Scharff, J. S. and Scharff, D. E. (1994). *Object Relations Therapy of Physical and Sexual Trauma*. Northvale, NJ: Jason Aronson.

Scharff, J. S. and Scharff, D. E. (1998a). Chaos theory and fractals in development, self and object relations, and transference. *Object Relations Individual Therapy*, pp. 153–182. Northvale, NJ: Jason Aronson.

Scharff, J. S. and Scharff, D. E. (1998b). The geography of transference and countertransference. Object Relations Individual Therapy, pp. 241–281. Northvale, NJ: Jason Aronson.

Scharff, J. S. and Scharff, D. E. (1998c). *Object Relations Individual Therapy*. Northvale, NJ: Jason Aronson.

Scharff, J. S. and Scharff, D. E. (2000). *Tuning the Therapeutic Instrument*. Northvale, NJ: Jason Aronson.

Scharff, J. S. and Scharff, D. E. (2005). *The Primer of Object Relations: Second Edition*. Lanham, MD: Jason Aronson.

Scharff, J. S. and Scharff, D. E. (2006). *New Paradigms for Treating Relationships*. Lanham, MD: Jason Aronson.

Schore, A. (1994). *Affect Regulation and the Origin of the Self: The Neurobiology of Emotional Development*. Hillsdale, NJ: Lawrence Erlbaum.

Schore, A. (2002). "The Right Brain as a Neurological Substrate of Freud's Dynamic Unconscious." Keynote address, International Psychotherapy Institute conference on Freud at the Millennium. Georgetown University, Washington, DC, October 1998, and published in *The Psychoanalytic Century: Freud's Legacy for the Future*, ed. D. E. Scharff, pp. 61–68. New York: The Other Press, 2002.

Schore, A. (2003a). *Affect Regulation and the Repair of the Self*. New York: Norton. Hillsdale, NJ: Erlbaum.

Schore, A. (2003b). *Affect Dysregulation and Disorders of the Self*. New York: Norton.

Searles, H. F. (1965). *Collected Papers on Schizophrenia and Related Subjects*. New York: International Universities Press.

Shi, Q. J. (2004). Understanding the Chinese Oedipal complex. *Journal of Nervous Diseases and Mental Hygiene* 02: http://translate.google.com/translate?hl=en&sl=zh-CN&u=http://scholar.ilib.cn/Abstract.aspx%3FA%3Dsjjbyjsws200402031&sa=X&oi=translate&resnum=1&ct=result&prev=/search%3Fq%3Dhttp://scholar.ilib.cn/A-sjjbyjsws200402031.html%26hl%3Den%26rlz%3D1G1GGLQ_ENUS282%26sa%3DG (in English). Last accessed 2007.

Shi, Q. J. and Scharff, J. S. (2008). Social change, intercultural conflict, and marital dynamics in a Chinese marriage in brief concurrent individual and couple therapy. *International Journal of Applied Psychoanalytic Studies* 5(4): 302–321.

Shi, Q. J., Zeng, Q. F., Sheng, X. C., and Senf, W. (Eds.) (2006). *Psychotherapy Theory and Practice* (in Chinese). Beijing: Chinese Medical-Pharmaceutical Science Publishing House.

Shuttleworth, J. (1989). Psychoanalytic theory and infant development. In

Closely Observed Infants, ed. L. Miller, Margaret Rustin, Michael Rustin, and J. Shuttleworth, pp. 22–51. London: Duckworth.

Slade, A. (1996). Attachment theory and research: Implications for the theory and practice of individual psychotherapy. *Handbook of Attachment Theory and Research*, ed. J. Cassidy and P. R. Shaver. New York: Guilford.

Spruiell, V. (1993). Deterministic chaos and the sciences of complexity: Psychoanalysis in the midst of a general scientific revolution. *Journal of the American Psychoanalytic Association* 41: 3–41.

Sroufe, L. A. and Fleeson, J. (1986). Attachment and the construction of relationships. In *Relationships and Development*, pp. 51–71. Hillsdale, NJ: Lawrence Erlbaum.

Steiner, J. (1993). *Psychic Retreats: Pathological Organizations in Psychotic, Neurotic and Borderline Patients*. London: Routledge.

Stolorow, R. and Atwood, G. (1992). *Contexts of Being: The Intersubjective Foundations of Psychological Life*. Hillsdale, NJ: Analytic Press.

Strachey, J. (1934). The nature of therapeutic action of psycho-analysis. *International Journal of Psycho-Analysis* 15: 127–159.

Suomi, S. J. (1994). Influence of attachment theory on ethological studies of biobehavioral development in nonhuman primates. In *Attachment Theory: Social, Developmental, and Clinical Perspectives*, ed. S. Goldberg, R. Muir, and J. Kerr, pp. 185–200. Hillsdale, NJ: Analytic Press.

Suomi, S. J. (1995). Attachment: Overview, with implications for clinical work. In *Attachment Theory: Social, Developmental and Clinical Perspectives*, ed. S. Goldberg, R. Muir, and J. Kerr, pp. 407–475. Hillsdale, NJ: The Analytic Press.

Sutherland, J. D. (1980). The autonomous self. In *The Autonomous Self: The Writings of J. D. Sutherland*, ed. J. S. Scharff, pp. 303–330. Northvale NJ: Jason Aronson, 1984.

Tomkins, S. S. (1995). *Exploring Affect: The Selected Writings of Silvan S. Tomkins*, ed. E. V. Demos. Cambridge, England: Cambridge University Press.

Trevarthen, C. (1989). Development of early social interactions and the affective regulations of brain growth. In *The Neurobiology of Early Infant Behavior*, ed. C. von Euler and H. Forssberg. New York: MacMillan.

Trevarthen, C. (1990). Growth and education of the hemispheres. In *Brain Circuits and Functions of the Mind*, ed. C. Trevarthen, pp. 334–363. Cambridge: Cambridge University Press.

Trevarthan, C. (2009). The intersubjective psychobiology of human meaning. *Psychoanalytic Dialogues* 19(5): 507–518.

Tronick, E. Z. (1989). Emotions and emotional communication in infants. *American Psychologist* 44: 112–119.

Van Eenwyck, L. S. (1997). *Archetypes and Strange Attractors: The Chaotic World of Symbols*. Toronto: Inner City Books.

Volkan, V. (1981). *Linking Objects and Linking Phenomena.* New York: International Universities Press.
Volkan, V. (2006). *Killing in the Name of Identity.* Charlottesville, VA: Pitchstone Publishing.
Vygotsky, L. S. (1988). Thinking and speaking. In *The Collected Papers of L. S. Vygotsky, Vol. 1,* ed. R. W. Rieber and A. S. Carton, pp. 39–288. New York: Plenum Press.
Weber, M. (1949). Objectivity in social science. In *The Methodology of the Social Sciences,* ed. and trans. E. A. Shils and H. A. Finch, pp. 89–99 and 110–112. New York: Simon and Schuster, The Free Press.
Winnicott, D. W. (1945). Primitive emotional development. In *Through Paediatrics to Psycho-Analysis,* pp. 145–156. London: Hogarth Press, 1975.
Winnicott, D. W. (1947). Hate in the countertransference. In *Through Pediatrics to Psycho-Analysis,* pp. 194–203. London: Hogarth, 1975.
Winnicott, D. W. (1951). Transitional objects and transitional phenomena. In *Through Paediatrics to Psycho-Analysis,* pp. 229–242. London: Hogarth Press.
Winnicott, D. W. (1958). *Collected Papers: Through Pediatrics to Psycho-Analysis.* London: Tavistock, 1958. Reprinted by Hogarth Press, 1975.
Winnicott, D. W. (1960a). Ego distortion in terms of true and false self. In *The Maturational Processes and the Facilitating Environment,* pp. 140–152. London: Hogarth Press, 1965. New York: International Universities Press, 1965.
Winnicott, D. W. (1960b). The theory of the parent–infant relationship. *International Journal of Psycho-Analysis,* 41: 585–595, and in *Maturational Processes and the Facilitating Environment,* pp. 37–55. London: Hogarth Press, 1972.
Winnicott, D. W. (1963a). Communicating and not communicating leading to a study of certain opposites. In *The Maturational Processes and the Facilitating Environment,* pp. 179–192. London: Hogarth Press, 1975.
Winnicott, D. W. (1963b). The development of the capacity for concern. In *The Maturational Processes and the Facilitating Environment,* pp. 73–81. London: Hogarth Press, 1975.
Winnicott, D. W. (1965). *The Maturational Processes and the Facilitating Environment.* London: Hogarth Press.
Winnicott, D. W. (1971). *Playing and Reality.* London: Tavistock.
Zelnick, L. and Bucholz, E. S. (1990). The concept of mental health in the light of recent infant research. *Psychoanalytic Psychology* 7: 29–58.
Zepf, S. (2006). Attachment theory and psychoanalysis: Some remarks from an epistemological and from a Freudian viewpoint. *International Journal of Psycho-Analysis* 87: 1529–1548.
Zhang, T. (2008). "The Chinese Oedipal Triangle." Unpublished paper. http://blog.sina.com.cn/s/blog4503004901000b5t.ht (in Chinese). Last accessed 2008.

Zinner, J. and Shapiro, R. (1989). Projective identification as a mode of perception and behavior in families of adolescents. In *Foundations of Object Relations Family Therapy,* ed. J. S. Scharff, pp. 109–126. Northvale, NJ: Jason Aronson.

Index

About the Authors

Dr. David Scharff, M.D. Co-founder, International Psychotherapy Institute; clinical professor of psychiatry, at Georgetown University and at Uniformed Services University of the Health Sciences; teaching analyst, Washington Psychoanalytic Institute; supervising analyst, International Institute for Psychoanalytic Training; psychoanalyst, couple and family therapist, Chevy Chase, Maryland; author, *Refinding the Object and Reclaiming the Self, The Sexual Relationship*; co-author with Jill Scharff, *Object Relations Couple Therapy, Object Relations Family Therapy*; editor *Object Relations Theory and Practice*; co-editor, *Fairbairn, Then and Now, The Psychoanalytic Century, Fairbairn and Relational Theory, New Paradigms for Treating Relationships;* series co-editor with J. Scharff of The Library of Object Relations at Jason Aronson; and expert teacher and clinician of "Object Relations Child Therapy" and "Object Relations Family Therapy" in the *Psychotherapy with the Experts* educational videotape series.

Jill Savege Scharff, M.D. Co-founder, International Psychotherapy Institute and International Institute for Psychoanalytic Training; clinical professor of psychiatry, Georgetown University; teaching analyst, Washington Psychoanalytic Institute; supervising analyst, International Institute for Psychoanalytic Training; psychoanalyst, couple and family therapist, Chevy Chase, Maryland; author, *Projective and Introjective Identification and the Use of the Therapist's Self*; co-author with David Scharff, *The Primer of Object Relations (2nd edition), Object Relations Therapy of Physical and Sexual Trauma, Object Relations Individual Therapy*; editor, *The Autonomous Self: The Work of John D. Sutherland, The Psychodynamic Image: The Work of*

John D. Sutherland on Self and Society; Foundations of Object Relations Family Therapy, co-editor, *Tuning the Therapeutic Instrument, Self Hatred in Psychoanalysis, and The Legacy of Fairbairn and Sutherland*; and expert teacher and clinician of "Object Relations Individual Therapy" and "Object Relations Family Therapy," both in the *Psychotherapy with the Experts* educational videotape series.